LIVING THE DREAM

LIVING
THE DREAM
My Life and Basketball

HAKEEM
OLAJUWON

WITH PETER KNOBLER

LITTLE, BROWN AND COMPANY
BOSTON   NEW YORK   TORONTO   LONDON

For world peace.

To my father, my mother, and my daughter

— H.O.

To Jane and Daniel

— P.K.

In the name of Allah, most gracious, most merciful.

CONTENTS

ACKNOWLEDGMENTS

WE WOULD LIKE to acknowledge gratefully the help and support of many people whose memories, good work, and good wishes were of great value in the writing of this book. Our great thanks to Pamela Greaney; David "D.H." Nordstrom; Rose Pietrzak and the entire media services staff of the Houston Rockets; Rudy Tomjanovich; Les Alexander; Lynden Rose; Reid Gettys; Ralph Adams; Scott Brooks; Jim Foley; Ralph Greene; Margie Yemoto; Fredi Friedman; Esther Newberg; Bob Levine; Nancy Rose; Chris Begala; Hasan Tulbah; Fayeez Gwuari; Jamaal Badawi; Jacquie Miller; Geoff Kloske; Yvonne Crum and the attendants and crew on the Rockets charter; Don Sperling and Paul Hirschheimer and NBA Entertainment; Rick Polter and the University of Houston athletic department. Special thanks to Ajmal Khan and Carol Lee. Thank you to my brothers Akins, Tajudeen, Afis, and Yemi and to my sister Kudirat for their support.

I especially want to thank my collaborator, Peter Knobler, who was the point guard of this book. It was wonderful working with Peter and fun traveling with him, a highlight of my career. I couldn't have worked with anyone better. I've made a lifelong friend.

LIVING THE DREAM

1

THE FINALS

MADISON SQUARE GARDEN WAS CRAZED.

It was game three of the 1994 National Basketball Association Championship Finals: my team, the Houston Rockets, against the New York Knicks. We had split two games at home in Houston and now we were in New York City for three games straight. If we couldn't win at least one of them our season was over. We all knew that this first one was the most important.

The Rockets had played all season to gain home-court advantage, to have the extra game in the NBA finals played in our gym, in our city, in front of our crowd, and the Knicks had come to Houston and taken that from us. Going into the Garden, the Knicks' home arena, we could have felt as if our backs were to the wall, but we chose not to. The way we saw it, now the pressure was on the Knicks, they had to win. They were at home in front of their fans; how disappointing it would be to lose this advantage so soon after they had gained it. Let's secure our position, we said, let's secure that we're going back to Houston.

I had played in the Garden before and sometimes the crowd got so involved I'd say, "Oh, wow, I don't think we can pull this one out tonight." You can actually see from the moment you walk on the court how the game is going to be. If the crowd is intense it's going to be a hard night. Sometimes the crowd is intense but the Knicks players have doubts — then it's even. But if the players are without doubts, that's a different ball game. If the players meet the intensity of the crowd, you know you're in trouble!

The Knicks' center Patrick Ewing is an intimidator. On the court in pre-game warm-ups before game three he looked mean, aggressive, anxious to get things going. He was stalking around like a wounded tiger.

I felt very calm. Even though it was a big game I was extremely relaxed. I had gotten my rest, eaten my pre-game pasta, gotten some sleep, and when I came to the floor I found I had a lot of energy. It's a mystery; some days you have it and some days you don't. Some days you look for that spark and you can't find it; you do everything right but it's not there. But that day in warm-ups I was active and flexible and loose. I felt the power. I knew it was there. That day I felt so confident, and the confidence gave me calmness. I didn't show it, I didn't do some super slam through the net, I just jumped happily by myself. Only once I took a lay-up and went way, way above the rim and let the ball fall straight down through the hoop. I felt so light. The more I warmed up, the more I felt charged, on a higher level.

I saw Patrick and I accepted the challenge. This was going to be a battle and I was not about to wait for his attack. I attacked him.

The Rockets came out aggressive, the Knicks came out passive. They didn't meet our challenge. In the first half they were down sixteen points. Our shooting guard Vernon Maxwell started us off. He went to the basket strong, he hit three straight baskets early in the game and set the tone. We were loose and flying and we were going to give it all tonight.

The Knicks were down from the beginning, but finally, in the last quarter, they came back. They were tough and the game got close. That's when it's time to do your absolute best.

Someone on my team shot the ball and when Patrick went for the rebound it went over his head and came right into my hand. He turned around. We had an even start.

I squared up on him and began driving right. The key to blocking that move is to cut me off; Patrick has to cut me off or I am going straight to the basket. But that was a set-up. I wanted him to cut me off and think that he had shut me down. As soon as he moved to his left I spun around him, a reverse pivot before he could react. That's when I used my quickness and speed. I was by him in a flash. Anyone coming from the weak side had no chance because by the time they could get there I'd already be coming down. I went in untouched and slammed the ball home.

The crowd, even the Madison Square Garden crowd, went absolutely wild.

It was one of my best dunks ever. A highlight-reel dunk. It was spectacular and I felt so good running down the court. You know that feeling, when you're out there, when you've done something out of the ordinary. I played it down but I felt *good!* As I ran past the Rocket bench my teammates were up and shouting, "Major-league! Major-league move!"

Rockets guard Sam Cassell was just a rookie but he came in and sparked us. He's got the personality to do that. He hit all three of his three-pointers and scored fifteen points, including our last seven. Knicks fans hated him but he was having fun.

We won game three, 93–89. Man, that was a relief. We had had two days in Houston before we came to New York and we'd been thinking positive, but every once in a while we had to consider the possibility that we could lose the series in New York. Now we had secured our position. We wanted to win at least another game on the road but we were definitely going back to Houston.

It was tough, it was a battle, but the championship finals, the entire series, was the most wonderful fun of the whole season. I was battling against Patrick but I was playing very loose, flexible, just playing my game. Even when we were losing I was very content, I felt no pressure. I had the feel.

This was the dream match-up I had thought about since I first saw Patrick play in college, when he was at Georgetown and I was at the University of Houston. This was going to be the most difficult task and I wanted to enjoy it and be competitive and respond. Whether we were losing or winning I was going to challenge every one of Patrick's shots. Always challenging, always a battle.

For my entire career the Rockets had played New York only two games each year, one in Houston and one in the Garden. Now that we had time to play each other on a consistent basis, we got to really know one another's games and feel comfortable on the floor.

Patrick and I became familiar with each other's moves. Every center has a hook shot that's his trademark. Kareem Abdul-Jabbar's hook began in his legs; when he took his giant step he went away from you and when he rose up there was nothing you could do about it. Patrick has a running hook shot. He puts his head down, dribbles to his left, rams his shoulder into you, and shoots. He is so quick and strong that he can go right over or through most centers in the league. It had been very effective for him all season long.

But when Patrick takes his hook he takes baby steps, he's not covering ground. I found Patrick's move could be taken away if I stayed in his way, stuck my chest out and challenged him. He would bounce off me to one side or the other, and because he was not covering ground I could catch up with him. He could be stopped.

Early in the series I would look for that move. I waited for it, and every time he shot his hook I would challenge it. As the series went on he knew I knew that move and he used it less and less. But when Patrick was frustrated and struggling, when he just wanted a basket, he would go to it.

On Patrick's turnaround jump shot I played right up in his face. If he jumped low he would get it blocked, so he had to jump high every time and it was a tough shot to make. I didn't mind him taking that because I knew he wouldn't make too many of them.

But Patrick is a smart player. He found one weak point in our defense and he milked it. He and Knicks guards John Starks and Derek Harper began really working the pick-and-roll.

Starks or Harper would bring the ball to the top of the key or slightly to the side. Ewing would come by and pick off their man and then explode to the basket, and I had to make a decision. Either I stayed with Ewing or I went out and helped with the guard. If I went out and helped, Ewing spotted up in the corner for an open jump shot and when the guard passed him the ball I had no time to get there. If I stayed with Ewing, Starks or Harper went directly in for the lay-up. I'd rather give up a jump shot than a lay-up, so Ewing was always open in the corner and he would hit it. They were very smart; they used that play over and over again. With me challenging Patrick's inside game, that jump shot was how he got most of his points. Every once in a while he would power inside and make a tough shot, but he was not going to win this series like that. Reporters criticized him for taking outside shots and not working inside, but that was his best shot in the series and he was smart enough to recognize it and maximize it.

The pick-and-roll, it's as old as basketball itself. It works. There wasn't anything I could do except encourage my teammates to switch to Patrick whenever they saw the play developing. I got frustrated with our guard Kenny Smith for a while when Ewing was getting all these wide-open jumpers. "I'm going to your man, you can run to Ewing. You don't have to block it, just run to him, distract him. Don't just stand here."

Sam Cassell came into the game. He told me, "Don't worry about Ewing, just be aggressive on defense!" Sam's a very emotional player and I like it when he tells me what to do out there. He got two steals and made Patrick miss some shots. Even if he couldn't block them he ran at Ewing and created a distraction.

Game four was tough and competitive. Up and down. The Knicks beat us, 91–82. Game five was the same way except worse. They jumped on us early; we were down 17–4 right away. I didn't even get a chance to shoot the ball. We turned it over and they would go in and score. The crowd was going crazy. But I was calm. I was so confident. This is going to be a long game, I thought, so just calm down, let's just play our game. We can beat this team. I was so relaxed that when I looked at Patrick as I went down the court, he looked surprised. Like, "He must know something I don't know. The way this game is going, the only way they're going to win is if we burn out."

But I knew we were just rushing our game. The Madison Square Garden crowd, which was really wild that night, was dictating what we did.

As confident as I was, we still lost game five 91–84, and we went back to Houston down three games to two. If we lost one more game we lost the championship, but we had two games at home.

The media was full of talk about how this was an "ugly" series, how neither team had yet scored more than a hundred points in any game, how we were grinding these games out instead of going with a flow. "It is boring," they criticized. "It is not championship basketball." But this is America, this is a basketball country — I thought they would know better.

Anytime you see a match-up where you have to work for every point, *that* is championship basketball. There was quality play every time down the floor. There were no easy baskets. There was no free-stroking, just-do-whatever-you-want play, like street ball; this was a championship game! Every game was close, there were no blow-outs, they went all the way. Every shot was contested. If it was not a flamboyant series it was intense basketball from the beginning to the end. When the championship is on the line, every time you make a decision it is *big,* every time you take a jump shot you have to make it. If somebody on the other team scores a basket it hurts you that he scored. *Every point hurts you.* This is how a championship game should be.

When we arrived back in Houston, the city loved us. They were so happy that we'd brought the series back. When I drove on the freeways I saw that people had painted the windows of their cars with Rockets slogans. The way the city appreciated us, we felt it was our obligation to win for them. We were all living in "Clutch City!" "Believe it!" was the slogan, and we believed it.

The Knicks were on *our* turf now. The championship trophy had been flown to Houston from the NBA office in New York, and just thinking about it getting put on a plane and flying back made my heart drop.

Game six was the first time in the whole series that I felt pressure. Up until then I'd been playing freely, but now the championship was on the line.

I didn't want to think about having to win two games. Just win one. Just win this one, then we'd worry about the next. Just win game six.

The Houston Summit, our home arena, was packed. Music was blaring, people were wearing their Rockets shirts. These were the faithful and they believed! The Knicks didn't want to play us in game seven in Houston, they wanted to close it out now. The same way we'd had to win game three in New York, they had to win here now.

They played to win. They played good enough to win. The game was tied at the end of the first quarter, we went up by ten at the half, and we led by three at the end of the third quarter. The game couldn't have been tougher. The Knicks were less than a game away from their championship. Under the boards no shot went unchallenged, and the rebounding was brutal. Carl "Amigo" Herrera hit all six of his shots to keep the game tight.

Patrick was playing hard and well, and in the fourth quarter John Starks took the game in his hands. Starks kept putting up shots. He scored sixteen points that quarter and showed no fear. With two seconds left we were up, 86–84. The Knicks had the ball. Anthony Mason inbounded and curled down low to rebound. Starks got the ball.

When the game is on the line and the ball is in your hands, you have three choices: You can win it, you can tie it, or you can lose it. John Starks was going to kill us with a three. He had already hit five of eight three-pointers that night. He didn't want to tie the series, he was going to *end* the series. He was going for the most dangerous. He had no conscience.

The biggest mistake the Knicks made was letting Patrick set the pick, trying to free Starks for his jump shot. I was guarding Patrick and that brought me close to the ball. If Knicks power forward Charles Oakley had set the pick, our power forward Otis Thorpe would have been there instead of me. I understood the Knicks' thinking: they wanted to get Ewing close to the ball for the pick-and-roll, their most effective play.

We were prepared. In our huddle, Rockets coach Rudy Tomjanovich had said, "Switch everything! Switch everything!" I was going to take the shooter, and the team would rotate to cover Ewing.

But when Ewing started to set the pick I switched only halfway, I didn't go all the way to Starks. If they gave the ball back to Ewing I wanted to be close by.

The distance I gave Starks looked like it was too much for me to make up. The Knicks' Pat Riley, an excellent coach, had called the right play and they had executed it perfectly. Starks got separation. He looked wide open.

But he wasn't wide open, he was still within my range as a shot blocker. I knew I could recover. I wanted to be close to Ewing — I didn't want Patrick to beat us — but one step and a leap straight up and I had Starks.

Still, Starks is the kind of player who can adjust. If the ball was still in his hand and I leaned and he saw me coming, he would give it to Ewing. I would be out of the picture and Patrick would have the championship on his fingertips. Also, with the amount of space I had given Starks, I couldn't meet the ball in his hand. I had to hit it at an angle after he released it. I had to meet the ball in flight.

I made sure Starks was taking that shot before I leaped, but as I was flying toward him I slipped. I was out of control. He had me stretched out completely.

I deflected the ball! It took everything — luck, experience as a shot blocker, destiny — for me to make that play. The ball never got to the rim. The game was over. The series was tied, 3–3. Houston went wild.

I couldn't sleep the night before game seven. I took this championship personally. I had been having fun, but now we were so close and I was feeling the pressure. They could not take that trophy out of Houston.

I needed to sleep because I needed my energy to perform, so I tried to focus and picture myself doing all good things. I saw myself from all different angles, being aggressive, succeeding. No negative thoughts, not a single Maybe not. Only positive. Mentally, I was tough. Finally, I got a few hours of sleep in.

When I arrived at the Summit the locker room was all prepared for celebration. There was crepe paper and signs on the walls and rolls of plastic hung so our clothes would be protected when we sprayed champagne on everything. On the TV monitor was the Knicks' locker room, and it was dressed up too. I got very emotional. I thought, We can't come back here sad. The city had never won a championship; everything was on the line.

I prayed. During my regular morning prayers I had put it in God's hands. I was going to do my very best and I prayed for victory, but if it didn't happen the way I planned, that would be God's will. I wanted to win very badly, but if I didn't I wouldn't be ruined; there had to be balance. I accepted that as part of fate and thanked Allah for the opportunity to get there. Still, I was going to do everything I could to win.

I didn't usually speak up in team meetings or before games. I felt comfortable with the team. We were doing our best. Most of the time I would stay in the background and let others do the talking. But now somebody had to take charge and let the team know this was important. Before game seven I felt I had to reinforce everybody's confidence, make sure we were all thinking alike and that there was a meeting of the minds. We all had to think very strong.

Rudy had been saying all year long, every important game, "This is the biggest game of the year." There were many crucial games, and he would say that each time. I'm sure he was right but after a while it sounded like a broken record. "This is the biggest game of the year." This was the first time I really heard the meaning of his words. This time I felt it. I felt the weight of the game. Just one game, and it was at home.

I was calm when the game began. So was Patrick. We both wanted to do more than usual, to carry our team, to dominate. Even the first jump ball was important. Let's get the jump ball, let's start it from the beginning.

We got the tip. Maxwell went to shoot; they were going to block it; he passed it to our forward, Robert Horry. Robert swung the ball around and it came in to me.

I had an open jump shot but I didn't want to take a jumper. The game was young. I wanted to take this in with authority, I wanted to make a statement. I took one bounce. I was going for the dunk.

Ewing challenged me. He was way up there, we both met way above the rim. I might have dunked over him but I didn't want to take the chance of getting blocked — that could have a disastrous effect on the game, getting a dunk blocked on our first shot. As I was coming down I saw Robert Horry running down the lane full-speed. There was this wild look in his eyes. I dished the ball off to Robert.

Ewing was already committed. I was truly looking for the dunk and he had met my challenge and jumped with great force to stop me. He came down and tried to go back up again to challenge Robert.

Oh, my God!

Robert was coming hard, with *momentum*. He saw the opening and he got hyper. It was a perfect set-up, perfectly executed. We couldn't have done it any better if we had planned it.

You don't get that kind of opportunity very often in a regular game — a running start down the lane, a huge jam in front of you, a chance to go through everybody and state clearly and simply that we will not be denied. Now this was the first play of game seven of the NBA championships and here it was. It was crazy.

Robert took the ball with two hands and dunked so hard over Patrick that Ewing staggered out of bounds.

You don't see that kind of dunk every day. In your career you might see maybe four or five of those dunks. It's not something you forget.

Ewing had gone after me from strength. When he went back up after Robert he was coming from weakness and Robert was coming from strength. I understand Patrick's effort — you've got to give him credit for trying — but it was not a wise decision. He had no chance, no chance at all.

Robert came down on Patrick with elbows and knees. Patrick almost fell. I felt sorry for him. That was a punishment!

This was the first basket!

Patrick didn't recover from that dunk until the second half. He scored only four points before the break. People might not have known what was bothering him, but I knew it was that dunk. It set the tone for the whole game. He could tell himself it happens to the best of them, but it was still an embarrassment.

As a shot blocker, when you get dunked on like that it's not something you just shake off. Not that kind of dunk; it was such a powerful statement about the game.

We led almost all the way but the lead was never very large or very secure. The only difference between the teams was that we were taking the ball in with authority.

Patrick was challenging all my shots, and when he wasn't guarding me, Pat Riley rotated their forward Anthony Mason. They never gave me a moment's peace. Ewing was pounding me and when Mason came it wasn't time for a rest. Ewing would lean his 250 pounds on my back in the post but at least he let me post up. Mason wouldn't even let me get that position. Mason knew that because I was so much taller than he was, once I got the ball his defense was finished; I could shoot over him. His strength was that he knew where I was trying to get the ball, so he would get there first and take the spot. If I didn't have the ball I couldn't score. Mason was aggressive and relentless. I had to fight him, and he was tough. He really made me work. He played strong, hard defense. I've got to give him a lot of credit, he did his job well.

In the second quarter, with the twenty-four-second clock almost running out, I was going to shoot in traffic when I saw Kenny Smith behind the three-point line at the top of the key and passed him the ball. Kenny, who had been having a hard series, shot it up. The ball bounced straight off the glass and into the basket. So we were blessed that night, too. Kenny did a good job. Another time, I was going to shoot when Patrick challenged my shot again. I was off balance and I surprised Maxwell with a pass. He put it up and the ball went in for another three. Max scored twenty-one points that game while playing tough defense against John Starks, who shot two for eighteen and missed all eleven of his three-pointers. (People blame Starks for the misses but they forget to credit Max for his defense.) Sam Cassell scored thirteen points in eighteen minutes, eight in the fourth quarter, stepping inside the defense for jump shots and generally playing like a veteran, not a rookie.

Our lead never got above eight points and we were never down more than three. It was a close, hard, anxious game all the way, never a moment to rest, never a moment when either team felt safe. And at the end we won, 90–84.

I happened to have the ball in my hands the moment the final whistle blew. I kept it. I have it at home right now.

People rushed onto the floor. Movement, color, like big roaring waves, Rocket fans coming from every angle and all directions. I took a few steps, cradled the ball, and sat against the scorer's table and just watched. Everybody was jumping and stomping on the floor, hands up, shouting, grinning. People were so happy. I had never seen anything like it. That was so beautiful to watch. My celebration was to watch everybody being ecstatic, rejoicing, jumping on tables and hugging each other, showing emotion in their own way.

That morning I had prayed that if it was God's will, we would win. So now I knew: this was His will. And in that moment I gave thanks that He had willed it.

My daughter, Abisola, was at the game and I held her. Players had their families with them as we held the championship trophy. Everybody wanted to put their hands on it. I held back a little. I knew if I grabbed the trophy none of my teammates would take it from me and I really wanted to share this with them. We had worked so hard and come together so beautifully. Everybody had played a role in this victory, from the bench players who practiced hard and were ready whenever they were called to the regular rotation who complemented each other's talents and added to mine to the coaches who conceived the victory and worked to make us bring it home. We celebrated with the entire Rockets family. We were all part of the championship. This was a tremendous feeling.

I was also happy for the Rockets' new owner, Les Alexander. People didn't know much about Mr. Alexander when he bought the team, but he turned out to be a very nice man. He and his wife were a nice couple. Mr. Alexander was not afraid to make a deal for the benefit of the team. He was willing to step forward and he was willing to pay the price to win, which I respected. I admired his desire to win, his hunger for a championship.

The locker room was churning, thick with media and friends and sweat and hot television camera lights. I couldn't sit at my locker because there were two hundred people in a room that was supposed to hold twenty. Nobody knew what the championship crush would be like and it was wilder and more demanding than anyone had imagined. The NBA had organized a press conference in the concrete guts of the Summit, and I answered questions and smiled and answered more questions and smiled some more. I talked to reporters and then slipped back into the shower room for some privacy. It was only when I finally took off my clothes and let the water run over me that it occurred to me: from that night on, all my teammates and I would be NBA champions forever.

2

GROWING UP IN LAGOS

THE LAST THING my parents wanted to see when I was growing up was me playing. When my father and mother, Salam and Abike Olajuwon, were at work they expected me to be doing something valuable, like homework or housework or studying. Playing, for them, was a reward after you've done all of that. For me it was what I really loved to do. There was a field right outside our door and I was on it every day. My parents would tell me, "This is what you love to do, play. You're not serious. People who are going somewhere, who are successful, they work. There must be balance." They made me feel so bad that I wanted to play rather than study.

When I was born, in 1963, Nigeria was only three years independent of Great Britain. Lagos was the capital, an international port city filled with business, particularly the oil business, and when the government needed land for new office buildings they had to find homes for the people they moved from downtown. My parents and lots of others were moved to new residential areas.

The neighborhood was well planned, with new one- and two-story homes. The homes were modest but clean, and the government financed the houses so people could afford them. They were all arranged around a large, central grass field with some palm trees. Mothers could look out the front window and see everything that was going on.

Because people moved into these homes all at the same time and then started raising families, my neighborhood was filled with kids my age. We all grew up together and we all played out there. Mostly soccer.

We thought of the field as our soccer field. And every time we played we would look out for our parents. If you saw your parents' car coming, you ran into the house the back way, sat down, and tried to look as if you'd been studying. It happened with everybody. We would be kicking the ball and running back and forth and then all of a sudden we would need some substitutions because two of the players would see their parents coming and just disappear.

I had a half-brother named Yemi Kaka who was an ideal older brother with qualities we all admired. He was fourteen years older than I was and an excellent student, winner of a scholarship from the Nigerian government to study abroad. That was the goal of all Nigerian students, to study abroad. Yemi Kaka went to school in England. I had a lot of respect for him and his accomplishments, but it was discouraging for me to want to walk in his footsteps. My mother would bring it up at every opportunity: "Can't you see what your brother has done? When your brother was your age . . ." he was never a problem; he was the nicest kid you'd want to have; he helped around the house. Yemi was hard-working and quiet and patient. He was the ultimate role model. I couldn't even compete.

If my mother tried to stop me from playing and make me do things around the house, they never really got done. I was very stubborn. You could not refuse your parents, you had to obey, but you did it with attitude. Groaning around the house. But as long as I was doing what I was supposed to, my mother would ignore me. At the end of the day I had to make friends with her and be nice.

If things got very tense she would call my father. That was the last resort. She'd say, "I'm going to report you to your father."

"No, no, no, no . . ."

Then I'd straighten out. My father never hit any of us but he had a very short temper and he wanted things done perfectly. "Go to the fridge and get me the Maggi," he would say. Maggi was his favorite bottled food flavoring, like ketchup or Worcestershire sauce, and you put it over rice. I would open the refrigerator and see so many things, but even if the bottle of Maggi was right in front of me sometimes I wouldn't find it right away. I would grab something else and bring it to him. He was not really tolerant of mistakes. But if you brought him exactly what he needed then he would smile. To get him to smile and be very happy with you, that was the ultimate!

My father was the head of the home. He ate first and the children served him. Sometimes we ate all together, but mostly the kids ate separately. Afterward my sister, Kudirat, would stay around the kitchen to help my mother, and I would go out to the field and play. When my mother needed something from the store she would send one of my brothers to get me. Of course I didn't want to leave the game.

I was lucky I had three younger brothers — Akinola, Tajudeen, and Abdul Afis. Everything was determined by age, and unless it was an errand that required a more responsible person, I would assign it to one of them. Or make them tell her they couldn't find me. "We can't tell her that," they'd say, "she's looking at you." So I had to go inside.

My mother would get upset and tell me I should run this errand just on principle, because she had asked me. "Send Akins," I'd say. Then she'd spank me. I got a lot of spanking growing up.

But handling four growing boys wasn't easy for my mother and as I got older she began to put me in charge. Instead of telling the boys she was going to call my father, she would say she'd call me. I became the enforcer in the house. Akins was only a year younger than I was and because we were so close in age I could not send him on errands. I would *ask* him, as a favor. I could send Taju and Afis. Akins could send Afis but not Taju. And Taju always had an attitude.

I began to see this more clearly when I went away to boarding school and came back on the weekends. Taju would be sent on a mission and say something over his shoulder as he left. "Next time I'm not going," something like that. My mother would hear it but not do anything. I took it personally.

"What did you say?"

"I didn't say anything!"

Then I would have to discipline him. Knock him on the top of the head with my knuckle. Sometimes he'd test me and talk back again. It's a trait all the Olajuwon brothers have: we're all real stubborn.

Afis was friendly with us all. He was the best person to send on errands because he was the baby and he loved to run them, he'd never refuse. Sometimes I'd have to step in for Afis because he was running too many errands. Taju and Akins could do them themselves but they were being inconsiderate of their younger brother.

"Taju, what are you doing? How come you can't do it?"

Because Afis was closest in age to Taju, sometimes he would refuse and Taju would discipline him. I wouldn't allow that and would give Taju a knock. Taju would say, "Afis, you wait till I catch you when Hakeem goes back to school."

My father was the ultimate authority. When something got out of hand it went to him. He just wanted to know the facts, then he would say, "Don't take it into your own hands. Come report to me." Then he would tell Taju, "Next time, do as you're told."

My mother and father were both in the cement business, a big, big business at that time, with Nigeria independent and expanding and a lot of building being done. My parents would contract to buy bags of cement in bulk from the foreign shippers and then sell them to whole-sale contractors, builders, and individuals in Lagos. My mother would make a down payment on, say, one thousand bags, and then sell the paper to five or six different buyers. When the ship docked, her job was to make sure she received her shipment and that the people unloading the bags delivered the proper number to each client. That was her strength. She paid the people who did the unloading; shipments could get sidetracked if you weren't careful. Then she would collect the money. She had to be very street smart because if you looked away people would take more than they paid for.

Sometimes she would take me with her to the dock. It was a world of its own.

The whole industry was spread out down by the water at Apapa Wharf, where maybe a hundred and fifty cement sellers set up shop in temporary trailers that looked like mobile homes. There was nothing permanent about these structures, but they never moved.

Lagos is a port city and people would drive their trucks from all parts of the country to get their cement so they could go home and begin to build. You never knew when the ships were going to come in, and so much building was being done that ships full of supplies could wait in the channel three days or more before being able to dock. The people with cargo on those ships could do nothing but wait for them on shore. At night they slept on mats under their trucks, but it was very hot in the afternoons and they had nothing to do all day except play cards in the shade and talk. Some local traders sold cigarettes and cola nuts. There was a constant hum of activity as bags were unloaded, deals were made, stories were told.

My mother was very selective about whom she sold to, and she had a lot of repeat customers. She was known for her generosity and graciousness. She would not do her business right in her office; there was a restaurant on the wharf where she would take her customers. While her loaders were carting the cement, her customers would order what they liked — at her expense — and she would count their money.

I never really wanted to be there because I wanted to be playing at home in the field, but sometimes during school vacations she would take me anyway. The other traders would say, "Ah, you brought him to work today! How nice to meet you." People liked my mother and they were nice to me just to make my mother happy. They gave me money, five *naira,* the equivalent of eight dollars in Nigerian currency, which was a lot of money for a little boy. But they weren't really giving it to me, they were giving it so my mother would be pleased, because she had done so many good things for different people. I would carry her bag filled with work papers and she would say, "Stay here, I'll be right back," and go off to do business for an hour. I would look around.

Half the people would be wearing traditional Nigerian clothes, the *buba* top, the *chocoto* pants, and the *agbada* coat. Both my mother and my father dressed very traditionally every day. Different tribes have different styles and in the ship channel you would see them all. The men layer the cotton fabric in folds over their shoulders for comfort and looks while the women hold the material in one hand and hitch it around them. Because the fabric shifts, every ten steps you see Nigerian men and women folding and wrapping, folding and wrapping their clothes around them. There was constant movement in the street. It was almost like a dance.

There were western clothes too, because Lagos was so international. The city was a big melting pot. Nigeria has three major tribes: the Yoruba, in the west; the Ibo, in the east; and the Hausa, in the north. There are many smaller tribes as well, each with its own dialect. My tribe is Yoruba — pronounced "Yo-roo-*bah.*" The language we spoke at home was Yoruba. The Yoruba are a mix of Christians and Muslims, the Ibo are all Christians, and the Hausa are Muslims, and they all came together in Lagos. Living in the city gave you a tolerance for dealing with all kinds of different people from different backgrounds and cultures.

Lagos is the smallest city in Nigeria by area, and the most populated. Very congested. People from all over the world came there to trade, including the oil industry and fashion, and they brought their families. We had lots of Chinese, Lebanese, English, Italians, and Americans in the city. Clothing designers would have showrooms in Europe, London, New York, and Lagos. There was a lot of business being conducted. The British were still there, people were going to and from Hong Kong, Germany was doing most of the bridge and infrastructure construction. We got the best of all different groups to build the country.

I would walk around the wharf and watch the people, but I never went too far because my mother might need her bag. It had her spending money, which she trusted me with. Her real money she tied in a wrap and carried around her waist at all times.

My brothers and sister and I used to think our parents were rich because every evening when they came home from work we saw them counting their cash. They had two, maybe three thousand dollars in their belts, and each night they would separate the principal and put the profits from the day under their mattress. What we didn't know was that that was the whole amount they had in life, their entire bankroll, their portfolio, and they were handling it every day. When we wanted twenty dollars it seemed like so little when we saw how much they had, but they had their life savings in their hands every day and they were not going to give it to us kids.

My mother was very generous. She had a big heart. For example, transportation was very difficult in Nigeria and when someone came to visit our home to give her a message or deliver a package from some friends she would give them money for a bus or a taxi home. And if somebody came with a message for my dad she would push him to do the same thing, which he usually didn't feel like doing.

My father was very straightforward, very principled. You would get something from him only if he thought you deserved it. I loved him for that because when he gave me something I knew he really meant it. He would always tell us that this money was not his money; he had built a unit of apartments a long time ago and borrowed against that to get money for his business. If he didn't pay his mortgage he would lose this building, which was everything he owned in this world. He was a warm and friendly man, but he had to think about money all the time.

My parents were very traditional people and they are Muslims. One of the big holidays each year was Ramadan, which celebrated the month in which the Qur'an was revealed to the Prophet Muhammad, Peace and Blessings Be Upon Him (PBUH). During Ramadan we were not allowed to eat from sunup to sundown, and at the end of the month each family prepared a huge feast. In Nigeria the culture and Islam are intertwined and Ramadan is a public holiday, so everybody looked forward to it. A lamb or goat was killed and even though some neighbors might be Christian they came and helped my mother cook and serve. We all ate together because we were all brought up together.

Everybody is supposed to dress their best for the Eid celebration that ends Ramadan. My parents always had a hard time with the kids. They wanted us to wear traditional clothing and we wanted to dress western. Everything you wear that day must be new, your most beautiful clothes. And Yorubas like to dress, they like to enjoy life; we're very famous for that. My mother knew that to look your best you cannot beat traditional wear. She would make certain we had wonderful fabrics with excellent detail work, and that they fit us perfectly. My mother wanted to be proud of her children on this special day. She knew that when you wear shirt and pants you look very plain and very simple compared to the majestic look of the traditional.

We didn't see it that way and we didn't want any part of that. I felt shy, as if my friends would laugh at me if they saw me in something traditional. We didn't wear traditional clothing all year long, why should we do it now?

My generation grew up trying to be cool, to look toward the future. The traditional people didn't go to school, the traders didn't go to college. The educated people who studied abroad wore suits and ties, and that's who we looked up to. Religion was for the older crowd. Everybody I knew wanted to go to England or America to complete their education; the traditional people didn't want to leave Nigeria except to go on a pilgrimage, a *Hajj*, to Mecca. Even though I would rather play than study, I wanted to be up-to-date. I wouldn't even try on these traditional clothes.

It happened every year, and my mother would make a deal with us. She would buy us two sets of new clothes, one traditional, one western. She would say, "Okay, you wear the traditional to the mosque, but when you come home to change and get comfortable then you wear

your western, then you can go out to see your friends." That was okay.
When we went out in the morning we weren't around our friends
anyway and nobody would see us.

We put on the traditional clothes.

My father was so impressed. "Do you see how you look?" He was
giving all the kids these compliments that I had never heard from him
before. "You look excellent!"

The tribes play an important part in Nigerian culture and each tribe
has its own attitude. Individuals in each tribe are different, of course,
but overall the attitudes hold true. The Ibos had a reputation for being
strong and hardworking. They will do any kind of work to earn their
living. Their sense of pride does not stop them from working in the
lowest job and being proud of it. There is a Yoruba phrase for the Ibo:
Aje kuta ma mu omi. It means, "Can eat stone without drinking water."

When I was very young there was a war in Nigeria in which the
Ibos tried to gain their independence. Many Ibos in Lagos and the south
moved back to Biafra to fight in this war. When they lost, it was a big
setback for them. In Ibo culture your standing in the community is
based upon the size of your farm; a man without a title is not a man
at all in Ibo land. Most of the Ibos in Lagos had sold their possessions,
and the houses they had moved out of were now occupied by somebody
else. When they returned they had to start all over and take any jobs
available. But they are a proud people and because of their strength,
perseverance, tolerance, and determination, they grew back fast.

The majority of the Hausa people are very poor and far removed
from civilization. They are the people who live in the past, the most
traditional. They are very devoted, peaceful, simple people who follow
the fundamental Islamic faith. They are not driven by business; they
are more devoted to family.

If you are Hausa either you are extremely wealthy or very poor, and
the majority of them are poor. The wealthy, successful businessman is
supported by the whole tribe, and he gives back to the people. The
Hausa are farmers and ranchers in the north where there is a lot of rich
land. The wealthy Hausas are in the transportation business, importing
and exporting agriculture and bringing cattle and crops to the south.
They control the economy and most are loyal to their tribe, bringing
that money back to their community.

The Yorubas love their own traditions. We have values and pride in our heritage, pride for being Yorubas. We like to work but we love to enjoy life more. Music, dance, fashion, education — when you see Yorubas in times of pleasure, that's when you really see the richness of the culture.

My father came with his three brothers from Dahomey, the country next to Nigeria that is now called the Republic of Benin. In our home there was a big color photograph of five people, with one man, the head man, seated on a horse like a ruler. This was my grandfather, my father's father. He was royal in the way he dressed and sat and seemed. His robes were traditional and he gave the appearance of a man in charge. It was he who moved his entire family to Nigeria, and this picture was from before they arrived. When I was old enough to understand, I would look at that picture.

I was fascinated. Here is my father when he was eight years old, here is my father's brother who comes to our house all the time. They were all children in another land. My grandfather passed away before I was born so I never got to know him, but he was a very important man, and very successful, and that picture showed the family pride and the heritage of a ruler.

I began to learn English in primary school when I was six years old. My father spoke English and French and some dialects of Yoruba. My mother didn't speak English, only Yoruba, but she was determined that all her children were going to be well educated.

We had all different kinds of people in my neighborhood — Yoruba, Ibo, Hausa — and many different outlooks. Some people were westernized, some traditional, and there was a continuing argument between them, not in words but in ideas. The people who had been westernized called the traditional people illiterate and their values backward, not civilized. The traditional people were very sensitive to their history and they accused the westernized Nigerians of losing their culture and trying to adopt the ways of the colonizers.

Some of it was true, some traditional people were uneducated and didn't send their children to school. Some kids my age didn't even know how to write their name. Maybe they had been sent to religious training and learned how to read Arabic so they could read the Qur'an. They had religious knowledge. They were trained to be mechanics or traders, but they would not go to school for education. Not all traditional people were illiterate, these families simply prized traditional values over the western ones they saw around them, and they tried to preserve that tradition and pass it down to the new generation. Some westernized families, on the other hand, turned their backs on the history of their tribes.

My parents were traditional, but education was very important to them and they drummed it into us all the time. My mother was particularly serious. She was the oldest in her family and all her sisters and brothers had been highly educated, but not her. She was bitter about that and she stressed that education was the key to success.

By the time I got to secondary school, at age eleven, we were not allowed to speak anything but English in class. The first day we got there we saw a big sign: "Speaking vernacular is totally prohibited." Nobody knew what *vernacular* meant. The teacher told us it meant dialect. The schools were left over from British rule and they wanted to refine and polish our education, so if they caught someone speaking Yoruba or Ibo or any of the Nigerian dialects he would get punished.

From the beginning the whole point of going to school was to be able to go to university and communicate, so you had to pass English. That was compulsory; you don't pass English, you don't graduate. To repeat any class would be shameful. That would be big news, to say that you had to repeat. English was also the only common language, the only way Ibos or Yorubas or Hausas could communicate with one another.

I was a very good student in math, was all right in English and general science and history. We learned world history and talked only sometimes about the influential people in Nigeria. I liked African history if somebody told it to me, I liked listening to our history, but if I had to remember what happened in 1902 I couldn't. They taught us which Europeans came and "discovered" Africa, and they talked a little about great African kings and heroes of the past. Mostly, I studied enough to pass the tests.

My favorite book was *Things Fall Apart,* by Chinua Achebe. It was about the Ibo culture. This book was a standard among Nigerian kids; everybody read and loved it. When you finished that book you knew everything about the Ibo culture and their beliefs and character. It was like somebody was telling you a story. Every day the teacher called on a different student to read it out loud. I really enjoyed that course, except when it came my turn to read.

I was very shy in front of the class. That was my weakest point. I could not read to the class or answer questions. Even though I would know what the book said or have the answer, I was very nervous. First of all, I would have to stand at my seat when I read, and the picture of everybody staring at me made me uncomfortable. I have always liked when the attention is away from me and turned on other people. I like to fit in.

I have always been tall. I was a big baby and didn't stop growing. While everyone else can feel comfortable and walk around different places freely and unnoticed, everywhere I go I am noticeable. People always stare. I can never fit in; the more I try not to be noticed the more I am found. There's always somebody looking.

Kids used to call me names. There is one word in the Hausa language that would always start a fight. It is the Hausa phrase for tall people. It's not an insult in Hausa, it's their language, but in my tribe and in Lagos in general it's a big insult. It causes fights. It will cause a fight to this day. So of course kids had to call me that.

I had a lot of close friends on the field. My closest were Segun, Femi, and Ifayin. One of our favorite ways to spend an afternoon was to go plugging fruit.

The land behind the last row of houses in our neighborhood was filled with almond and guava and apple and banana and palm trees. Once we got back there it was like a different world. The underbrush blocked out all view of the houses and we could get twenty feet inside and be completely gone. The land was undeveloped and wild, and the deeper we went the more alone we became. It was quiet, kind of spooky. The whole area was only two blocks deep but we were in the jungle.

We didn't want anybody to find us so every day we would block the road that we came in and out on. Anyone passing by would think nobody had ever been in there. And if they stumbled inside, we also blocked our path. We had a getaway road just in case.

Segun, Femi, Ifayin, and I built a house there in the trees. We used dead palm leaves as the roof, and banana leaves as the floor. The rest was long dry grass. Outside the sun was hot but in our house it was very cool. We'd go there, it was quiet, nobody would know where we were, and we would talk. We found a little natural spring that we would run into when we wanted to swim, and we made a grill out of some cinderblocks that we had carried away, and roasted cassavas, which are like big potatoes, and plantains. It was the best.

Each of us had his own catapult. In America they're called sling-shots, but to us they were catapults. We made them by wrapping V-shaped branches with red and black tire from inner tubes, which took days to find. We used leather thongs to hold the stones, and then we tested them. With practice we could shoot long-distance with these things. Way off. We got so excited.

Catapults were forbidden by our parents; to them it was like having a gun in the house. So I would hide mine in the bathroom, far back under the tub. When I wanted to use it I shoved it under my shirt and hurried outside.

Each of us had a little bag and we would go pick up stones on the ground very selectively, like we were choosing bullets. Then we would go into the brush.

To plug a fruit you had to hit it with a stone from your catapult and make it drop. This was how you gained respect; we all four aimed at the same fruit and whoever plugged it, that was his. When you got a whole tree full of fruit somebody called, "Look at this, look at this!" and we would all aim for the best.

We would plug fruit for two or three hours and when we came back we would have this big bag full. We brought it out to a table and split it up. All the kids saw the bounty and wanted some of it, but they couldn't touch it because they weren't part of our foursome. Then we would pick. Whoever plugged the most fruit would be the first to choose, then the next, then the next. It was like draft picks. Round one, round two . . . We picked for about five rounds and then left the rest for everybody else. We couldn't take this crop into the house — our parents would ask where we got it, and we couldn't tell them — so we ate every bite before we got home.

School went from eight in the morning until two in the afternoon, and I would walk there and back with my friends every day. In Nigeria we related to the days according to their feel. You could tell what day it was just by going outside and looking at the people. Monday morning, everybody we saw was serious. It's almost a crime not to be serious Monday morning in Nigeria: this person is a failure, he has no ambition. Monday morning everybody is going somewhere, everybody has things to do, children are running to catch the bus, nobody has time for play. First thing Monday morning is the time to take care of the most important thing. The homework assignment from Friday, the one that you have not finished, you want to get to school and do it before the bell. People are going to work, carpooling, the streets are full, the whole city is active and alive. Monday is a workday.

Tuesday it continues. It's not as hectic, but it continues. Wednesday is mild. On Thursday people are building up, looking forward to Friday.

My favorite day was Friday. A lot of kids were happy because there was no school the next two days, and the people going to work knew this was the last day, there's no work on the weekends. Because Nigeria was an Islamic country, Friday was also a holy day, which made lots of people happy.

Monday through Thursday when I walked to school I would pass Hausa gate men in front of different houses. That was a job Hausas were famous for, standing guard. Each guard would have a radio, each one tuned to a different station, and as I walked past one and then another the songs would change like I was walking up a radio dial. On Friday there was one station that played the rhythmic tone of the Qur'an being recited in Arabic, and every Hausa radio would be tuned to it. All I would hear was one long Islamic chant all the way to school. It was fantastic.

On Friday, Muslim students who were going to the mosque would leave school early. On the way home I would hear the Call.

The Call is a Muslim call to prayer. It is made five times a day, every day, in every mosque. In large mosques there is a minaret; that's where the caller goes to proclaim to the whole city and its people that it is now time to pray. In the local mosques the caller is not a professional, just a brother who knows the prayer. But the same path of Hausa radios that I had walked in the morning would now be playing the most beautiful Call you ever want to hear. It is done by a professional, and it is the example of how the Call should be. I would wait to hear the whole thing.

The caller takes a long breath, stretches his voice, drags the notes, and prolongs the Call to Prayer. It is high and haunting. It rings in the street, from all these radios playing at once. The voice comes from everywhere, and it is so beautiful I would just stand and wait and hear the whole thing. The Call lasts several minutes. It froze me. Anytime I heard it I just stood and listened.

After the Call people go to the mosque. I would stop by one near school and we would recite the Qur'an. I loved the rhythmic and flowing recitation. This was a surprise to me. I didn't even tell my parents about it. Everybody in the mosque was happy because they understood the prayer and they loved the whole rhythm and impact.

My parents were practicing Muslims and I learned Islam from them. Devout Muslims pray five times a day and sometimes I would wake up before sunrise to go to the bathroom and I would find my mother on the prayer mat. I would jump! If she was not in the middle of prayer she was getting ready or had already finished and was just sitting there, contemplating. I would look outside. It was still dark out, and I'd think, Wow, this is a real commitment. Weekend afternoons I'd see her getting ready as I was going out to the field to play, and I would play for a long time and then get hungry and come back inside and see her still sitting there. What kind of religion is that? I would always wonder. I would never have the patience to do such a thing.

My parents didn't force Islam on us. They did not know I was even involved with the faith. It was never really something that we would sit down and talk about, but our values and training and discipline came from their home. My brothers and sister and I didn't know the difference between the Nigerian culture and Islam because in Lagos everything was mixed together. What was consistent was the respect for my parents and their values. They were the source and the final authority. We could be stubborn but when they got serious we had to back off.

Every neighborhood was built around a mosque; it was the cultural center of the community. We would be playing in the field and elderly people walking by would stop and ask, "Where's your dad?" We would tell them he had just left, and they would continue on to the mosque. We wouldn't snicker at them — you respect elders always — but we could not relate to them. Their program was to pray, ours was to play.

When I was twelve years old my parents sent me to boarding school. About three quarters of all Nigerian students go to boarding school; it makes them grow and mature faster. The school I got into was the Aladura Comprehensive High School. *Aladura* means Church of Christ. It was a missionary school. My parents tried to get me into a Muslim program, but this was the only school available at the time and they decided it was more important that I got educated than that I got Islamic training.

The school was in a different part of town, more in the midland of Lagos, pretty far away in the middle of nowhere. I couldn't come home now — it was much too far — so my parents came on visiting day, the last Saturday of every month.

The school was new, and most of the buildings were not permanent. It was like going camping for the whole semester. My dormitory was about a thirty-minute drive from the classroom building. We had to take a van to get there. The classroom building was temporary and built within a lot of trees, and if my friends and I were behind in our homework or weren't prepared for class, we would hide behind the van, ducking down so the teacher wouldn't see us, and one by one give each other the signal — "Okay, my turn . . . *now!*" — and run over more than twenty yards of open ground into the bush.

We just clicked the fence open and within ten steps we were far away from civilization.

I made a lot of friends at school, and some of the kids came from the old country. They had grown up on farms, and once we got into the bush we would dig up yams or potatoes and cook them over a fire and some rocks and just talk. The birds were singing; nobody was around; it was quiet; it was nice.

The bush was thick and sometimes I would get nervous. The other guys were used to it, they weren't afraid, but I was from the city and when I was with them I always stayed in the middle: two of them in the front, then me, then I would get somebody to stay in the back. They knew. One time we saw a snake and they chased that snake and killed it. I didn't go with them. I *ran* back to school.

When my friends returned they told stories of how some of them had been bitten by snakes before and it wasn't a big deal, they knew how to treat it, they were bush doctors, they had all this leaf medicine. I admired their bravery. They were not afraid of the bush, but from then on if we were out there and they said they were going back to class, *I* was going back to class.

After classes it was time to play, and there were a lot of sports at

Aladura. We all played soccer. It was always competitive pickup games and I was a goalkeeper, but I lived to play fullback. I have always been coordinated, and being tall was an advantage because if somebody tried to kick the ball by me I could just stretch out my leg and reach it. Nobody was used to playing with someone my size. They always thought the ball was too far away for me to reach, but I would just slide and *boom,* kick it away. Most fullbacks are not really skillful, they're just fast and tough; once they get the ball they simply kick it out. But sometimes I would take the ball at midfield and work it in. I had the dribbling skills, and I liked to scheme and try the goalkeeper and score. Like a sweeper. I liked to score.

During my year at Aladura a state official came to talk to us with a warning.

In addition to Muslims and Christians, Nigeria had many people who still believed in different gods: the god of thunder, the god of iron. They were idol worshippers. The missionaries and Islam had tried to wipe out all of that, but some people still held on to their idols and maintained that African tradition. Most of them lived in the country.

Christians and Muslims lived side by side in Nigeria, but they all stayed away from the idol worshippers. My parents would not let me go to an idol worshipper's house, but once I did go. There were strange things hanging on the walls, mystic symbols, very heavy. The idol worshippers have rituals. I didn't trust them; I felt uncomfortable. The main reason is, in their tradition they use human sacrifice.

They use the word *kidnapper.* The kidnapper has a piece of power, maybe a ring in his hand, and he goes up to you, hits you in the chest, and you are no longer able to talk; you just obey and follow. They take you out of the state and into the country for their sacrificial rituals.

It sounds like legend but it's not. So many times people were just missing. Children would disappear; they went to school and never came back. That's what this official came to tell us. He was going around to all the schools. There had been an outbreak of disappearances and we had to beware.

The man trained us. "If somebody calls out to you to come get some candy, what do you do?"

"Run away!"

"If someone offers you money, what do you do?"

"Run away!"

Our dormitory was far from the school and every once in a while the van that took us back and forth would break down and we would be given money to catch the public bus. School started at seven in the morning, so to catch the bus we had to leave around six. I didn't want to ride the bus, I wanted to keep the money and walk. It would take a good forty-five minutes to an hour to get there, and a group of students was willing to do it. Early in the morning there would be a trail of kids along the road.

One morning not long after this man had come to talk to us, the van broke down and somehow I got left behind. Maybe I started late or was walking slowly, but I got separated from the rest of my friends. It was not much past dawn, still a little dark outside. You had to walk on the side of the road facing traffic so the drivers could see you and take care not to run you down, and up ahead I saw the bus station, a little hut where people stood out of the weather and waited for the bus. From a distance I saw a man standing there. He was wearing traditional clothes and holding a briefcase.

No one in the country who wears traditional clothing would carry a briefcase. He would have a satchel or a cloth bag, never a briefcase. Very contradictory. I looked over my shoulder; if one of my classmates was there I would just wait and walk with him. No one was coming. The man was standing right down the road. In order to get to school I had to walk right past him.

I didn't want this man to think I was aware of him. He was just standing there, reading a newspaper. I walked a little out into the road.

He moved with me.

It was nothing obvious, just a little shift, a foot or two, but he had cut down my angle.

My hair started to stand on end. I moved farther into the road.

He moved with me.

I didn't want to get anywhere near him. I kept veering to create space. If a car came it would have to swerve to miss me. I was in the middle of the road, and he was closing on me. There was no question.

He made a move.

As soon as he shifted his weight toward me I jumped way out in the street. I wasn't thinking about getting hit by a car, my eyes were on him, and I ran to the other side of the road and kept going.

He was a burly man, not athletic but large. I looked back and saw three of my schoolmates coming. I started screaming, "It's a kidnapper! That man's a *kidnapper!*"

The bus was coming. It stopped at the little stand. The man picked up his briefcase, got on the bus, and it drove away.

3

STAND TALL

THE NEXT YEAR my parents enrolled me in Muslim Teachers College. I didn't want to be a teacher, but it was explained to me that this was a general school that gave students the opportunity to teach if they wanted to pursue that as a career, but the rest of the courses were like any other high school. The dormitory was only about a ten-minute walk from home, so I was comfortable in my old neighborhood.

I made friends quickly at my new school. My two best friends were Johnson and Ola. Ola was short, I was tall, and Johnson was medium-sized. We were all athletes and we went everywhere together.

Every morning the students at Muslim Teachers College, who ranged in age from thirteen to seventeen, assembled to be addressed by the principal before going to class. Of course before the bell rang everyone was running around playing and shouting and having fun. That was the toughest part of every day for me. I couldn't move around like everybody else, partly because the other kids would laugh at me because of my height, and partly because if I was running around the teachers would see me. Everybody else would be causing a commotion, but I would be the one who got caught. So instead, I would stand beside a tree, and Johnson and Ola and I would talk. If they started playing around too, I'd be by myself. As soon as the kids saw a sign of the principal coming, there would be all this movement as classes fell into straight lines in size order. For the other kids that meant the fun was over; for me it meant the pressure was off. We would march to class as the school band played.

Kids teased me because of my height all the time, and at one period of time I was fighting someone different every day.

One day, money was stolen from the locker of the boy who sat next to me. He told the teacher, and the school administrators locked the classroom and began to search it. Nobody moved. Money was missing, they were searching . . . and I was the closest person to the crime. I was the prime suspect, the person with the most opportunity, right there. I wasn't the one who took it, but I felt everyone was suspicious of me. So I went to the boy privately and offered to reimburse him.

The kid took my money. He didn't know who'd taken his, and he thought maybe this cash belonged to him.

When the boy reported that the money had been found the teacher asked him where. He said, "Hakeem gave it back to me." The teacher called me into his office. He was very upset. He thought I had stolen from this boy.

I told the teacher that I hadn't but if the money was never found people would say, "Who's closest to you? *Ah!*" Because I was the closest, people might think I had stolen it, so I'd reimbursed him.

The teacher wasn't satisfied with my answer. He brought me back to the classroom to make an example of me in front of the whole class.

In the hall on the way there we met the boy who had been robbed. "We found it!" he said. The thief had gotten scared and returned the cash. The teacher realized I had been telling the truth, but he still wanted to make an example of me. This time, though, it was as an example of a good citizen. Still, he said, "You don't have to do that, because it's not the right thing to do." For me it was. Just the idea in people's minds that I might steal . . . I'd rather pay this guy the money. Otherwise people might think I had a lack of home training.

Lack of home training. Where I come from there isn't a lot worse you can say about someone. People are proud of their background and their homes. Everywhere you go you represent your family, and if you show a lack of home training you are insulting not only yourself but your mother and father and your entire line. So you have to behave in public and in private in a way that brings honor and not disgrace upon you and your family. That's a requirement.

People with lack of home training talk to elders without respect. They're called hooligans, they're from the street, they're just lost. You can't mix with them or you'll become an outcast. My father and mother wanted to know who my friends were, and if they found one with no home training they wouldn't allow me to associate with him.

It wasn't only street people who didn't have home training. There were a lot of rich people in the city of Lagos when I was growing up, and many of their children were spoiled. I would walk past big houses in the wealthy parts of town and wonder who lived inside. Sometimes I would meet them and be disappointed. These kids wouldn't go to school; they traveled abroad in the summers and relied on their parents' money. I would see the rich kids driving their first cars at a young age, or having their drivers take them wherever they wanted to go. To most of us, having a car in Lagos in the mid-seventies was a sign of great accomplishment; it meant you had finished school, gone to university, graduated, gotten a good job, saved for many years, and finally built up enough assets to afford something worth having. There was no financing for working people in Nigeria; you had to buy a car for cash. But for the wealthy other rules applied. These kids were driving without having earned it. They were not serious. They were living on their parents' reputations, not on their own identities.

Once when I went home on a weekend, an elderly man, a friend of my parents, came to our house. He was almost as large as I was but he was stooped, almost deformed, from years of bending his neck and folding his shoulders trying not to be so tall. I watched him. When he left, my mom and dad called to me. They had seen me stay away from the doorway and knew it was because I felt when you stand by a door and are taller than the door, you emphasize your height. They knew I was having problems, trying to hide, and they tried to reassure me.

"Stand tall in the Nigerian culture," my father told me. The traditional clothes, he said, look best on a man of great height; these people are very unique, these are the men the Yorubas make their leaders. "When robes hang from such a man he looks like a king and is treated with respect." I should be proud of my height, he stressed, not fold up because of it.

I didn't mind standing out in sports. I never felt alone on a soccer field; I felt natural and coordinated and good. I played all the time for my school. For my first two years I was goalkeeper on the soccer team and I ran track. In my junior year the Nigerian sports authority sent a coach to teach us team handball. Team handball was a new sport in Nigeria. A few schools were very good at it, but the game was not widespread. Lagos was the important trade and international center of the country and they wanted to establish the game in Lagos and then spread out from there. Muslim Teachers College was selected as one of the new schools in Lagos to be taught how to play.

At first I wasn't interested. They announced at assembly one morning that they were teaching this new game, but all my time was taken up with soccer and I didn't go. The kids who did go came back the next day very happy. They were all excited and teasing each other about some of the things that they did, and I realized, Wow, I missed something! The next day I went.

They taught team handball in the National Stadium, which all by itself was a reason to go play. The Stadium had been built in 1972 when Nigeria had hosted the All-Africa Games, a kind of Olympics for African countries. It was designed and built by a German company, and it was a huge project — it held about seventy thousand people — and was very beautiful. There was a big soccer field and indoor and outdoor basketball courts; this was a whole complex. The Nigerian national soccer team practiced there. The guards wouldn't let just anybody inside, but if you had a school uniform — not a sports uniform, the uniform you wore to class — you were allowed through the gate. Even then we weren't allowed indoors.

There were twelve states in Nigeria and each one had its own sports teams. The man who had been sent to teach us, Coach Bello, was the team handball coach for Lagos State. Right away I liked the game.

Team handball is tough, competitive. The ball is about the size of a volleyball but heavier; there are goals half the size of soccer goals on each end of the court, and you can dribble, pass, and shoot. There is a goalkeeper you try to throw the ball past and a lot of defenders who try to keep you from scoring. Team handball has its own three-second rule: you can only hold the ball for three seconds and then you have to dribble it again. There's no double-dribbling. There is a zone where you can shoot and a line six meters from the goal that you can't go past. The average game score is about 15–12. I didn't know the rules at first, but I knew it was fun.

The team handball court at the Stadium was concrete. They lined us up in two rows and we practiced.

A lot of people would run or dribble and try to get as close to the goal as they could before shooting. When they were in the nine-meter area they didn't even look at the goalkeeper, they were still working the ball, trying to get closer. They would dribble in, the defense would close down on them, and they had to pass the ball out. But when I got to the nine I always watched the goalkeeper and sometimes I faked a shot. Sometimes I took the shot. I liked fakes. I knew that when the ball hit me in the face it hurt, and I knew if the goalkeeper took the ball in the face it would hurt him too. I realized immediately that this could be a dangerous sport: you don't see the ball, it's so close, there's so much speed, you have to take care of yourself. When I faked a shot at the goalkeeper he tried to block it; when I faked a shot at the goalkeeper's face he covered up, he tried to protect himself. Then I could shoot over him.

Always in soccer we aimed at the goal post. You never shoot straight because the goalkeeper has the better angle; you try to get it as far away from him as possible and then bounce it off the post in the upper corner and into the goal. Most of the time in soccer we would shoot for the post and miss. It was the same idea in handball, but I had better control of the ball with my hands than with my feet, and now that I could palm the ball I could hit more. In the first few minutes I got the idea.

Coach Bello saw me, tall and active, and liked me right away. He asked me, "You played this game before?"

"No."

He put me in the middle, at center. When I got the ball I attacked the goal. You can hold the ball for two and a half seconds before you have to shoot it, but if you dribble you have another three seconds. I was moving, and when I faked, the players ducked. My hands were so big I could wave the ball one way and the other, fake a pass to the left and come back and shoot across my body from left to right. When I had the ball the goalkeeper was watching me; he didn't know where I was going to shoot. My teammates were moving to get the passes. I was passing and shooting, distributing the ball. This was a good game.

My school took up handball that semester and we became one of the top teams in the state of Lagos. Back then the competition between the states was big; there was a lot of rivalry in all areas to see which was best. Team handball was a new sport to Muslim Teachers College but not to Nigeria. Each year there was a nation-wide tournament to crown the Nigerian team handball national champion. That year, when the coaches picked the talent that would represent the state of Lagos in these championships, they picked eight guys from the experienced St. Fimbas team, Johnson, and me. I was given a track suit with *Lagos State* on the back. That was a big honor to wear. I couldn't believe it. Imagine me representing Lagos State!

The national tournament was a couple of months down the road. Before that was the Teacher Training Sports Festival, which was among all the teacher training schools in Nigeria. All the teams — track, soccer, field hockey, basketball, volleyball, handball — would leave campus and go to the competition. The only sport our school was very confident about was team handball. We knew we were going to get a medal. We had gone to the finals and played well against the best team in all of Lagos, there was no way any teacher training school had a chance against us. We practiced for two weeks getting ready and we were sharp.

Two days before all the teams were supposed to get on the bus and leave for the tournament Coach Bello gave us bad news. Because handball was a new sport and we were almost the only teacher training school that had a team, the handball competition had been canceled. The whole team would have to stay home. We could compete next year against regular schools, but there weren't enough teachers' schools to have a tournament.

This was devastating. I could not accept the picture of all the other athletes in the school getting on the bus and going off to this competition without me. I had to find a way to go; I had to find another sport to get into.

I had been so happy with handball that I had neglected other sports, and I hadn't qualified for any other team. The soccer coach had tried to get me to play both but I was having such a good time I had stuck with handball. The first sport that came into my head was basketball. The handball and basketball courts were right next to each other outdoors at the Stadium, and I'd had to pass one to get to the other. I would see the basketball team playing pickup games. I never really stopped; I'd just look and keep going.

The only game I knew that was like basketball was net ball, and only girls played net ball, so I hadn't paid any attention to it. Net ball was played on grass or clay; the players didn't dribble much, just passed the ball around and tried to shoot it through a net that was attached to a pole with no backboard. It didn't look like a lot of fun.

The basketball coaches would sit and watch me play handball, which impressed me: no one had ever paid that kind of attention to me before. And after the game they would talk to me. They always tried to get me to play for them, but I was getting a reputation as the star of team handball and it was fun, so I wasn't interested in changing. They would see me walking by and say, "This is your sport, this sport was made for you!" Every time the head coach saw me, at the Stadium or on the campus, that's what he would say. I would laugh and go away.

This time I went to him. I had to find a sport to play.

The head coach's name was Ganiyu Otenigbade, and when he saw me coming he laughed at me. It was a friendly laugh. He welcomed me. "I told you all along this was your sport!"

I said, "I want to play."

He looked at me. I was 6′8″. He said he had room for me on the team. "Don't come here thinking you're just going to this tournament. This is permanent." I didn't know about that, but at least now I had a game to play. This was wonderful.

The basketball team was at one end of the court and the first thing Coach Ganiyu did was take me down to the other end and teach me how to shoot a lay-up. He showed me the steps: one, two, and go. It looked easy when he did it, but I couldn't get my feet together, I was more worried about scoring. He said, "Don't worry about that, just get the form, the technique."

I looked down at the team at the other end of the court and I saw that even for our team, making a lay-up was a big deal. Some guys who had been playing basketball the whole semester had to concentrate to do it, and when one went in everybody would clap. I saw some others who had been playing for a while: they would drive and put it up, make free throws. One guy was just idly dribbling, putting it between his legs, behind his back, without looking at the ball. How did he do that without looking? I thought that was pretty cool.

Coach Ganiyu was not only the Muslim Teachers College coach, he was the head basketball coach of Lagos State. He had been a guard on the Nigerian national team, an excellent ball handler and passer. He knew how to play, and he showed me how to shoot. Then he gave me the ball. I shot a couple of air balls. "Don't push it," he told me. "Shoot it with the wrist." Ganiyu was very sound with his fundamentals; he loved fundamentals.

And all the while that he was showing me, he was talking. "This is what you play now," he said over and over. "This is your sport, it's a big man's game." He was selling me this game. Coach Ganiyu told his assistant coach to work with the team, and he and I worked alone together for two hours. I was very impressed with this extra attention: the head coach of the whole Lagos State team was working with *me*. And he kept saying, "You are the kind of player, the kind of person, that we need in basketball. If you knew how valuable you are to the sport you would not even think about any other sports. This game is played in *America*."

When he mentioned America he saw my eyes light up. All the cool guys had T-shirts with American college logos on them. Whether it was in academics or athletics, for a Nigerian kid America was the goal. "This is an American game," he said. "There are a lot of tall people there."

"Taller than me?"

He started talking about American games, American sports. Everything sounded so cool.

Coach Ganiyu looked down the court. "You see all these guys right here? They've been working night and day just trying to improve, but you can cover in two days what they've been doing for years. There are some things that you'll be able to do that they will never be able to do." The players couldn't hear him but Ganiyu had assigned his point guard, the best player on the team, to come to our end of the court and rebound the balls for us, and *he* was agreeing with the coach. It all seemed too good to be true. Now all I had to do was learn to play this game.

That first day Coach Ganiyu laid a foundation. He knew from seeing me play handball that I was active and coordinated and had the aggressiveness to play. I was a competitor. What I had to learn was the rules and the fundamentals.

"You see this zone right here?" he said, stamping an area around the basket. "This is big man's territory. The little guys are not supposed to come into this territory. Anything that comes here, you throw it out. Anytime the ball goes up, you box out, you rebound. When you get the rebound you never bring the ball down, you look around for these little guys."

He tossed the basketball to the point guard. "Shoot the ball."

When the shot went up, Ganiyu backed me away from the basket, making sure I could not get around him. When the ball bounced off the rim he jumped and grabbed it with both hands and held it at his chest, his elbows straight out from his body like thick, sharp branches. He was a little man but I could see that he played big.

"You rebound *wide*. Real big and wide, and look around." He twisted his body fast and hard; anyone who got caught by his elbows or forearms was going to get hurt.

"Now you try it."

The ball went up. I jumped and got it and stood there.

"No matter how you get the ball you've got to protect it," he told me. "The big man cannot just get the ball and be careless. Just getting the rebound is not enough, you still have to *fight* to clear it. *You have to clear.* That's why you use your arms; if the other guys get caught with an elbow they will back off. If they're not afraid of you, every time you get a rebound they will come and slap it from your hand. You have to clear the ball firmly, then they will know you; when you get a reputation those guys won't come close."

Ganiyu showed me how to pivot, come down with the ball and make one big step around. "Pivot *big*," he said. "*Wide*. Real big men make people think they're even bigger. 'This is a big man!' "

Every time he explained I understood. The picture was very clear.

I already had some of the basics. Handball has three-second and double-dribble rules, and you bounce the ball to dribble it. But the handball itself is much smaller, and we always passed with one hand, not two. Coach Ganiyu flicked a pass with two hands that hit my chest.

"You have to be alert."

I was amazed that with just a snap of his fingers he could make the ball go full-speed and direct. I tossed it back to him. *Boom.* He snapped it to me again. I loved the snap of the wrist and the speed of the ball. I tried to do it like he did. "You can feel the ball leave your fingers.

Snap it!" Back and forth, with speed, he taught me to do a chest pass. "With a big man you do that with an overhead pass." I snapped one at him with two hands from over my head. It was so much fun.

In handball you throw the ball to shoot, so when I tried to get the ball in the basket I threw it. "No, no, you have to release with your fingertips and shoot with your wrist." I tried a couple. Then he showed me how to post up. "Right here," he said, putting me a few feet from the basket. "Now, when you get the ball, turn around and shoot it. Don't even bring it down, just turn around."

We practiced, just me and the coach and the point guard getting the balls, for about two hours and then went back down to the other end of the court to where the team was scrimmaging. "Watch the center," Ganiyu told me, "watch what he's supposed to do." The center wasn't tall, he was just the tallest guy on that team, but he was doing everything the coach had just got through telling me.

When practice was over Coach Ganiyu and I were talking. He was very happy with my form, my jumping and balance. He said, "You would be a unique player for this sport. A player like you doesn't come along very often. Your potential here is tremendous. I've never had a big man like you to work with." I was excited but I didn't think I had done very well. I was disappointed that I had missed so many shots. "Don't worry," he told me, "you'll make those soon. When you get the form down, that's going to be a lay-up. The form is what's important." I didn't think I was that good and I certainly didn't see the potential they were seeing. I thought, Can they be serious? But they motivated me to do even better.

Ganiyu made a big impression on me, even the way he dressed. His warm-up suit was different from any one I'd seen. It had an American college logo on it. I had seen Lagos State, Oko State, all the Nigerian teams, but he was wearing something that came from the United States. His shoes were Converse All-Stars. Chuck Taylors. Everything about him was different. His T-shirt was from an American college. He told me that when his former players traveled outside the country, they brought him back gifts from wherever they'd been. He listed players who were now in the United States, in cities like Chicago and Miami. I didn't know if they were studying or playing basketball, but I wanted to follow right in their footsteps.

I was excited. This *is* the sport. I can't wait!

As well as learning the game I also had to learn to be accepted by a new group of people. There was competition on campus over who was the best sports team, and since I represented handball some of the basketball players weren't very glad to see me. I was worried that my friends on the handball team would be disappointed in me because I had decided to go to a different sport, but nobody stood in my way.

Two days after I stepped on the court we left for the teachers college tournament. At these tournaments people always went nuts. The Hausas are very knowledgeable about the game; they're serious about basketball and a lot of sports. The north wants the best, and they have been the best in sports for a long time. Lagos gets its players from different parts of the country, but the north are always the best. When they played in the finals the north always won. I didn't know anything about this since I wasn't into the sport, but I learned the whole background on the way there.

When American coaches and players come to Nigeria they almost all go to the north, where they are taken very good care of. Coach Ganiyu was a fantastic coach, and he was an African, so there was a lot of politics. He had to get serious with everybody; he had to report back to the Lagos State committee on what happened, and the team's winning or losing was a reflection on him. This tournament was in preparation for the national sports festival, where the best guys from these regional championships competed to represent the country on the Nigerian national teams in the African championships. When you looked at the Nigerian national team, most of them came from the north.

The major lesson I learned at the teachers college tournament was that I had a lot to learn.

I didn't start for my team. I just had the basics, just what I had learned in two days. I could box out, I could pivot. In the games I blocked a lot of shots and got a lot of rebounds and helped the team on defense. But I was always in foul trouble. I wanted to get everything and the other teams would get me up in the air with head fakes and I would come right down on them. On offense, almost every time I shot the ball I got it back in my face. I didn't know about faking, I just turned around and tried to shoot. It had worked against my teammates because, just as my coach told me to do, I never brought the ball down and they weren't tall enough to contest me. But the other teams' centers stuffed it almost every time I tried to put the ball back up.

The team to beat was Kano. They had tall guys who could play, they had good guards, they could run the floor, they had tricks. And they had the best center in the tournament. He was very skillful, an excellent player on offense who had a lot of nice post moves. On defense he was powerful, an intimidator. He had been playing for a long time and he struck fear into all the teams. I never did know his name; everybody just called him Big Man. He was very proud of that nickname, Big Man. I had always tried to hide from my height and he impressed me; this was the first time I had ever heard somebody be called a big man and be proud of it.

When we played Kano in the first round I got a chance to play against him. He was 6'5", so I was much taller than he was, but he was Big Man and he really played big. I did well enough on defense, I contested his shots and he had a problem shooting over me, but on offense I wasn't effective. He was very active, very physical; he put his hands in my face and made me work. I would get the ball, turn around, and shoot just as I had been taught the week before, and he would block my shot *every time.* Kano was so superior, they beat us easily. In fact, Muslim Teachers College did not advance past the first round.

But we wanted to see who was going to win the tournament; it was either going to be Kano or their big rivals, Sokoto, another northern state school. My teammates and I were really looking forward to this match because we knew it was going to be very tough. We all sat together at the finals and watched how the game played as it was supposed to be played. Big Man was powerful underneath the basket and intimidating all around it. He posted up and defended and rebounded, and no one could stand in his way.

Kano won, they were the champions. And the difference was Big Man.

4

THE INTERNATIONAL GAME

COACH GANIYU PICKED ME to play basketball for Lagos State! Coach Bello picked me to play handball for Lagos State! Coach Bello wanted me to give up basketball.

I told him, "No."

I had just come back from the Teacher Training Sports Festival and I knew I couldn't give it up. I saw how important the big man was to the team, and I realized that what Coach Ganiyu had been telling me all along was true: basketball was a big man's game. I told Coach Bello, "If I had to choose one, I think I would choose basketball."

He got nervous. They made me captain of the Lagos State intermediate handball team. (There were the intermediate and the men's teams; we were the younger.) That was a high honor, which I accepted with pride, but he kept pressuring me to quit basketball and I kept refusing. Coach Ganiyu put me on the intermediate team also and was saying to me, "With time you will quit handball naturally. You will see that your future is right here." The coaches talked and decided that I could play both.

I could not believe it! All of a sudden my status had grown from somebody who was just trying to make the team to someone who two big sports were fighting over. Each of them gave me a team jersey, though I only got one warm-up suit and one pair of tennis shoes, since it's all for the same Lagos State. But that warm-up suit was *prestige*. You could not buy this; to have one you had to be a real player — to represent the state! And you had to be doing it right then; once you were no longer on the team you had to return it.

By March of my senior year we were training for the national sports festival. Ever since I had begun playing on the state teams I was in and out of school. The principal loved it; it put the school's name on the map.

We practiced for two weeks and the routine became very difficult. The handball team trained in one camp and the basketball team was in another. I had a bed in both and had to shuttle back and forth. Johnson had been chosen goalkeeper for Lagos State, and I was glad to be with him.

My handball game changed. With my new basketball skills to draw on I became more confident, I had more strength; the one tournament I had been to gave me experience in competition. I felt there was nothing I couldn't do in handball. The whole team knew we were good. If any team was going to win a gold medal for Lagos State, it was going to be the handball team.

In basketball I had a lot to learn, and I was learning every day. I didn't feel any pressure; handball was my specialty, this was just my second sport. This was a team that didn't really need me, they had always gone to the finals and played Kano. Sometimes they won. It was a strong rivalry.

These were quality players. All of medium height, the forwards ranged from 6'1" to 6'5", and the guards were very quick and smart. They would penetrate and dish off or pull up and shoot jumpers. They were happy to see me because now they had what they needed: height.

On the court in practice what I loved the most was blocking shots. The guards would drive or the forwards would post up and shoot, and I would wait until the last second and pin the ball on the glass. That moment was the ultimate, when they would come and you had perfect timing and just *erased* them. Especially when a guy was going for a lay-up and thought he was home free. Not many of our players dunked; they would lay the ball on the glass and I would come out of nowhere and just smack it right there, *bam,* against the backboard, and then snatch it away.

I started playing tricks with them. I would let them go by me and think they were in and then turn around and pin the ball over them. Once they saw they couldn't go over or around me they started testing my skills, my reflexes. I used my reflexes in soccer and in handball, and they were sharp; the more they were tested, the better. Players tried to shoot over me, lots of arc, but when I went up and got those balls they accused me of goal-tending. They couldn't believe I jumped that high. The guards tried to penetrate and dish off, but I caused a lot of three-second calls because once they got into the paint nobody really wanted to shoot and get stuffed, so they looked around, faked, dished off, and couldn't get back out. I would jump and recover and jump and recover; my confidence was soaring.

My defense was solid, and Coach Ganiyu began working on my offense. There was only one guy who could dunk on our team and he had to take a running start from half court to do it. The guy showed me one time but I couldn't get the hang of it. Coach Ganiyu told me how — take two steps as if you're going in for a lay-up and then jam it through the hole — and gave me the ball. I could get up high enough but I did not have the technique to throw it down once I did. He tried to teach me for weeks but I got so nervous when I couldn't do it that I would put pressure on myself — "I'll try not to miss it next time," I told myself — and when the next time came I would miss it again. I kept worrying about the steps and could not get my feet to take the right ones. If I planted my feet I could not get high enough; if I had to run I would miss my steps.

One day at practice the coach was talking to all the players and I was standing under the basket, holding the ball. I was listening and looking at the basket, listening and looking. I was 6'8"; that basket looked so short. I stepped under the goal, bounced the ball one time, jumped up, and dunked.

The coach was talking, so he didn't see. The players saw.

"*Wow!*"

"What happened?" the coach asked.

They told him.

Coach Ganiyu stopped the whole practice. "I didn't know you could do that. Do it again!"

I got really shy. I was afraid that I didn't know how I'd done it the first time. I didn't want to fail in front of everybody.

"No, no, you have to do it again."

While he'd been talking, everything he said had begun to make sense. I just did it naturally, and it was very easy. I was not running, the basket was right in front of me, all I had to do was take one step and put the ball in. I did it.

I must have dunked a hundred times that day; that's all I wanted to do after that. From then on my offense was just to dunk the ball. And I just loved it. I would post up very deep, as close to the basket as I could get, and when I got the ball I would take one bounce and finish it. In practice I would just dunk it, dunk it. Block a shot on one end, dunk on the other. That was the best feeling, to pin the ball, run fast down the court, and dunk it. I was very aggressive, very confident, very happy.

Now I had some offense. Every once in a while I would turn around and shoot. I would miss. My shooting was still a gamble and my teammates playing against me would give me that shot all the time, take away the dunk and give me any other kind of shot at all. Once in a while I would take it; most of the time I would miss.

With my new offensive skills I was ready for the national sports festival.

The festival was held on the campus of the University of Ibadan in Oyo State, and it was like going to the Olympics, so many different athletes playing so many different sports. The whole place was in use, all the fields, all the courts, and here were athletes from all over Nigeria. It was wonderful.

Lagos was the favorite team to watch, both handball and basketball. Newspapers were writing about us, people were talking. Everybody started saying that Lagos was going to win the gold medal in these two sports.

They were talking about me, as well. I was new in both sports. Last year at this tournament, I wasn't even there, I wasn't in sports at all. Now all of a sudden the crowd was hearing about this guy from Lagos. I didn't think of myself as a celebrity, I was too busy finding out about the guys I would have to play in these games. I was fascinated by this sport.

We got to the finals in handball and basketball, and they were both held on the same day. The coaches made a deal with each other: Since the handball final started first and the basketball team had been good before I ever played with them, I would play handball first and then join the basketball team.

We played the handball final against Anambra State. They were Ibo from the east, very strong, very rough, very physical this tribe. They didn't have a lot of skills but they had strength and they had gotten to the finals without technique but with power. They tried to wear us out. When they shot the ball they tried to hit us in the face. They came with the elbows, very dirty. The referee kicked two of their players out. It wasn't a difficult game but it was a tough one, and we won. We won the gold medal.

I was so happy. I couldn't believe we had done something so big. All my teammates were jumping up and down but I didn't get a chance to celebrate. The basketball finals were going on and I jumped into a van and left for the other gym. I pulled off one jersey and put on another. Johnson came with me; he wanted to see the game. The van plowed down the middle of the street and — *pah, pah, pah* — horns were telling everyone to clear the way.

The court was outdoors, very primitive, and the crowd parted as the van took me straight to the sidelines. The second half had already started, and when I stepped out the whole stadium started screaming. Oyo was in the south, and they always disagree with the north. So even though a lot of people didn't like Lagos — we're too diverse, too worldly — we were from the south also and they supported us.

We were playing Kano State. They always won, or almost always, and we didn't want it to happen again. My teammates had been down by a lot early in the game but they had pulled to within four points when I arrived. As soon as I climbed out of the van, Coach Ganiyu called a time-out and put me in.

The crowd took over; they were wild, and it was for me. I hadn't realized this would happen; I was so surprised. I didn't even think of myself as a basketball player, I was a guy learning how to play. But the crowd had been waiting for me and gave me a lot of energy, and I did my best not to disappoint them.

It was our ball and the whole tone of the game changed. My teammates' confidence was up. You could see it in the way they pushed the ball down the court, really aggressive, with the crowd behind them. And I was very happy to see how happy they were. We didn't want Kano to win this time.

Kano was a very smart, structured team. They had played together for a long time and they held the ball, they didn't make mistakes. You had to beat them; they didn't beat themselves.

And they had Big Man.

It had been three months since I had played against him at the teacher training games and I respected him a lot. He had been physical and intimidating, and he had dominated me totally. So far in this game he had been dominating our entire team.

So why, when he tried to bull me inside, was he so easy to stand up to? In three months I had gotten used to the physical game. A half hour before, in handball, Anambra had been more physical than Big Man. I moved him aside. I was very surprised when he got the ball in the paint and turned and tried to shoot over me. No fake, no move, just tried to shoot over me. I swatted it away. It was very easy to block Big Man's shot.

The crowd buzzed and hummed; they were astonished. No one had done that to Big Man.

He was overshadowed for the first time and I think it took a lot out of him mentally. From that play onward it wasn't the same Big Man. He was not aggressive and he stopped taking his shots; he would make his move and rather than go strong to the hole he would pass to a guard. It wasn't the same Big Man I had played three months before.

Kano's guards, realizing their center had been shut down, took charge and tried to drive on me. That was exactly what we wanted. Our guards played very good defense, and Coach Ganiyu had structured our offense so that when someone got by them I would come from the weak side and block the shot. Our guards would get the loose ball and run down the court and score. Kano was getting a lot of shots blocked, and every blocked shot would result in a lay-up. We intimidated them, our confidence grew even more, and we built a lead quickly.

But Kano was a smart team. They called a time-out. Then they came back. Big Man started playing a little better, but their guards gave up trying to drive and started shooting from the outside instead. And they were good. They cut into our lead. The game was very close all the way.

We were up by one point with only seconds left to play. Kano had the ball. If they scored they would win. A guard drove. The referee called him for traveling. The clock ran out. Lagos State was the champion. We won the gold.

It is a great honor to stand on the court and receive the gold medal in the national sports festival, but we didn't get that honor. As the horn sounded, Kano supporters streamed from the stands and began beating the referee. They believed he had cheated them. The players ran too. We ran to the van while on the court people from the south were fighting people from the north and the referee was running for his life.

Officially, we won, but there was no ceremony, no celebration; all we got was a riot. They sent the medals to us in Lagos.

My mother could not believe it. There were articles in the newspapers every day about how Lagos State was doing and a picture of me with two gold medals on my chest. My mother had been keeping the clippings.

For weeks after I got home I couldn't wait for school to be over so I could run right over to the Stadium. Before the finals, if Johnson and I wanted to play ball we had to create stories for the guy at the gate so he would let us off campus. We would tell him anything, just make up stories about how it was really okay for us to leave. We were always nervous that someone would catch us — it was against the rules for students to go off campus. Now we had the perfect excuse: We were representing the school.

I was in love with basketball. At the Stadium there were some of my teammates from the Lagos State team and other good ballplayers, and I played three-on-three half-court pickup games four hours a day for the whole month and really began to develop my skills. Mostly I worked on my inside moves as a center in the post. I worked and worked and worked. If you lost you had to wait for the next set to play, and I didn't like losing or waiting.

Late one afternoon a man was watching me play. He was dressed in traditional clothes and stood in the corner of the Stadium and watched the three-on-three games for a long time. When they were finished he called to me. He was very complimentary. "You play well," he said. "Very well. What's your name?"

I told him. The guy was 6'10" and I could tell from his accent he was an American. We talked basketball for a while. He had played in America and he knew what he was talking about much better than I did.

"Where do you live?" he asked.

I told him my house and my school. He asked if I wanted a ride. I said sure. I didn't want to go back to school because I wasn't supposed to be off the campus, so he drove me home.

He drove the National Sports Commission's car, the car they give the coaches. It was green and white, the colors of the flag of Nigeria. His name was Richard Mills and he was from San Diego, U.S.A. We talked in the car and he seemed like a very nice man. He loved Africa, our culture and traditions, and in his time here he had become more like the natives than most people I knew. He no longer wore tracksuits or T-shirts with college logos, he dressed traditionally. He had changed his name to Olawale. It means "He returned home." Olawale was the head coach of the Nigerian national sports coaching institute.

When the car pulled into my neighborhood all the kids knew it had to be either a coach or some official in the government. Just for that car to be in our neighborhood was a really big deal. When it stopped in front of my house, all the people playing in the field stopped and stared and came over. When I came out they were very impressed.

Inside our house Olawale was very respectful to both my parents and me. He spoke slowly, just pointed and waited a while and said something else. He told them, "You have a unique son." He paused. "Have you seen him play?"

My parents said, "No, we have not."

"Your son . . . has a lot of potential. He will be . . . somebody. This will be the beginning."

My father was amazed. He had been reading about me and my gold medals; now the national coach had brought me home and was talking about me.

"He will be a great player," Olawale told him. "One day he will go to America and play." My father looked at him. "Not now. In the future I will take your son to America with me."

I couldn't believe he was saying such a thing. He had been complimentary in the car, but he opened up much more strongly to my parents. "One day I will take him to America with me, for college."

Wow! I was full of energy. I didn't know he felt that way. My father was excited too. He was impressed with how Olawale had adapted to Nigerian culture, and he was happy that Olawale was taking a special interest in me.

As he was leaving, Olawale told me to come to the Stadium the next day.

That night I couldn't sleep, and I had trouble concentrating in class all the next day. I got to the Stadium as fast as I could. When I got there Olawale told me I should practice with the national team.

The national team. This was not the intermediates or the juniors. These were men, the best basketball players in all of Nigeria. They played *inside* the Stadium on hardwood floors, not outside on concrete. This team played in the African championships that determined which nation would represent Africa in the Olympic Games. I walked to the sidelines.

"Who's this?"

Olawale had been hired as head of the national coaches' institute to teach Nigerian coaches about the different parts of the game in the classroom and on the court. As part of his contract he could coach the Nigerian men's team. So he wanted to coach the men's team, and he had invited me to try-out camp.

What he didn't know, and what the directors of the coaches' institute didn't tell him, was that the same coaching job had been promised to another American coach who had been working in Nigeria for fifteen years and knew the whole network of people and already had players in camp. His name was Oliver Johnson.

Oliver Johnson had seen me at the intermediates tournament but hadn't invited me to try out. Olawale told me to go change and get in there and practice. When one of the government officials realized that the two coaches were fighting he called them to the side. While they were talking I looked around.

The best basketball players in Nigeria were on the floor playing three-on-three. Until recently I hadn't known anything about basketball at all. I hadn't seen any games on television, I didn't know about foreign players or Nigerians. Now that I was playing I was in the grapevine, and fans on the sidelines would tell me about the great players in Nigerian history. I had heard about these guys but I had never seen them up close. Here they were.

Everyone who followed basketball knew they all had nicknames. The small forward was called the Big Four; I didn't know his name but that was his number. He was about 6′5″ and very, very strong. He would go into the paint and *occupy space.* Next to him was a man they called Stone. He was tall, Stone, and very skinny. Skinny guy and a sharpshooter. He could drive, too. If he hit you or you ran into him and there was contact, his elbows were *sharp.* He was all bone, very bony but strong. When he got a rebound the crowd would say "*Stone!*" and everyone under the boards would back off because when he cleared the ball he had cut people.

But the man I noticed most was the idol for all Nigerian basketball players, a very big, very strong, very skillful 6′10″ center with a beautiful jumper and excellent moves. His name was Yommy Sangodeyi, but no one ever called him that. When he took his jump shot everyone in the stands would shout "*Yommy!*" And when it went in — it always went in — they would shout "*Basket!*" That's the only name anyone ever called him: "Yommy Basket!"

I had heard about "Yommy Basket! Yommy Basket!" for months now but I had never seen him in person, I'd never seen him play. To me he was a legend.

They took me over to meet him.

I was so shy I could hardly talk. He shook my hand and said something to me but I wasn't really listening, I was looking at his arms. They were huge. He was about five years older than I was and you could tell he was a weight lifter because his chest was so big. He was an athlete; I could understand right away why he was such a great player.

I practiced with the men that day and I knew they were *men.* They banged like men, they played fast and hard, they played a physical game that I had not experienced at the intermediate level. They were very tough. It was only when they were talking to each other that I noticed the respect that one gave to another. It was more than the respect you give another teammate, it was a matter of rank. And discipline. They were a disciplined team. When practice was finished they went to the baths, and as they came out and were dressing in the locker room I saw that most of them were putting on uniforms. Sergeants. Generals. It was only after the practice was over that I realized most of these men came from the Nigerian military.

That was a different ball game. In Nigeria the military is the final authority. People who go into the military are very tall and strong, and they can handle you. People get nervous when they see soldiers in Nigeria; anytime you see soldiers you straighten up. They have that much power, and they're strong and they will beat you. None of my friends had ever gotten arrested by the military but we would see soldiers in the street walking around the neighborhood and we would always give them room. The military had a basketball team, the Scorpion, and most of the national squad came from there. Only a very few civilians, like Yommy Basket, were allowed on.

At the end of the day the coaches came back. They had made a deal: Richard Mills — Olawale — would take the junior team and Oliver Johnson would coach the men. Olawale was disappointed, but the junior team tournament was coming in a few months so he would have his chance. And he had used his power to get me on both teams, the junior team and the men's. He told me, "Most of the players here, except the established ones, still have to make the team. You are on it; regardless of how you play you'll be on the team. You're a project. You have more potential than any player here and you're so young, we will train you early and you will represent the country for many years."

I was very shy. Particularly with girls. Way before I started playing sports there was a girl in my high school who I really admired; her name was Joyce. She and I were connected, I never understood how. If I was in class and would look outside the window, as if by natural instinct, she would be walking by. All I saw was Joyce. And when I would look at her she would look at me. But only for a moment.

She had a very innocent look; you could tell she was good. That was part of what I liked about her. I saw how some of the other girls behaved, all giggling or smart-talking, and I saw how Joyce was, and I thought Joyce was the best girl I had ever seen.

We never spoke. Just smiled at each other quickly from a distance and that was it. I didn't know how to approach her, to talk to her, so I wrote her letters. My best friend Johnson was in Joyce's class so I would write a letter, put it in a book, and give it to Johnson to give to her. She would reply through the book, give it to Johnson, and he would give it to me. In our letters we would talk about school, or just "How are you doing today?" She was smart and was always concerned about how I did on my tests. She was shy and I was shy and there was a likeness.

If I wrote Joyce a letter in the middle of the day I could be sure of getting an answer by the time school was through. I looked forward to writing to her and I looked forward even more to seeing Johnson because I knew he had the book and I knew what was in the book. Johnson spoke to her and I would always ask him, "What did she say? How did she act when she received it? Was she smiling?"

I had heard her voice when she talked to other girls, so I knew how she sounded, but I couldn't talk to her. When I looked at her she looked the other way; when she looked at me I couldn't even meet her eyes. But our relationship was beautiful. I was satisfied with the excitement and anticipation of getting her letters. I would receive one and read it and read it again and again. Sometimes I'd write two letters in a day, one at lunch break and one again after class, so I would receive one back in the afternoon and get a reply before I went to the dormitory at night. It was very exciting.

Joyce brought joy to my life without any effort, just by being who she was. I looked forward to seeing her walk by. And the more attention my sports activities got at school, the more important it was to me to have the attention of someone I admired so deeply. As I got famous she didn't step forward and say she was my girlfriend, she stepped back and became even more reserved. I admired and respected her. She became someone very special to me.

In early summer, when school was on holiday, the men's team gathered for two weeks at a training camp to practice for an international tournament. The camp was not far from school but they had us all check into a hotel. I had never been in a hotel before. This was like a big house with a lot of different rooms and a nice dining room. It was very personal. Johnson would come by all the time and we would hang out.

The men were always sending me on errands. They wouldn't buy from the hotel store because it was too expensive and right on the street it was much cheaper, so two or three times a day they would send me to pick up some minerals or juices from the store, or down to the traders to buy them things. I was the baby to them and I couldn't say no.

They also liked my position on the court; I was a project, I wasn't competing with anyone for playing time, so I was not a threat. They could see how I was trying to block shots, how I was making people change their shots. They could see improvement, they could see that I could compete.

But I couldn't win. They were too strong and they would take advantage of me. I was skinny — by this time I was 6'10", 180 pounds — and they knew how to use their bodies. For instance, if I caught one of them under the basket and there was no way for him to shoot over me, he would just jump in to me. I would bounce off and they would make the basket. They might miss the basket sometimes but I would never block it.

I wanted to block everything and they knew it. They faked, I jumped; I would jump at everything, so they would get me up in the air and dish off and I would jump again. I jumped about three times on every shot and I would get tired. Then they would score easily. Even though these people were smaller and older than I was, they had been playing for years, they were smarter, and they had more experience.

I didn't get too discouraged, though, because they did the same thing to Yommy Basket. He was a shot blocker but he wasn't blocking shots easily, they made it very difficult for him and he had to work for it. I watched Yommy Basket and he was patient, he knew how to position himself and when not to jump. I was too anxious; when they faked I would just go.

I got my blocks from the weak side when I could surprise them. It wasn't like on the junior team when I could block any shot; the men had to make a mistake for me to succeed, they had to come in and not see me. Then I would pounce. I was a boy but I made an impression. They could see that I would not give up, that I kept on fighting.

The team training was very disciplined, very military. Each morning the trainers would wake us up, the van would take us somewhere and drop us off, and we would run three miles to the Stadium. Everybody was supposed to follow the leader and run at the same pace to get there but I was always last. I had never run miles in my life! It was dark outside, I didn't know my way, and I didn't want to get left behind. But these guys, this was a vacation for them. When they were on duty in the barracks they'd go about eight miles in the morning. That was standard! After that they would go lift weights. When they came for breakfast they would eat *big!* This was an army.

After two weeks of training we went to France to play some friendly matches.

We played some club teams and they beat us. I didn't even get in the game. Then we arrived at the international competition in Morocco. This was all of Africa we were playing against. That's when I saw all these *big* teams. Big guys! The Sudanese — I couldn't believe it — tall, *tall* guys, much taller than I was. The Egyptians had *two* seven-footers. I thought I was tall but that was the first time I saw so many others my height. I had no confidence.

Our first game, I warmed up and did all the stretching and shooting before the whistle, but I was a backup to Yommy Basket and he was the best. I just sat down and got ready to watch.

Halfway into the first half Yommy Basket got his third foul. The coach didn't even look down the bench, he just called my name.

I couldn't believe it. This was an international tournament and he had called me. I was shocked. I was very scared. I took off my treasured warm-up suit. When you're nervous everything tenses up, and my back was tight. I went in.

The arena was very noisy, the crowd was loud. Of course the home crowd roots for the home team, and each country has its own fans, but in international competition people come from all over and at most games they're not for any one team, they just love the game and watch any team that's playing. There was tremendous noise in there.

I felt like I'd never played the game before. The whistle blew and the ball came in bounds and I saw opportunities, but I was so nervous I was just lost out there. The ball came out, I got the rebound, put it up to the backboard. I couldn't believe it went in. This wasn't a game where I was dunking and running, it was a different feel, like everything was going on at once and I wasn't ready to play.

We lost but the coach was very impressed with my performance. I wasn't. I didn't think I'd played that well. I saw that basketball could be played at a much higher level than I'd thought and I wanted to play the game at its best. When I sat and analyzed the game I saw things I could have done differently. It was encouraging to know that if I hadn't been nervous there were things I could have done. My biggest question was whether I would be able to do it when the opportunity came my way again. I felt I could play at this level but I would need a second chance to prove it to myself.

When I got home I got letters from several Nigerian universities saying they were interested in having me attend and play basketball. Representatives came to my house and offered scholarships and made promises to my parents that they would make me feel comfortable. I was going to college!

A few months later Coach Richard Mills, Olawale, selected the junior team. He called me up and said, "You're my captain." Playing against the men had been difficult, international competition against men had been difficult, but when we started practice, playing against other kids under eighteen, everything was so easy. It was fun; against the men it had been work. All the things I had seen the men do and hadn't been able to do against them, I now had lots of openings and opportunities to work on. I started dunking so hard that people were getting out of my way, so I had more space and could dunk even harder. I looked skinny, but after training and practice I was stronger than I looked. I was dominating the junior team. I hadn't expected it and it was exciting.

We had a solid team, all these tough Hausa Kano and Sokoto players, smart and experienced point guards from Lagos and Kano who could push the ball and make good decisions. Good drivers, good shooters, good defenders. People were telling us, "If you guys don't win something, don't come back to the country."

The junior tournament was played in Angola, and after the first game I was big news in all the papers because I had dominated. I scored a lot of points, mostly on dunks; I blocked shots, got rebounds.

Tournaments in Africa are tough and the only team we were afraid of was Angola. The home team was supposed to win, and if they didn't it would be a disaster for the whole tournament. I was new to international competition; I didn't know this. The coaches and more experienced players knew — they said if the games were played in Nigeria it would be the same way — but everybody played hard anyway. We watched Angola play the first game and we knew they were going to win. The cup had been brought there and you knew that one way or another they were not going to let it leave the country; they were going to keep it.

I had a great time. It was so much fun playing with a good team, dunking, blocking shots, rebounding, winning. I scored sixty points in one game against Togo — my best ever, with fifteen dunks! — and in the early rounds we dominated.

In the semifinals we played the team from Central Africa. I had seen four of their players in Morocco on the Central Africa men's team and they were experienced and tough. Their two top guys were Anicet Lavodrama and Fred. Lavodrama was a shot blocker, aggressive, very physical, and he could jump. Fred was very short and very skinny. At the hotel we saw the whole team eating together and we saw this little boy. Who is this little boy with the team? we thought. Before the game the little boy was taking lay-ups. "You see that kid? He's going to play." We laughed. Then they called the starting five. He was starting?

Even before the game began the crowd loved him. He was so small he was like a mascot. Then the game started and he destroyed our guards. We had two very tough guards but they couldn't keep up with him. Fred. He was the most exciting point guard I had ever seen — the most exciting point guard I have ever seen *still*. He had a good shot and his ball-handling skills were excellent, pushing the ball down the floor, penetrating, dishing off, throwing lobs. He was throwing alley-oop lobs to Lavodrama — this was the first time I'd ever seen that done.

I played well but Lavodrama was tough and he neutralized me while Fred dominated everybody. It was a good game, close, tough, but they had the better team. It was like playing against men again, and they beat us. I was disappointed that we lost but I knew there was no way we'd beat Angola. I was glad that Central Africa was going on to play Angola because I didn't want to play them, it wasn't a game you could win.

The finals were classic. When Angola was leading, everything was smooth, but when the game got close and it looked like Central Africa might take the cup, then we started getting scared. The crowd wasn't throwing ice on the court, they were throwing stones. That was a warning. Everybody plays to win, but during the course of the game we knew that if Central Africa beat Angola there would either be injuries or some player might get killed. It was a common practice. English soccer crowds are not very different. The referee was scared for his life. Literally for his life. He wasn't calling traveling when Angola traveled, he let them foul when Central Africa went for the basket, he stopped calling any fouls that might prevent Angola from winning.

It was life-threatening. Still, the game was close and toward the end I saw that more and more police were being brought out to surround the court. Then things got out of control. Even with the army there, people were throwing things and trying to get on the court. *But the army was Angolan* and they wanted their team to win, so the army was on the court swinging and hitting the officials too! It was not a game you wanted to win. Angola came away with the championship.

5

COMING TO AMERICA

I WAS IN MY ROOM after we lost to Central Africa when some-one came in and said, "There's a white guy waiting for you downstairs, he wants you to come down."

"Who, me? Nobody knows me here."

"He asked for you."

"Okay."

I didn't go down. I thought it was a mistake.

A few minutes later the guy came back and gave me a note. *I am Coach Christopher Pond,* it read. *I coach Central Africa. We played you guys this evening. Would you please come downstairs and talk with me?*

Christopher Pond was around forty-five years old, about six feet tall, not an athlete. A T-shirt-and-sneakers kind of guy. He might not have looked impressive but Central Africa had just beaten us and they were obviously well coached. He asked me to join him at his table in the hotel restaurant and I was curious.

An American coach! All African basketball players paid attention to American coaches. This was like speaking to an oracle, basketball from the original source.

"You played a good game, a tough game tonight," he told me. "I was impressed with the way you played us. We brought a men's team and you played us very well. With a little more experience you could beat us." He was very complimentary.

"I hear you are a student?"

"Yes."

"And you just started playing seven months ago?"

"Yes."

He couldn't believe it. Coach Pond told me he came from North Carolina originally and traveled worldwide just to teach and promote the play of basketball in different countries. Most recently he had been in Africa but until this year he hadn't seen me in any of the tournaments. Even at the men's tournament he hadn't noticed me. But from what he had seen here he was very impressed. He asked me, "What are your future plans?"

"Well," I told him, "the biggest goal now is just to finish school."

"What year are you?"

"This is my senior year."

"Have you been approached by any universities in Nigeria?"

"Yes."

"No. Don't go to college in Nigeria. Go to college in the United States. That's where your future is, that's where you should go."

I liked that. I liked what he was saying but I didn't know anybody in the States, I didn't have any contacts in the States. "That would be nice. I would like to go."

"Really? What do your parents do?"

"They sell cement."

"If I arranged for you to have a scholarship and a visa would your parents buy you a plane ticket?"

"Oh, yes."

He was talking crazy. To get a visa in Nigeria was *big*. Everyone who finished high school and wanted to go to college automatically tried to go to the United States. They worked in Nigeria and saved all their money just to try to go to the United States. It was *the* destination, the measure of success, the championship. Business, education, fashion; the new generation felt that whatever you wanted you could find it in the United States. But the American embassy was very strict and made it very difficult; they didn't want you to come and just stay, they didn't want any illegal aliens.

To get a visa you had to provide proof that you had already been accepted to college and could afford to pay school fees. I knew so many who had gotten rejected. Getting a visa was something people always talked about, so when this guy told me that a visa was not a problem I couldn't believe what he was saying. "What do you mean the visa is no problem?" I told him, "It's the biggest problem in the whole country."

"Okay, tomorrow morning, ten o'clock, meet me here and you and I will go to the American embassy in Angola. Can you get your passport?"

"No, the team has it."

"Okay, that's all right, don't worry about it, you just be here, I'll take care of everything."

I couldn't sleep. I couldn't believe what I was hearing. This man had everything — visa, contacts. No, it was too much for me to handle. I wasn't worried about the plane ticket. I had to make my parents buy it for me. I knew they could afford it, and even though it was a lot of money for them I was 100 percent confident that if I got the visa my parents would come through. I was much more worried about the visa.

The next day we drove to the embassy and we were expected! Christopher Pond had already been there that day. They gave me a badge so we could walk around inside and we strolled past the cafeteria and up to the consul general's office on the third floor.

Christopher Pond, though he was coaching Central Africa, was an American, and like any American with a problem overseas he went to his embassy for help. He had traveled the world and was truly a basketball ambassador. But he was an unusual man. Unlike most other people, he was not interested in the material or financial, he was not looking to make money on a deal; he really wanted simply to spread the game of basketball. He loved the game and he taught the game and he scouted talent all over the world. He knew coaches all over the world and sent players wherever they could do each other the most good.

In his travels Christopher Pond had met many important and influential people. Sports would get him through the door, but after that people just liked him, he would make friends, he was a very likable guy. I had known him for less than twelve hours and I liked him already.

The consul general himself greeted us. The top guy.

He was a big basketball fan. He closed the door to his office, loosened his tie, and he and Christopher Pond talked sports like buddies. He was familiar with the tournament. Mr. Pond said, "This is the young man I was telling you about. This man, in America, he will be able to get a scholarship."

"What do you want me to do?" the consul asked.

"Well." He reached into his bag and pulled out his address book. This Christopher Pond was an unusual man. You could tell he was a traveler; everything he had came from different parts of the world. This book was very heavy, very different — it was thick and almost falling apart from use. In it he had names and numbers for American basketball coaches from Division I to junior college, as well as names of international coaches from all over the world, and he said he knew them all. "I have a lot of friends who coach in the United States," he said. The way he said it, I had no reason to doubt him. "I know if I call two or three of them we can get Hakeem here a scholarship."

Christopher Pond didn't have any money but the consul gave him a telephone with a direct line to the United States. I couldn't believe it. I was sitting there and this man was calling coaches across America saying, "I've got this African guy."

I didn't know the schools. The first couple said their head coaches were at lunch, could Mr. Pond call back in two hours. He called St. John's University and whomever he was speaking to said, "Your player can visit." They didn't commit one way or the other, all they said was, "He can visit."

"If he visits and you like him will you offer him a scholarship?"

"Well," they told him, "he can visit."

Christopher Pond had met Coach Guy Lewis of the University of Houston over the years and had sent him one player who had not worked out. The last time they had seen each other Christopher Pond had said he was going to Africa and Coach Lewis had told him, "If you see a player that can play, send him to me." So he called Coach Lewis.

"Coach, this is Christopher Pond. I'm in Africa and I've got a young man who is seven foot standing right here with me." I was 6'11" but seven foot sounded better. "He's seventeen years old. If he was in America today he would be All-American, you could not even talk to him because so many schools would already be ahead of you." He went on like that for a while.

"But we have a problem. The only problem we have now is the law — U.S. law. According to the embassy he cannot get a visa unless they know that if he is qualified you'll agree to give him a scholarship."

Coach Lewis said, "Well, if he's everything that you say he is, then I'll give him a scholarship."

That's what the consul general wanted to hear. He liked Christopher Pond, he believed him, but he didn't know him before that day and he wanted to confirm from America that this man had credibility. The consul spoke to Coach Lewis directly.

"Hi, this is Coach Lewis, head basketball coach, University of Houston. I know Christopher Pond and if this guy is actually what he says we will consider him for a basketball scholarship."

That was all he needed.

"This is what I can do," said the consul. "Because Hakeem has a Nigerian passport I cannot give him a visa from Angola. But I will call the consul in Lagos and we can arrange it from here."

So as we were standing there the consul got on the phone to the American embassy in Lagos. The consul's name in Lagos was Mr. John Bennett. "I am sending you Hakeem Olajuwon, a young basketball player, a Nigerian citizen . . ." He explained the situation, that he had talked to Coach Lewis, that everything was set. "When he comes, please take care of him."

When he got off the phone the consul told me, "When you meet with Mr. Bennett at the embassy in Lagos take your plane ticket and your passport and you will get a visa." He gave me his card and wrote *Bennett* on the back. "Show him this card and he will know who you are." Then he asked me, "Have you ever seen American basketball?"

"No."

"Let me show you."

They had a video at the embassy of one college game, an NCAA championship between UCLA and some other team. I watched a big white seven-footer play center; I didn't know who. I tried hard to believe what I saw. The crowd, the arena — it was all so huge. I'd been hearing about UCLA because I had seen players wearing T-shirts with those letters on them. I didn't know what it stood for but I knew that UCLA was world-famous. I saw only a little part of the game but I was impressed. I was so happy.

When we were driving back to the hotel I couldn't come down from the amazement. All this was a dream. Christopher Pond said, "Don't tell anybody on the team about this. If the officials know, they will not want you to leave. You're a project; they want to develop you to represent Nigeria for a long time. Once you leave what are the chances of you coming back to play? So you have to be very quiet." He warned me, "Don't let anybody know."

Christopher Pond said he would make some more calls and arrange for me to visit several schools to make my chances of getting a scholarship even greater. He said he would be taking a team through Lagos in about three weeks and would meet with me then, and we would go to the embassy together.

I was in an oceanfront hotel in a beautiful country and all I wanted to do was go home so I could tell my parents. But there were still a couple of days to go. My life was changing right in front of me. Things that I thought were impossible were happening, one after another. I was representing my country for the second time and I was getting used to it. I was getting publicity, the fans liked me. It was all very difficult to believe. I turned the consul general's card over and over in my hand. When I took this to the embassy this was a visa; this was *gold!* And somebody on the other side of the ocean had promised me a scholarship. Now, how could I tell my parents this and have them believe me?

I was Most Valuable Player of the tournament in Angola. The team's progress was reported constantly in the Nigerian newspapers, and my parents were excited and proud and the whole country was happy. All my parents' friends were congratulating them, neighbors started coming to our house just to talk to them and discuss when I had started playing. It was such a high honor to be on the national team and represent Nigeria. No one in the neighborhood and maybe only two people from the entire Lagos State team were on the national. I didn't realize that my parents were getting all this feedback until the National Sports Commission van dropped me off at home and the whole neighborhood rushed over to meet the players.

I was comfortable with the celebrity because, from handball skills to basketball, it had grown slowly, without my really realizing it. I had always stood out because of my height but now I was becoming comfortable with my athletic reputation.

When my father came home from work he began asking me questions about how the tournament went. They had been keeping newspaper clippings and he had read that I had scored sixty points against Togo. It was the most points I had ever scored. Togo sits right next to Nigeria, and my big game made news. My father asked me, "How do you score sixty points against a defense?" I was very shy. I was surprised that my father was asking because he usually said nothing about sports. He followed sports and had played when he was growing up, but he followed soccer, not basketball. I told him that from the beginning I had been very excited — just up and down, dunk, dunk, dunk — and after a while the players were just backing up and getting out of my way. He was so proud.

I had to ask my parents for a great sum of money. I knew my mother would do anything for her children's education. She had made a promise and commitment that all her children would be educated, and if you asked her for something having to do with school she would always give it to you. For your personal use she could say no, but for school she always said yes.

My father was another story. You really had to prove you needed something before he would give it to you. I didn't want to talk to him about this alone, so I talked with my mother first.

"I have something that's very important for all of us to discuss," I said. She went to my father and said, "Your son said that he would like to say something, he would like to discuss something with us. Let us hear what he has to say." They were shocked; I had never approached them this way before.

But before I spoke, they had news for me. They didn't know about sports, they knew about academics, and while I had been gone three college coaches had come to visit and offer me scholarships to schools in Nigeria. They were excited. "Well," I said, "that's one of the things I was trying to discuss with you. I met a coach, an American coach, he's a white man." If you say "a white man" in Nigeria they take you more seriously. "He is from the other side so he must have contacts. Everything he tells me he has done there is legitimate. His advice to me was to not go to college in Nigeria."

My parents had been excited that I was going to college, but once

I said *not in Nigeria* they could not picture it. They didn't say anything, they were listening, but the expression on their faces was not favorable.

"He said I should go to school in America."

"In America?" said my mother. "You don't know anyone in America."

I told them about the phone calls and the scholarship. Now they had to take my word.

"Do you know how difficult it is to get a visa?" my father said. He told the story about his first son's terrible problems getting one. I had heard that story many times.

"This man has already arranged everything," I told him. I showed them the consul general's card with the name Bennett on the back.

"What if they don't give you a scholarship?" I knew my father was thinking of the bottom line.

I didn't get an answer that night. My father wanted to wait until he spoke to Christopher Pond.

Three weeks went very slowly. When Christopher Pond's Central Africa team came to Lagos I went to the court where they were practicing. I saw the boys I had played against. They didn't know what was going on, they just waved.

Christopher Pond came and hugged me. He told his assistant to continue practice and we went inside.

He said, "You look very happy, what happened? Did you talk to your parents?"

"Yes, I talked to them."

He was excited. "Did they buy you the ticket?" The way he asked, I couldn't say no.

"They said yes."

"Really!" He gave me a high five. "Did you bring your passport?"

"No. I didn't know if you'd be here."

"Okay, got any money with you?"

I had about ninety dollars, a lot of money for me to have in my pocket but it was left over from the allowance the team had given us at the tournament. My parents had also given me some spending money, so I had given half back to them and kept the rest. "Okay," he said, "we're going to the embassy. Did you bring the card?"

"No, I didn't bring anything. I didn't know if you'd be here."

"It doesn't matter."

I remembered the name Bennett. It would stick with me forever.

John Bennett was happy and excited to see me. He was a basketball fanatic and had been reading the Nigerian newspapers and heard many good things about me. Christopher Pond was like my press agent, he kept saying, "You have not seen anything. This guy started playing basketball eight months ago."

"No!"

"If you saw how he moves . . ." I was very surprised that I had impressed him so much with my playing. "In a couple of years," Christopher Pond was saying, "you will be hearing about this guy. This is history right now that you are watching."

"Do you have your ticket and your passport?" Mr. Bennett asked.

"I —"

"He didn't bring it," Christopher Pond interrupted, "but that area is covered. We just came to visit because I will be leaving tomorrow and I wanted to make sure that you two met and everything would be taken care of."

"Oh, there's no problem. All Hakeem has to do is show us his passport and ticket and we will do the rest," Mr. Bennett told him. "You do have your ticket."

"Oh, yes, sir."

We agreed I would return on Monday with both.

When we finally left, Christopher Pond and I caught a taxi and he told me the other schools he had contacted that would like to see me. There was Houston and St. John's, and he had added Providence, North Carolina State, and Georgia. "You can buy a ticket to visit three or four if you want. We don't know which will give you a scholarship, but the one you should definitely visit is Houston. You'll like the weather there and Coach Lewis is a good coach and a good friend of mine. Have you heard of Elvin Hayes?"

I said no, so he started telling me the history of Houston and Elvin Hayes, how they beat the big man Lew Alcindor and UCLA in 1968 in the Astrodome in one of the great games of the century, and how Coach Lewis had coached all these players who had gone on to the pros. "You'll like Coach Lewis," he said, "he's a great man."

He wasn't worried about the coach liking me. "Coach Lewis will give you a scholarship," he told me. "I have seen you play. In fact, you should not even play your first year. You should redshirt and just work out. Beef up a little, learn the system, then you'll have four good years."

By the time Christopher Pond dropped me back at the Stadium he was so happy he was hugging me and giving me high fives. The taxi didn't want to drive inside so I jumped out in traffic and started to run. As I was running Christopher Pond stuck his head out of the window and shouted, "*Houston, Houston, Houston!* I'll see you there in January. *Houston, Houston, Houston!*"

Inside, some of the players were choosing up a three-on-three game. I knew I wasn't supposed to say anything but I could not hold it in. "I think I'm going to be going abroad," I told them.

"Oh sure, yeah, sure." They didn't believe me but they picked me anyway.

My play was different. I was playing with joy! The whole day ran through my mind and I thought about basketball on another level — Houston versus UCLA, big arenas, thousands of fans, championships, the U.S.A. This was all in my head and I totally dominated that game, grabbed everything, dunked everything, ran the floor like I was flying!

Our team beat everybody. It was winner-stay-on and we stayed on the floor a long time. Teams were taking turns coming at us but they knew they were going to lose. As they sat on the sidelines waiting, two guys looked at the game and said, "You should go to America."

I said, "I am."

Everything I saw was America. Walking home I was smiling, picturing competing in a big tournament. My heart would not rest. The long walk was very short; I looked up and I was almost home. I jogged across the field and my toes barely touched the ground.

I was confident that there was no way my parents would say no to me. It was all in their hands. I came in so excited.

"Where have you been?" my mother asked.

"Remember that coach I told you was coming to Nigeria?" I asked. "I saw him today."

I could tell from her expression that she was not pleased. She didn't want to talk about it. She sent me on some errands right away. I wanted to talk but she kept the day full — do this, go there. Then my father ate his dinner.

If my mom didn't want to talk about it maybe my father did. I went to him.

"Remember the man I said was coming? Well, he came."

"Really," he said. "Have you talked to your mom?"

Finally I got them together. I told him about the five schools that wanted to see me. My father didn't know any of them. He said, "I have other obligations to be concerned about. It's difficult to make this commitment to you alone." I knew he had to pay my sister Kudi's school fees to the American University in Cairo. "There is no guarantee that any of these schools will give you a scholarship and this is a lot to spend."

I was scared. I had been taught never to go outside the family for money and now I had nowhere else to go.

My mother stood up to leave the room. She touched me on the knee to come with her. In the kitchen she said, "I will talk to your father more about it."

But of course I worried. My future was in their hands and if they said no I had no other solution.

Everybody went to bed that night except me. I sat on the couch in the living room with the lights on and watched television. After a while I turned the TV off. I couldn't sleep; my mind was jumping, dreaming of America. I had energy, my heart was pounding, and I couldn't rest.

Sometime around three o'clock my mother woke up and was walking to the bathroom when she saw the light. She went to turn it off when she saw me sitting wide awake in the same clothes I had been wearing when we'd spoken.

"How come you're not sleeping?"

I didn't say anything. I couldn't. I could hardly move. But she saw, she knew. She said, "I will talk to your father in the morning. If he says no then I will give you the money for the ticket myself. Now go to sleep."

I couldn't believe I heard those words from my mother. Throughout my life my mother never wanted her children to doubt her; when she made a promise to us it would always happen. It was a guarantee. I was so happy. I was going to America.

Within a minute I was asleep.

I was the first one up the next morning. My mother wakes up every day at six o'clock to pray and she was surprised to see that I was awake and had brought her the kettle of water to wash before prayer. Normally all the kids slept right through it. She prayed and then went and talked to my father. Between them they decided what to do. My father would give me spending money — if I was studying in America I would need to have money in my pocket — and my mother would buy me the ticket.

My mom called to me and I sat with her as she counted out the cash from her bankroll. This was principal, savings, money you did not spend. The ticket cost around $4,500. She gave me all the money she had.

I took the cash to the ticket office immediately, unrolled the money from my sock where I had hidden it, and bought an airline ticket: Lagos/New York/Houston/Atlanta/North Carolina/Providence/New York/Lagos. It had to be round-trip, that was what the embassy required. They wanted to be sure I was coming back.

Before I left the house my mother told me, "Make sure you give yourself at least ten days before you leave." She knew that the way I was feeling I would get on a plane that afternoon. So I scheduled my flight to leave in exactly ten days. I looked at the ticket. It said *Lagos/New York. New York!*

I went from the ticket office straight to the embassy.

The line for visas at the American embassy in Lagos went on for a city block. They open applications at nine each morning and stop at eleven, then you have to come back the next day. Some people sleep there just to be first in line. It's always like that, every day. I walked past people in their best hopeful dress, all fighting with one another, trying to impress one another that they have connections. They didn't like to see me walking by and they assumed that I, like everybody else, would be turned around and sent to the end of the line. "Where's he going?" "He'll be back." "What does he think he's doing?" Policemen were patrolling up and down, back and forth.

The soldier posted as security at the embassy door didn't blink. He stood so still you wouldn't think he was human. I walked up to him and asked for Mr. Bennett. He didn't speak but the look across his face said, How do you know Mr. Bennett? I showed him the card of the consul in Angola and he saw it was a genuine American embassy calling card, then he turned it over and saw Mr. Bennett's name on the back. I said, "No, no, I'm sorry." I exchanged the card for the one Mr. Bennett had given me. The soldier was very impressed that I had two. He radioed to someone inside.

John Bennett himself came down and met me at the door. I was worried that he wouldn't remember who I was, wouldn't let me in, but he was excited, happy to see me, and shook my hand. "How're you doing today?" He gave me a badge that let me walk around inside the embassy. "How's everything? You practice today?" He was asking me all kinds of questions and I was answering. I was very honored that he was treating me this way.

"Did you get a ticket?"

"Yes, yes."

"Good, good, good!" I gave it to him. "Where's your passport?" I gave it to him. Mr. Bennett called his personal secretary and gave her my ticket and passport — "Take care of this" — and kept on talking. Got it from me, gave it to her, he wasn't worried about a thing. "What do you think about your chances in the U.S.? Do you think you'll do well?" I tried to concentrate as I watched Mr. Bennett's secretary walk away with my entire life in her hands.

"I have not seen the competition but the way Christopher Pond was telling me, he thinks I will do fine."

We went to Mr. Bennett's office. The phones were ringing, we were talking; he told his secretary to hold all his calls. I wanted to talk about the visa — was I going to get it? — but all he was talking about was basketball. "Which cities do you think you'll like?"

"I haven't been to any of these cities so I don't know."

"Well, it's cold in Providence, it's very cold there. You like cold weather?"

"No, sir, I don't think so."

"Houston is warm, maybe you'll like that."

Mr. Bennett's secretary came back in. "Do you have $1.50?" she asked me. A visa application costs $1.50.

"Oh, don't worry about that," Mr. Bennett told her. He signed for it, then he signed my visa. I looked at the piece of paper. It was a multiple visa; I could go in and out. And written by hand on my passport was: "Prospective student, under consideration for basketball scholarship, University of Houston." I didn't see the word *considera-tion,* didn't see it at all. What I saw was *student* and *basketball schol-arship.*

Before I left the embassy I secured my passport, ticket, and visa in my clothes. When I walked by the line everybody was looking at me and I pretended nothing had happened. I took a taxi home.

It was the middle of the day and no one was in the house. I took out my ticket and passport and visa, looked at them, read everything — *New York!* — put them back, then hid the whole package under my mother's bed and went to the Stadium.

I was playing loose, I knew for sure I was going. That's when I told the guys, "I got my visa today."

"You got a *visa?* To where?" They didn't believe me. People say it all the time, it's everybody's dream.

"To America."

My mother couldn't concentrate at work. She just made sure her customers were delivered their goods and then came home. She asked my brothers if they had seen me today. They said no. Then she got worried. When I got home she was cooking in the kitchen.

"Did you buy the ticket?"

I made the saddest face I knew how, but when I saw she was going to believe me I said, "I'm just kidding. I got it!" I went to her room and reached under the bed. "These are the tickets." She looked at them. She couldn't read English. "Did you get a visa?" she asked.

"This *is* the visa. Look!" I read it to her. Then I read her the passport: "Student, under consideration for basketball scholarship." She knew what *scholarship* meant. She started crying and praying. "This is from Allah, this is from God! How many days do you have before you leave?"

"Ten days."

"That's good. You did well."

When my father read it he shook his head. He said, "This is God's will." My father does not show much emotion, he's very subtle, but he smiled. They were proud of me. And because my parents were proud of me I was very fulfilled. I was proud of myself. That kind of feeling is a blessing. There has been nothing in my life before or since that compares with the feeling of that day.

I couldn't concentrate in school. People's whole lives depended on how they did on their final exams — they were scared, would they go on to university or go out and get jobs? — and that was what I had expected for myself. But now it didn't matter, all I had to do was pass. I tried to prepare and study, and I did all right, but I was already gone. News started spreading around campus, and my best friends Ola and Johnson were both happy and sad. We had all thought we would always be together. I would miss them, but they were glad for me that I was going to America.

Yommy Basket's Ogun State men's team came to play Lagos. I saw him and said, "I have some news for you."

"What is it?"

"In a week I'll be leaving for the United States."

He looked at me. He didn't know me very well but I'd said it so casually that he had to believe me. All his life he had been trying to come to America. He knew he should be a professional player and he had been promised so much so many times by people who had not come through for him; clubs that told him they would send him abroad to play, and had let him down. He had been disappointed often. He didn't trust anyone.

"Have you told anybody?" he asked.

"No."

"Don't. Don't tell any of these people. You have a ticket?"

I told him the whole story. He couldn't believe everything had happened so quickly. This was his dream and he'd almost given up on it.

"Don't forget me."

I promised him I would do my best. "This would be the first time," he said. Then he started talking like a ballplayer.

"Make sure when you get there that you fight hard. Let them know there are ballplayers in Africa. And that we are tough. You go ahead, I'll be right behind you. Just pave the way and I'll come back you up." Yommy Basket hugged me.

The hardest part of leaving was that I had to tell Joyce. I wrote her a long letter. I said I was going to the United States in ten days, I told her how much I had enjoyed our relationship and everything we had meant to each other. It was like a fantasy. I wished her the best of luck in school. I didn't know if she was going to become a teacher or not but I wished her the best of everything. I gave her my address at home in Nigeria and said she could write me there and keep in touch through Johnson.

I didn't get a letter back.

On the last day, as school was closing, Joyce was determined that we should talk. We were both outside on the schoolyard and I saw her walking toward me. I walked toward her and almost tripped, my feet missing my steps. I didn't want to speak, I was afraid of saying the wrong things. I knew her through her letters but I didn't know how to talk to her.

She was medium height and when I walked next to her I towered over her, which made me even more uncomfortable. It's not like she had stood next to me every day and gotten used to it; no, it was very different. She'd always seen me from a distance — and I'd seen her from a distance.

We couldn't look at each other. When she spoke I looked at her face but she looked away, when I spoke she watched me but I could not look in her eyes. We kept walking.

"Did you get my last letter?"

"Yes."

"What did you think?" I could tell she was very sad but she didn't say anything. "I left my address. I would still like to continue to write you."

Joyce said she would give her address to Johnson and he could give it to me. Her family was from midwest Nigeria and she didn't know if she was going to stay in Lagos or go back home. We didn't talk for long. She was crying. I knew I would miss her.

6

HOUSTON! HOUSTON! HOUSTON!

NEW YORK! I had heard about and read about and dreamed about this city for so many years and now I was going to land in it.

The terminal at John F. Kennedy Airport was crowded, active, full of movement. I was amazed to see how everybody was in a hurry, and I didn't feel comfortable at all. I had a paper in my hand that told me where to go. My first stop: St. John's. I had a telephone number but I had no experience with telephones; in Nigeria you go to the address. I was simply going to go to the campus and find the basketball office. I stepped toward the glass doors and they slid open without my having to touch them.

It was cold! New York in October 1980. I had on slacks and a cotton shirt with a button-down collar, no sweater, and the way the wind hit me . . . I had never felt cold like that. I ran back inside.

Three taxi drivers were fighting to see who would take me. I didn't trust any of them. I had been warned, "Don't just get in a taxi, that's where a lot of the robberies occur." I said, "I'm waiting for somebody."

"Who are you waiting for?"

"Somebody's coming to pick me up."

Finally they left me alone. I stood in one place for ten minutes thinking, What should I do? I didn't want to get any farther into New York City. I had seen all I needed to see. Christopher Pond had recommended Houston highly, it was next on my itinerary; I walked to the ticket counter.

"Can I go to Houston today?"

The man behind the counter looked at my ticket. "You're not sup-posed to go to Houston for two days," he told me.

"Can I change it? Can I go earlier?"

He looked at his schedule. "Sure. The next flight leaves in about four hours."

"Okay." I checked my bags. Now I had my hands free and four hours to wait in New York.

I looked around the terminal. This is America! I saw people like me. I could tell they were first-time travelers too, that I was not the only one. I began to look at the people.

The first thing I noticed was that there were a lot of black people but they weren't African. They had a very different feel to them. I had met some black Americans in Africa. Most of them worked at the embassy. They would come to the Stadium every once in a while and play pickup games with us. We thought any American could play better than we could; most of the Americans could shoot. Now I watched people as they passed and thought everybody played. That guy is a point guard. He'd be a power forward.

But where were the giants? I had been told for the past year that America was the land of the tall people. I was expecting an entire nation of people my size — where were they? I saw height — Americans seemed taller than the average Nigerian — but I didn't see anybody even close to me.

The black people spoke a different language than what I was accus-tomed to. In Nigeria we all wanted to talk American street slang but I couldn't understand a word of it.

Someone passed by and asked, "You play ball, man?" I told him, "Going to the University of Houston."

In Lagos about 90 percent of the population is black, but there are also English, Chinese, Lebanese, Americans, Europeans. It's an in-terracial melting pot. At the airport I saw a mix of black, white, and other races. I saw more white people than I'd ever seen in one place before. I didn't know how they would respond to me but there was no problem, just something different. The hours passed quickly. Then my flight took off.

I looked down as the plane was landing in Houston. It was sunny, there was a lot of land, a few houses, trees. The airport was organized and people walked calmly. Everything was settled. I felt comfortable right away.

I would have found my way to Coach Lewis without announcing myself but I was not expected for another two days, so I telephoned.

"Coach Lewis, this is Hakeem Olajuwon."

"Where are you?"

"I am at the airport."

He was surprised. "Take a taxi to the basketball office, University of Houston. We will pay for it when you get here."

I don't say the letter *h* very well. I don't do it purposely but if a word begins with an *h* I drop the sound, and if it doesn't I add it. *Hand* becomes *and, ankle* becomes *hankle.* I got in the taxi and told the driver I wanted to go to *"University of Ostin."*

The taxi driver was Nigerian. That was a welcome surprise. "You are going to Austin?" I didn't know. "Let me see what you have." I showed him the paper with the address on it. "Oh, you mean *Houston."*

"Ouston."

"Houston." He made me say it until I got it right.

We found the basketball office and I got out of the car. Almost immediately a round black man came charging out of the building. "Let me help you with that." His name was Terence Kirkpatrick and he was an assistant coach on Coach Lewis's staff.

I thought I was expected but it turned out that the University of Houston didn't have high hopes for me. Christopher Pond was an international ambassador of basketball but the last prospect he had sent Coach Lewis, from Venezuela, was supposed to be a 6'9" forward and turned out to be a 6'4" guard who didn't make the team. According to Pond I was seven feet tall, but maybe I was 6'6". So as far as Coach Lewis was concerned, if I arrived, fine; if not, that was fine, too.

But he was looking out the plate-glass window as the cab pulled up and when he saw me unfold out of the taxi, all six feet eleven inches of me, he paid attention.

Coach Guy Lewis looked me up and down. I was young, I moved well, I seemed coordinated; with my body, my walk, I looked like I should be able to play. He was smiling; he had gotten more than he had expected. Coach Lewis was in his late fifties, about 6'4", and had played basketball for the University of Houston. He had a big, lined face and leathery skin that made him look like he had been through a lot. He spoke with the authority of a man who runs things, a teacher from the old school. I had to concentrate to understand his accent but he was being very nice to me. We talked in his office for a little while — "How was your flight? How's Chris?" Small talk — and then he assigned Terence Kirkpatrick to be my guide.

Coach T was a friendly, rather round black man from California and he talked to me like he just wanted to make my life comfortable. He laughed a lot and had an easygoing way about him. I liked Coach T right away.

There's a day in October before which basketball coaches are not allowed to supervise practice sessions. It's a National Collegiate Athletic Association rule. I didn't know anything about that rule — I hadn't even heard of the NCAA — but the coaches did. All of that year's Houston Cougar basketball recruits were outside running on the athletic field track, working on their conditioning, and the coaches were going over there to watch but not instruct. Coach T said, "Do you want to come with us?" I said sure.

Out on the track these guys were serious! There were about eighteen of them. They would run around the track three times, then stop, wait for everyone, and start again. When they finished they ran wind sprints. I had never really done any conditioning except for the two weeks I'd spent with the national team. This reminded me of when I was running with the soldiers.

When the running was done I was introduced to the guys. At home when I was playing at the Stadium I had been hearing for a year that "You're taking advantage of us because of your height. You're so tall you should go to America, that's where all the tall guys are. You think you're tall, you see guys much taller over there." I was worried that American players would tower over me, but I also had a satisfying picture of America in my head: "You mean I can actually walk on the street and feel comfortable and not out of place? Wow!" The first thing I noticed was that although some of the players were taller than I was, I was taller than some of them. I had enough height to compete.

The players had seen this tall guy standing in his street clothes next to the coaches. They didn't know I was coming, they had no idea who I was or if I could play — I'd just appeared.

Coach T made the introductions. Everybody shook my hand and

said the same thing: "What's up, man?" Down the line, everybody: "What's up, man?" That was the first American phrase I learned: "What's up, man?"

At home, when somebody asked you "What's going on?" you said, "Everything is cool." At home: "It's cool." So that's what I answered. To everyone.

"Everything is cool."

"It's cool."

"Cool."

"Cool."

I could see them start to laugh at me. Like, "Go ahead and say 'What's up?' to that guy and see what he says." Who is this guy? I started getting mobbed with "What's up, man?"

And I was bowing. That is what you do in Nigeria when you meet someone new. You shake hands and bow. It's a sign of respect. By the time I got done bowing and saying "It's cool" I was something these guys had never seen.

The players went to the weight room and I followed them. At home only boxers and wrestlers used weights and I was looking at these players doing sets, taking turns. You could tell they had all been thin and were developing muscles. I was just skinny. I was in my street clothes so I didn't even try to join in, but I could see this was a tough program.

From there the players went to the gym. Coach T asked me, "Do you want to play with them?"

"Yes!" I was very excited. "I would *love* to play with them!" I had been traveling eighteen hours from Lagos to New York to Houston but all I wanted to do was play ball. They called the equipment manager to take me to the locker room and give me shoes, shorts, and a jersey.

I was very discouraged right away. New shoes? I couldn't play in new shoes.

In Nigeria I played basketball, handball, soccer in size thirteen tennis shoes. I was 6'11" and my feet were much too big for size thirteen, every toe was folded under my foot at the last knuckle when I ran, but that was the biggest shoe you could find. Day to day I wore sandals, which were made locally, but they didn't make tennis shoes in Nigeria, tennis shoes were imported and you had to find them. Size twelve was the biggest they sold in the country, people went to Europe to get size thirteens and bring them back. Size thirteens were like gold. Just to find a size thirteen could take months, and then they could be on the whole other side of the country. You would hear about one pair on the grapevine and you would send for it, and it would take three weeks to arrive, if it arrived at all.

Yommy Basket had one pair of fifteens and the only other shoe bigger than thirteen that I'd seen was once at the junior championships, when Richard Mills gave me a used pair of his own size fifteens. Very generous. They had padding and cushion, very soft leather. That's how I scored sixty points against Togo. I wore those shoes gratefully until they gave out.

It usually took me about three months to break in a pair of size thirteens. And even then, at every time-out or when I was on the bench, I'd take them off. The rubber and canvas never really stretched; every time I ran down the floor I hurt. I just played in pain every day until I got used to it. I was going to bring my tennis shoes with me but Richard Mills had said I'd find plenty in the States. So when the manager said he would give me a new pair of shoes I felt that my college career was over before it began. I couldn't play against Americans in new shoes.

The equipment manager, Ralph Adams, gave me the shorts, jersey, and socks. "What size shoe do you wear?" he asked.

"Thirteen."

He looked at my feet. "Are you sure?"

I didn't know what to say. I didn't want to ask for something they didn't have.

Adams went into another room and brought out a leather thirteen. Wow, he has thirteen! And leather! Before I put on a new pair of shoes for the first time I always felt the pain psychologically. I began to put them on. Adams looked at me.

"That's too tight," he said.

"I know," I told him. "It's going to take me a while . . ."

"No, wait." He went back into the other room and brought out a fourteen. I had never seen a size fourteen shoe. I tried it on. It felt better than the thirteen.

"That's still too tight," he said. "Has your foot grown, like, in the last day or two?" He took the box away from me. Then he went and brought out a fifteen.

I was quiet after that. In the whole of Nigeria you could search and not find a fifteen for me. This was a miracle.

He had given me two pairs of sweat socks and when I put the fifteens on they were still too tight. "Wait a minute," I told him. "If I just take off one pair of socks —"

"No, no, no, no."

He brought out 16s.

My mouth was wide open.

I put them on and for the first time I had shoes that fit my feet perfectly. I didn't even know I was wearing shoes. No pain!

I didn't care who I was playing against then, I was so happy just to find shoes. I jogged down the hall. When I got to the gym I kept looking at my feet and jumping, jumping, jumping.

My jersey was white with a red *Houston Cougars* and a number on it on one side, and if you turned it inside out it was red with white. This is what was big at home, fashionable. White shorts. They gave me a wristband for this pickup scrimmage. In Nigeria we only got wristbands for tournament games. I would always look for wristbands because the rims we played on at home were iron and didn't break away and I would dunk so hard I'd cut my wrists on them.

When I came out I could see the coaches smiling. The way you wear your outfit is the way you think of yourself on the court, and the coaches know just from the way you wear your socks (rolled down midway, so you have flexibility in the toes) and the way you tuck in your shirt (loosely, so you can jump) how you play the game. I could tell from their grins that they liked to see me in their uniform.

There were a few juniors and seniors on the floor but mostly the players were freshmen recruits. There were Houston natives who were very popular in the city and a few junior college transfers and walk-ons, but mostly new guys from different places, new to one another, trying to prove themselves. A lot of mind games were being played because you weren't there unless you had a high school reputation. I was the newest of the new guys.

I didn't know any of them but they were all hitting their shots. I was under the goal looking for rebounds. There were four balls on the court and every time someone would shoot from a distance — *basket,*

basket, basket — he never missed. If everybody was at this level I was in trouble.

Finally a shot was off. They were human. Two players went for it but I beat them to the ball and dribbled back out between them. Usually whoever gets the rebound takes the shot, but I didn't want to shoot; I knew the coaches were watching — I could see them — and I might miss, I might shoot an air ball. I passed it back to the guy who had missed. At home we did that sometimes, depending on how we felt, if somebody missed we'd give them change anyhow. I kept on that way.

I concentrated on what I knew I could do. If someone was dribbling behind his back and through his legs, showing off his ball-handling skills, when he beat his man and drove to the basket like he was so cool I would challenge him, fake him, play around with him, make him miss. There was all this action and interaction.

Finally they chose up sides. They didn't pick me.

That was okay, they didn't know me, maybe they knew one another better than I thought. Out on the floor were high school all-state Clyde Drexler, all-district Larry Micheaux, high school All-America Michael Young, Southwest Conference freshman Newcomer of the Year, Rob Williams. I didn't know their titles and credits but everybody else did.

At home when we were playing soccer if someone didn't get chosen he had to go deal with the guy who was supposed to pick the next team. I talked to that guy. He looked at me. He wasn't sure if I could play or not. Then he said okay.

I sat and stretched and watched the game on the floor. It was fast, up and down full-court, and I saw a lot of things I could do. I saw guys getting the ball under the basket and shooting little lay-ups when they should have finished with a dunk. I saw the guards going to the basket and shooting it up like they were big guys. No, the big man should reject that. The coach at home had taught me the big man runs the paint and I saw guys penetrating straight in and trying to shoot. How could they go in straight? I knew they could never get those shots off me, I would block them, so I was very comfortable; I could play with these guys.

But when the game ended the guy who was choosing the squad wanted to take the big man whose team had just lost. He had picked me, but then he dropped me. I was disappointed that the guy hadn't kept his word; I had gone and done a sales job on myself in the beginning. But I understood his position: If you won you stayed on and he wanted to win, so he was going with someone he knew for sure could play.

All of a sudden the guy called me back and said, "Okay, let's go." I was surprised, very happy. I didn't know that the coaches had sent a message down that I should play.

When the game started I was filling the lane back and forth. My game at home was speed and jumping, and that's the way I played here. I ran down the floor a couple of times and the guys saw I was controlling the middle. They said I was goaltending because I went after every shot no matter how high. I knew I was making good blocks but these guys didn't think I could get there. I didn't know who any of these guys were but I knew when they came to the basket they weren't going over me.

One guy made a nice move in the backcourt, beat his man, and drove. He thought he was in when from the weak side I stepped in and — *boom!* — swatted the ball. It was something I had a lot of practice at because at home there came a time when people stopped driving on me and I wasn't blocking many shots anymore so I had to play tricks on them. I'd stick with the guy I was guarding and let them feel comfortable that the middle was open, and as soon as they beat their man I would come over and stick them.

So — *boom!* — I swatted the ball and it went straight to one of our guards, who started a fast break. I filled the lane and we made the lay-up on the other end so I quickly circled and ran back on defense.

There were a couple of dozen guys on the sidelines and when I got that block they all went "*Oooooh!*" Who *was* that guy? they were thinking.

The game was very active. They would shoot, I would box out, get the rebound, run the floor. I didn't get to show a lot of offense because all those guys were just looking to make an impression for themselves, they didn't worry about feeding the big man. I got a nice tip dunk but mostly I was posting up, getting in a good position to shoot, boxing out, and getting back on defense. I was just playing.

My team lost but the next guy picked me right away. I was happy to play but the coaches called me; it was time to take a shower and get settled in.

They were going to put me in a hotel for the night but I hadn't had a meal since before I landed in New York. "I have to have something to eat," I told them.

"What kind of food do you like?" Coach T asked. He wasn't familiar with African cuisine. I wasn't familiar with what there was to eat in America.

"Rice," I said.

He didn't know where to get rice so he took me right across campus to a restaurant called Nanny's. I looked at the menu and didn't recognize anything on it. "All I want is rice."

"They don't have rice." So he ordered for me. Chicken-fried steak.

The waiter brought a big, long plate to the table filled to overflowing with mashed potatoes and a huge slab of thin breaded meat covered with thick, speckled white gravy. Coach T said, "Go ahead."

"This is for one person?"

I couldn't believe it, I was in a state of shock. I thought it was for all three of us.

I dug in.

This was delicious. Now it was Coach T's turn to be astonished: I finished the whole thing. "Do you still want rice?" he asked.

"No." He laughed. Then I asked, "Can I eat here every day? I won't worry about rice again."

They checked me into a Quality Inn hotel right across the street from the campus. The last bed I had slept in had been in Nigeria, and I slept like a rock.

At around eight o'clock the next morning I was to have breakfast with Coach Lewis, and when I left my hotel room it was cold! It had been warm when I went to sleep that night. The first thing the waiter did when we sat down at the restaurant was fill our glasses with water and ice. That was a big surprise to me.

At home, ice water is what you drink when it's hot outside. Ice is very special, a precious commodity, it's not something you can get every day. If you had a refrigerator, which not everyone did, there was space for only a few cubes, and they had to serve the whole family. Ice water on a cold morning? Coach Lewis drank his and began to chew on the ice.

I looked at him like he was a different animal. *Chewing* on ice? I looked around the restaurant and on every table they *all* had ice. This was standard! I asked for hot tea.

Coach Lewis asked me, "What are your plans, son?"

"I plan to visit the five schools," I told him.

"What are you looking for?"

"I am looking for a scholarship."

"Do you like Houston?"

"I like Houston."

"If we give you a scholarship will you stay?" he asked. He saw my smile.

"Yes. I will stay."

He seemed pleased.

They didn't know a thing about me and they began asking me questions. Could I read English? What was my background? "How can we get you in school?"

I had been confident I could get a scholarship somewhere but I was happy it had happened so quickly. One day, one visit, one pickup game.

They took me to the admissions office and I was told I had to take a GED, general equivalency diploma, exam. Now the coaches were afraid; they didn't know if I could pass. They were very concerned, talking about "the test," telling me it was something I had to really, really study for. They wanted me to study hard so I could get into school. I felt pressure. I said I would do my best. They got me a special teacher.

When I saw the book I was supposed to study I couldn't believe this was what they were worrying about. It was material we had covered way back in my second or third year of secondary school. The teacher told them not to worry about me.

In Nigeria you couldn't just go from high school to college, you had to pass a whole year of courses at ordinary level, and I could not hope to pass the ordinary level exam without studying. To be accepted into university in Nigeria was a big achievement. When it is said about a student "He's in university," you know that student is really dedicated, a brain. Now I understood why everybody wanted to go study abroad: it was harder at home. This was something I could handle.

Coach T gave me his office telephone number and his home phone and told me, "Anything you need, talk to me." Not only didn't he want me talking to anyone from North Carolina State or Georgia, he didn't want me talking to anyone outside the basketball coaching staff.

Each day Coach T would come pick me up and bring me to campus, where I would play ball with the guys until evening. Then I would have dinner with him before he drove home. The athletic department moved me to the Holiday Inn downtown and it took some time for them to arrange a room for me on campus. I didn't like it at this new hotel, the area shut down each night around six o'clock, it was not very safe, and I was kind of lonely walking around by myself, but I didn't say anything. The guys and I started talking and I told some of them the story of my scholarship.

"Have you been to the other schools?" they asked. These weren't the other scholarship athletes, they were walk-ons. I said, "No."

"What did they give you here?"

"A scholarship."

"No, no. Didn't you tell them you were going to go to the other schools?"

This wasn't Clyde Drexler or Michael Young or Larry Micheaux; those guys just wanted to know how I'd gotten here. These kids were the walk-ons and students who were convinced that all the varsity players were getting some kind of inducements for coming to Houston — parents were being taken care of, money changed hands, you didn't come to this school for nothing.

I didn't know anything about that. When Coach Lewis had asked "What are you looking for?" I had told him exactly: a scholarship. That was a big offer, to be admitted to an American university.

They said, "With your talent you can get a scholarship anywhere. There's no school in America that wouldn't accept you."

So I tested Coach T. "I'm getting tired of Houston," I told him. "I might want to see the other schools."

They moved me into Coach T's house.

I rode home with Coach T the first night and he showed me a big bedroom and said, "This is yours." Coach T and his wife, Joyce, were friendly and warm and wonderful. They had four girls: baby twins, a five-year-old, and a ten-year-old. They were a beautiful family and had just moved to Houston from California, so they were almost as new to the city as I was. Each morning I would ride with Coach T to campus.

I would play all day with the guys and then we'd ride home together at night. It was relaxing going back and forth with him — he was a good guy, we would talk about all different things, and I felt very comfortable. I liked staying with a family in America.

I was seventeen years old and could not enroll myself in college; school system regulations demanded that all students under the age of eighteen be enrolled by an adult with legal standing. I was going to turn eighteen in January, two months away, and for a while it looked like I had a big problem. This was solved when Terence Kirkpatrick volunteered to take that legal responsibility. He called my parents in Lagos to discuss it. He told them he was in no way taking their place, this was simply a legal technicality that would allow their son to attend the University of Houston. My parents said they understood, and soon after Coach T became my legal guardian.

The basketball office was a center of activity. Players coming back from class would stop there for conversation before practice; if you wanted to use the telephone between classes, that was the place; lunch break, you go to the basketball office. Everybody loved it. People were talking, going in and out, it was the most fun place on campus. The coaches didn't know, but sometimes guys hung out at the office instead of going to class. In Nigeria when we cut classes we'd go to the bush; when you cut classes at the University of Houston you'd go to the basketball office.

Coach T loved to talk. He loved the players, he loved the game, and he could discuss basketball and nothing else for hours. I had played pickup games all day, I was tired, I just wanted to go home and take a shower and eat. But Coach T never wanted to leave. The basketball office was like a clubhouse and if it were up to Coach T he would stay there forever.

I took my test and was admitted. I was a student now at the University of Houston. That was wonderful.

I sent my ticket back to my mother. I gave it to Lois Thorn, Coach Lewis's secretary, to forward. It was the most exciting thing I had ever done. I wrote my mom a letter telling her I had been admitted to the university on a basketball scholarship. Very good news. The school gave me a basketball program, the one they sold at the games, which told all about the school. I took a picture of me on campus and Coach T wrote a beautiful note introducing himself and telling my mom they were very happy with her son. I sent them all to her. I felt so good to be able to recover almost three quarters of the money she had given me — I knew she wasn't expecting it; she thought it was gone — and to do it within two weeks. I was a Cougar.

A few weeks after I was admitted to school they moved me onto campus. The school year had started two months before but I could jump in as both a student and a basketball player. Coach T told me, "You have two options now. You can join the team or you can redshirt, wait this year out and play a full season next year."

I was eager to play. I had just come from Nigeria, I saw I could play with these guys, and I didn't think I wanted to wait. Pre-season had started and I went and practiced with the team that day.

The next day Coach T came to me in a different mood. He said, "Maybe you shouldn't play this year. If you join the team now you will have to learn all the plays, you will probably play only half games, you're going to waste a year. You shouldn't do that. You have a scholarship now, you're in school, this way you'll be a semester ahead and you can get your degree at the end. That might be better because you won't spend all four years in college anyway."

I remembered what Christopher Pond had told me, that I shouldn't play my first year. This made sense to me. I had seen practice and all the plays they called and I knew I had to catch up there, so I thought about it and decided I should wait.

Coach Lewis called me in and said he was proud of me, that I'd made the right decision.

That whole freshman year was so much fun. I took general courses in the beginning and some in African history. I learned more about Africa when I was at UH than I had in Nigeria! Classes were not difficult. I was a redshirt and by NCAA rules was not allowed to practice with the team, but every day after class I would go watch them practice. I wouldn't stay the whole time, though; pretty soon I would go upstairs and play intramurals.

I liked American food. I ate at the cafeteria where there was a special line for athletes; you could go back if you wanted some more. At home in Nigeria I ate rice almost all the time — a little meat or stew over a lot of rice, delicious spices and flavor. I loved that. But at the cafeteria there was no rice, they would give you a big steak and a baked potato. I'd eat a couple. When they didn't serve us steak it was chicken or some other meat. I would eat whatever they served me — especially ice cream, that was my favorite. I would eat as many of the little ice cream Dixie cups as they would put on my tray, and after each meal — lunch and dinner — I would take four more back to my room. I had a small refrigerator and everybody knew it was always full of ice cream. Vanilla. And when they ran out of vanilla I developed a taste for strawberry.

At home, breakfast would be either oatmeal or custard or bread and tea, that's Nigerian breakfast. Now I was eating pancakes. I had never eaten them, and now I had them almost every morning. Or eggs and sausage. On Sunday the cafeteria served only lunch, no dinner, so I went to the place downstairs where they sold hamburgers and french fries. I ate well and I liked it. By the spring I weighed 240 pounds. I had been comfortable when I'd arrived and didn't think I needed to beef up, but from the time I arrived in October to that spring I gained sixty pounds and was even more comfortable.

Campus life was the best. During the week the pace was busy, lots of people hurrying to classes. On weekends the campus cleared out, the gym was closed, and a lot of the students who were from Houston to begin with went home. Most of the weekend action would be in Hermann Park. The park was large and green, not at all like the rest of Houston, and boyfriends and girlfriends would go there to study together, people would sit under trees talking or lie on the grass. Very few students went there; it was mostly regular Houstonians. And the place was full. People were throwing Frisbees, just a very peaceful, beautiful lifestyle. There was always something happening in the park.

The first thing I saw was the cars. People had spent hours polishing these old cars to a high gloss so you could see your reflection; the spokes on the hubcaps were all chrome and shone brightly. There was a whole procession of these wild cars, real low to the ground — low riders, I found they were called — each one with the radio blasting, tuned to the same station that everybody else listened to, and they kept rolling by, they never stopped. And as they cruised in a big circle the cars were bouncing to the music. Bouncing! I thought this was the coolest. Guys were standing around looking at what was going on, their shades on, talking with their girlfriends. Real cool. I loved going to the park on Sundays.

I saw an outdoor basketball court and stopped to watch the game. It was nothing like the University of Houston practices. Some of the players were wearing cut-off jeans and very dirty tennis sneakers. They had Jheri curls and more than one of them had stuck an Afro comb in his back pocket. You could see it sticking up as they bent to guard their man.

These were park players, very competitive; they knew the flow. I saw incredible ball-handling, fancy work just to show the other guy up before you scored on him. Funny jump shots, some with two hands, with form that any coach would have drilled out of his team — but they wouldn't miss. No matter how strange the shot looked going up, it came down in the basket. The rims were all bent from people hanging on them but everyone seemed to know just how the ball was going to bounce off the backboards, they knew how to use them. The park was everybody's home court.

They were three-on-three half-court games, which I was used to at home. I realized that if these people played in the Stadium they would really dominate; this was a different level of competition.

I was standing there watching when one of the guys called to me, "You want to play?" I was wearing jeans and my new tennis shoes and I said, "Sure." I got in the game, blocked a few shots, dunked. And as the game went on, word got around. We started to draw a crowd.

"Who is this guy?"

"Next year he's going to play for the University of Houston."

"Yeah?"

The following Sunday I was prepared. I put on some shorts and played ball in the park all day. It was a lot of fun, the kind of competition I enjoyed, right in your face. Intramurals upstairs in the gym were tough and physical but in the park there was a lot of style and talk, the kind we used to hear about in Nigeria. Everybody back home wanted to pick up American slang — we thought that was the coolest thing — and on the court I heard it all. So this was how Americans had fun.

When the University of Houston coaching staff heard that I had been playing in the park games they got upset. Coach T called me and said,

"No, no, no, no, don't play in the park. You might get injured." They stopped me from playing. After that I just went there to mingle.

Everything was new to me, everything was different. New food, new friends, new studies. One of the first friends I made was a junior named Lynden Rose. Lynden was the starting point guard on the Cougar team. He was from the Bahamas, and we got along from the beginning. Bahamians have a similar culture to Africans, I found out; although there are differences, I could relate to him and his friends easier than to the rest of the guys.

The basketball players were all housed in the same dormitory and there was always a lot going on in Lynden's room. His friends were mostly Bahamians, not UH ballplayers, and his room was like a clubhouse, an international clubhouse. Lynden introduced me to everyone and said, "This is my homeboy."

Lynden was very smart. Most basketball players, I found out quickly, were there only to play basketball; Lynden was trying to use his scholarship to finish school and get his degree at the same time he was playing. Very unusual.

Lynden was also very sensitive to racial prejudice. As a foreigner and a black man, he was never really accepted by the UH community, the boosters and the alumni, and he had the perspective of an outsider. He watched me and saw things around me that I either didn't see or wasn't aware of.

For instance, after UH home games it was traditional for the players to go to a function the athletic department held for the alumni. I was happy to attend, to be part of the team, and I would come in smiling. By the time the season started Coach Lewis had made the announcement that I had signed with the school, and there had already been articles in the newspaper about how there was a seven-footer from Nigeria who was going to play on the team the following year. So many of the alumni wanted to meet me. I had always been taught to be respectful toward my elders, and when I was introduced I bowed to each person individually. It's the way you do things in Nigeria. You don't just go shake an elder's hand. You say "Good evening" and bow at the waist to show respect for the person's age and position. That's standard.

These people were older. Many of them were wearing their University of Houston Cougar red blazers, their hair was all white, they were very proud of their school and supported the team strongly. They would tell me, "We know you're playing next year. We can't wait to see you play." I thought that was very good. I didn't grow up in America, I didn't have feelings about slavery or servitude, I was just trying to behave properly and show good manners. Some of my teammates didn't see it that way. They saw all these white Texans standing around drinking with their buddies and lining up to shake my hand — "Billy Bob, let's go have this big black boy bow to us" — and thought I was being a Steppin Fetchit. I didn't even know what that meant.

If there was misunderstanding about my background, some of it came from the players. The second day I was in Houston I came to practice dressed in traditional wear. Even though I never wore it at home I wore it to practice. I wanted to establish my identity: I was an African; I was different. I had on the special robes my mother had made me buy, the latest fabric, called stone. It was like lace, light for summer, my skin showed through it and the garment had many stones sewn into it; they looked like diamonds.

Everybody started laughing. They didn't laugh in my face but I could hear them around corners or when they thought I wasn't listening. They looked for things about me that they could laugh about.

Maybe it was because Coach T had taken me under his wing and paid more attention to me than to the others; maybe it was that the newspaper articles took attention away from the players who were already on the team; maybe guys who weren't going to become pro ballplayers were frustrated at seeing someone who had a chance. Whatever it was, I wasn't fully accepted by some of the guys. A couple of them started calling me "Africa," or "the big African." Several of my teammates, especially the seniors, would ask me, "Do you live in a hut?" Some of this was innocent — a few people actually thought all Africans lived in the jungle, that we were all bushmen, that we ran around naked. Some comments were not. I understood this behavior without liking it. I was used to people picking on me, this was nothing new and I'd had a lot of experience at it, so I was firm and confident. I had a constant battle to establish myself and my identity.

I loved clothes. In Lagos you had all the best stores — European designers, American designers, all the fashions came to Nigeria. On campus everyone wore jeans and a polo shirt, either Izod/Lacoste or Ralph Lauren/Polo. Most people wore Izod since it was less expensive, so whoever wore Polo was the coolest guy on campus. Clyde Drexler wore Polo. I saw all the basketball players wearing Polo — it was the trend on campus, really in, but I didn't want to wear it, I saw it too much.

At home there was a store that carried Giorgio Armani and I had several Armani T-shirts. They were simple but beautiful, excellent colors, with only a single *GA* on them. I was wearing a *GA* T-shirt. These people had no idea what *GA* was, and they didn't want to know. I was surprised they didn't know Giorgio Armani, especially Clyde, who knew how to dress. If it wasn't Polo it wasn't cool, that was his attitude. He swears to this day that he taught me how to dress, and he didn't even know about Armani!

I called my family about once a month. A telephone was not something that was easily found at home. There was a lady who lived across the field in my neighborhood whose husband went on international business trips and she would sometimes receive calls, so they had a telephone. Very unusual. I called that number when I wanted to talk to my parents. The lady would answer and I would wait five minutes while she went and got them. In my mind's eye I could see her crossing the field where I had played soccer all my life, going into my parents' house, telling them I was calling.

They asked all about America.

"Oh, it's beautiful here. Everything's okay. How's everybody at home?"

"Everybody's fine. Your friends Johnson and Ola are always asking about you." Johnson and Ola had been at my house all the time when I was growing up and had established a relationship with my parents. They both came from poor families and when I'd left I'd asked my mom to take care of them. She'd said, "You know me." My mom and I communicated so well I didn't have to be specific, she got the message. When they came by to get word of how I was doing in the States she fed them and gave them pocket money. I was happy that my friends still had my family in the city.

The Cougars went 21–9 that season, tied for second in the Southwest Conference, and then beat Texas in the SWC tournament final to get an automatic bid to the NCAA tournament. But they didn't get any farther. Villanova, which had placed third in the Big East, held the Cougars to twenty-eight points in the first half and beat us, 90–72. The season was over.

Sometime after the tournament, the NCAA announced that I had lost one full year of eligibility. Because I had participated in one team practice I now had only three years left instead of four. There was no contesting their decision; this was the NCAA, you can't argue with them. I was disappointed and upset. Next season I would be coming in as a sophomore instead of a freshman. Then Coach T told me, "Don't worry about it. You'll probably only use two years out of those three anyway." That made me feel a little better.

One of the first things the coaches had asked me when I arrived was whether there were more basketball players like me back in Nigeria. I told Coach T there was somebody better: Yommy Basket.

"Better than you?" said Coach T.

"Yes."

"What's his problem?"

"He needs a visa."

Coach T told Coach Lewis. They asked me, "What is it going to take to get him?"

I wrote a letter to Yommy Basket and got one back by express mail. In order to make sure he didn't play for anyone else, he wrote, Ogun State had given him a job as assistant coach on the men's team. To get a visa he would need a letter saying he was invited to the United States to attend a coaching course to see how American coaches train their players. The coaches told me, You just tell Lois whatever you need in that letter and we'll get it to him.

The letter got written quickly and they sent one copy to Ogun State, one to the embassy, and one to Yommy Basket. It was written on University of Houston stationery and had an American stamp on the envelope. No one could doubt this letter; it was very impressive.

Ogun State approved. They were in favor of their player learning how to coach from coaches in America. Yommy Basket didn't tell them he had no intention of coming back. They bought his ticket and continued his salary for the six months he would be away. His salary would go to his family.

Within a month Yommy Basket arrived.

But when they looked at his papers there was a problem. Yommy Basket was twenty-three years old. There was an NCAA rule that stated no foreign player could play Division I basketball if he was over twenty-one. If the coaches didn't know about this rule when they invited him over, they knew now. Yommy Basket was ineligible to play for the University of Houston.

Coach T got on the phone. He called his good friend who was coaching at Sam Houston State, a National Association of Intercollegiate Athletics (NAIA) school in Huntsville, Texas. "I want to send you a player," he told him. "You want to take a look at him." The over-twenty-one rule didn't apply in the NAIA.

The first thing the Sam Houston coaches did was watch Yommy Basket play. They set up a two-on-two game, Yommy Basket and me against one of the Cougar guards and Larry Micheaux. They were very impressed. Yommy Basket was a sharpshooter, a rebounder, a fully developed basketball talent. They gave him a scholarship.

Yommy Basket played immediately — he played college ball before I did. Not only that, Huntsville was not a far drive from Houston and we hung out all of my freshman year. I was very excited. I didn't know him very well but I had such admiration for him. I had a fellow Nigerian ballplayer and, as far as I was concerned, a superstar to hang out with.

Yommy Basket became a star at Sam Houston University and turned pro after his junior year. He was drafted in the third round by the New Jersey Nets but he didn't stick. Unfortunately, Yommy Basket was a better basketball player than he was a friend. After a while we stopped seeing each other. He turned out to be a real disappointment. But I felt good about what I'd done. I had promised him I would not forget him, and I didn't.

The school year went by very quickly. I did well in my classes, I played ball all the time, I learned about America. When the second semester ended the dormitory was closed down, everybody went home, and I moved back in with Coach T and his family. This really prevented me from being homesick because Coach T and his wife were so enjoyable to be with. The adjustment was very natural. Even though he was an assistant coach, Terence was a lot of fun, like a big kid.

I was playing sports too much to watch a lot of it on television. At home in Nigeria the only televised sports was a show called *Saturday Sports,* and it only showed soccer games. Everybody watched the soccer game. So it was strange to be able to turn on the set and see basketball. I had heard all the stories: David Thompson jumped so high he could take a silver dollar off the top of the backboard; Dr. J, with his Afro, could take it off and make change. Guys said there were witnesses. After that I had gone and looked at a backboard, thinking, I have to see this. And every once in a while I would see the Houston Rockets play on TV. Calvin Murphy was an All-Star for the Rockets, and the big man, the center, the MVP, was Moses Malone. That spring Coach T had told me, "This summer you will play against this guy."

"Really?" I couldn't believe that.

"Yeah, he plays at Fonde." Fonde Recreation Center (pronounced "*Fond*-ee") was where everybody went to play in the summer.

"Wow! He plays with non-professionals?"

"Yeah. You'll see."

I noticed the cars right away. There were Mercedeses and Jaguars and Porsches. Everybody had one. I thought, These people must be very successful.

Fonde was a simple brick building on a major street in downtown Houston and it drew the best basketball players in the state. Professionals would come after their seasons were over, guys in the NBA and on teams in Europe; the Cougar team was on the court all the time; playground and street players were trying to impress everyone. It was the Mecca for Houston summer basketball.

Fonde was dark, two rooms, dirty windows, always humid and hot. It had fold-down bleachers and smelled like a gym, but they tried to keep it neat so people wouldn't be afraid to come and watch. There was a locker room but before games nobody used it; you came to play. Fonde had two courts separated by a blue plastic screen. One of them always had two half-court games going on between street players, and the other was for the Cougars and the pros.

It was summer 1981. Fonde started at four in the afternoon. Coach T was in charge of the first three games; he chose the UH squad and even if we lost we stayed on. This was the center's way of making sure we showed up.

Coach T put on the floor the team he thought would start the next few years: Clyde Drexler, Michael Young, Lynden Rose, Larry Micheaux, and me. Rob Williams, UH's first team All-SWC guard, was a special case.

Rob Williams and Indiana University's Isiah Thomas were being called the two best college guards in the country. Williams had fantastic skills, he was a sharpshooter, a great ball handler, and when he played he was so quick the pros couldn't stay with him. He was the University of Houston's main attraction. Williams was going into his junior year but the coaches weren't really counting on him too much that summer because they were looking to the future of the team and they knew he would be leaving, turning pro after the season. Williams would show up every once in a while. He had his clothes, his Datson 300ZX with the T-top sunroof you could take off and put in the trunk. He got all the attention.

So we would play against the pros. There would be five NBA players on the court and another dozen or so waiting to get in the game. A lot of the Houston Rockets lived in the city and you'd see Robert Reid, Allen Leavell, Tom Henderson, Major Jones, Joe "Jellybean" Bryant, plus Alton Lister, Jackie Dorsey, Cliff Levingston. Games were to fifteen, you had to win by two. We would challenge them and always play them tough; we weren't getting blown out.

Then Moses Malone showed up. He was a little late for the beginning of the Fonde season because the Rockets had just lost to the Boston Celtics four games to two in the NBA Championship Finals.

I had heard about Moses. Everybody knew about Moses. He was the ultimate, the best center, the best player in the league. So when Moses came to the gym the first time it was like, *"The MVP!"* I didn't know exactly what that meant, I didn't know much about the National Basketball Association or what being the most valuable player in it really signified, but I knew he was a million-dollar player and that everybody at Fonde got out of his way.

When Moses came to the gym I was excited. I knew he was known for his rebounding, that he was a hardworking player, real physical. To play against him was big excitement for me. He had just averaged twenty-eight points and fifteen rebounds a game against the best players in the world in the NBA. He dominated his whole league, so who was I? He was supposed to dominate me.

But I had a sense of pride. For the weeks before Moses arrived at Fonde, I had been playing against power forwards and been very effective, blocking a lot of shots. I didn't want him to embarrass me. I had to compete. I felt a combination of excitement, fear, and intimidation. I wanted to see how I measured up.

Now the pros had their main guy and Moses didn't give me a break. He realized immediately that I was a shot blocker and he used his strength and power to prevent me from blocking his shot. He was also much quicker than anybody I had ever played against. The other pros would back in against me and use their bigger bodies, but when they would put their shots up I would come back and still block them. The first time he tried to post up I pushed him, but he overpowered me and went through me like I wasn't even there. Moses's power was very quick; he would dribble and back me in, and every time he used his power move he would plant his right leg and seal me. He was so strong I couldn't go around him and so quick that by the time I got back from taking his hit and tried to get up and block him, he was already gone. I was jumping behind him, and every time I jumped he just bounced off me.

There was nothing I could do with Moses. If he sealed me and turned to the inside, he had a lay-up. If I tried to cut him off to the inside, he had a running hook so he just turned and made that. Moses was an expert in sealing his man; once he sealed you, you could only foul him. Terence was coaching me — Do this, do that — and I was competing very hard against him, but Moses scored on me anytime he wanted to.

And Moses would talk on the court. He never instructed me — not once did he tell me how to do something — but I watched the way he played and it was all-out. There was no weakness allowed. You did not call a ticktack foul at Fonde. You're going to the basket and someone slashes at your arm, you don't call a foul — you go in and dunk on him. Your man beats you on defense, now you want to call traveling? No, you got beat. "Be a man!" That was the phrase at Fonde. You heard it all the time. Moses would back into me, I would grunt, and he would back in again. And each time he hit me he would say, "*Be a man! Be a man!*"

But I never stopped competing against him, and as I got better I started to challenge his shot more often. I was quick enough to cut him off sometimes and force him to go with the running hook. I only hoped I could get it, or make him change his shot and maybe miss. I was bothering his shot!

I was so busy on defense that my offense was not productive. I would run and try to beat him down the floor and sometimes I would get a nice dunk, but when I tried to post up, Moses would just move me away from the box. I couldn't get close, I wasn't strong enough to pound against him, I would feel like I was running into a wall. I would get the ball, put it on the floor, do my turnaround, and he would challenge it. "Gotta be hungry for those blocks and rebounds," he said. "Eat 'em up." He was dominating me, that was very clear.

We very rarely won against the pros. Every time the game was close and we had a chance to take it, they would go to Moses down low and he would use his power move and score. If I blocked it I would be satisfied for days; coming close wasn't enough. I loved that move so much, but I couldn't copy it; Moses had great strength in both legs, he could explode off his left *and* his right, while I was strong only on my left. The drop step was his strongest move. I shot my jump hook off my left, my pivot foot. If I shot coming to my right I would get it blocked, but Moses was unstoppable whichever way he wanted to go.

Moses was serious, he wasn't playing around with me, but it was because I was pushing him, I was actually giving him a game. He knew if he gave me an opportunity I would take it over him, so he was trying to kill all opportunity. When I shot the ball he boxed me out, went and got the rebound, ran the floor, and made his power move real quick. He was doing everything *real,* in *real* time with *real* effort. He showed me the respect of playing hard against me.

That gave me confidence, mentally and physically. I began to feel, Wow, if I can play with Moses then college should be easy; there's no big man who can play like Moses.

Then Moses started talking about me to the reporters. When they asked, he started telling them about my footwork, my speed on the court. He said I ran like a deer. He told the reporters I would dominate college basketball easily. He didn't tell me, he told the reporters.

Moses was king at Fonde and all over Houston. During the NBA season when reporters swarmed all around him he was gruff and silent,

7

COACH LEWIS, CLYDE, MR. MEAN, AND THE GUYS

PEOPLE SAY that Houston coach Guy V. Lewis didn't really coach, he just rolled the balls out and let his players run with them. That's not true.

I had heard about the history of the University of Houston basketball team — winning the game of the century against UCLA in the Astrodome in 1968; Elvin Hayes, Don Chaney, and all the great players who had passed through the school. Christopher Pond was the first one who had told me the history, and people were still talking about it on campus. I loved those stories. Coach Lewis didn't say it but he carried around the attitude that he had coached too many great players to change things for you, you had to follow his program, and it was very disciplined. He was demanding, humbling, and you had to give him your best at all times. It was very tough to play for Coach Lewis.

I had been playing basketball for only a year and a half and I was still learning the game. The summer at Fonde had taught me about competition; this season at UH was going to be about technique and the work ethic.

The University of Houston had not been dominant for quite a while; Arkansas and Texas were the teams that did well. But this year there were a lot of expectations and all the media was picking us to win the Southwest Conference. Some newspapers and magazines were already predicting me to be Newcomer of the Year. I read about myself in the paper but I wasn't really worried about the press. I didn't think I had but at Fonde he was a totally different guy. He was comfortable, always standing in the middle of a crowd making jokes. People wanted to be around him, they would talk and laugh, fighting just to be in his presence, everybody trying to be his friend. Moses liked that. He's a very simple man, like a big kid; he likes to play and have fun. Play basketball and hang out, just what boys like to do. Being in a crowd having jokes made about me makes me uncomfortable, but Moses went out of his way to include me. He would joke about me and everyone would laugh and I would be in the inner circle, but for Moses even to mention me in front of the crowd made me more shy. Moses tried to bring me closer, and I would be in their company but I would feel isolated anyway. I wanted to be there but I didn't want to be hanging on like everybody else.

The players were always talking about clothes and it turned out that Moses and I wore the same size. One day Moses arrived at Fonde with a bunch of suits for me. Dress suits. He said, "Next week I'll bring you some more."

I was very grateful, very shy. I had pride, I didn't wear other people's clothes, but I was also excited and proud that Moses talked to me. The suits were custom-made of nice material. I took several to a tailor for alteration and then wore them thankfully.

Moses was very generous. He gave me five hundred dollars in cash and said, "Whatever you need, you let me know." My closets were full of suits and pants, and I bought some sweaters. I looked at Moses like he was a big brother. He wasn't like that with everyone, which made me feel like I was special to him.

proven myself; I hadn't actually played a game yet, I just wanted to play.

You were quiet when you came on the practice court, everybody was serious business. Coach Lewis had several plays that he had been running for many, many years and he taught us those. But they were just general guidelines. When you get a rebound or block a shot on one end, you push it and get a fast break, run the lane, and score. You can't coach that, that's just basketball, and that was 75 percent of our offense.

What Coach Lewis stressed was that we be unselfish on offense, that we distribute the ball, and that everyone have a chance to run down and score. You could never walk on the floor, there was no room for laziness. Coach Lewis got the maximum out of everybody. He also made sure we got back and played good defense, that we boxed out and rebounded and did what we were supposed to do. That was his strength. The running game looks undisciplined because there's so much activity, but everyone has to know where to run and where the other players are going to be. Coach Lewis made sure the balls went to the right people's hands in the right places and that we were taking good shots.

We never ran lay-up drills, that was too ordinary, too slow. We ran two-on-one or three-on-two fast breaks with guys going full-speed, trying to dunk on our teammates. The defensive players were encouraged to get run over, to take the charge and get the ball. If the guys on offense didn't score they got some punishment, like running the gym stairs. If the defensive guys got scored on they had something else they had to do. This was the way we would warm up for the day. Very active. Practices were tough, hard, and competitive. Coach Lewis divided us up into the red team and the white team. The white team wore white jerseys and were the starters, the red team — the rest of us — wore red jerseys.

The white team consisted of Rob Williams, Clyde Drexler, Lynden Rose, Larry Micheaux, and Michael Young. Very strong.

For the previous two years the team had been built around Rob Williams, he was All-America and it was his team. He was excellent at the half-court game. He would walk the ball up, very fancy, dribble between his legs, run the clock down, shake and bake and shoot and score. He had a crossover dribble that would make the guy defending him fall and twist an ankle. Anytime there was nothing there, he could create points. He would give up the ball if he was double-teamed and had no other option, he could set you up to finish with a nice dunk, and he did that very well. But that wasn't his first option, that was his last option.

Rob Williams's shot was one of the toughest for me to block because he knew how to shoot over a big man. He was not worried about the big man; he would penetrate, I'd see him coming, I'd establish position, and he'd still find a way of scoring over me. If he could not, he would pass off. Not many players can do that on a consistent basis. He also really had some range. You didn't think he would, but at the crucial time of the game he would pull up and shoot from very, very deep — and finish it. I truly respected his game.

Coach Lewis *loved* his game. Rob Williams must have bailed the coach out of many situations in his first two years — when they needed a basket, he would get it; that kind of player — because he was the only player to whom the coach showed favoritism. He got away with more than anybody. If someone bumped Williams too hard in practice he would get upset and go sit down. Nobody else could do that with Coach Lewis. Sit down? Coach Lewis was a tough man with a real Texan cowboy accent. He'd say, "Somebody give this boy a quiche. She can't play ball." But not to Rob Williams; Rob Williams had his own set of rules.

But everybody knew Rob Williams, who was a junior, was leaving school to turn pro at the end of the year. This was a team that was shifting away from him. He was a brilliant half-court player and now we had a new set of teammates who loved to run. On the other hand, with me on the team he now had someone to block shots and rebound for him and get him the ball. Once he had the ball Rob Williams was happy.

Clyde Drexler had been Southwest Conference Newcomer of the Year his freshman year, which was a surprise. He and Michael Young had both gone to high school in Houston; he had only been all-district while Michael Young had been All-America. And you could see immediately when we got back that over the summer Clyde had improved his game tremendously.

I loved Clyde's game. He was a small forward, about 6′6″, and he loved to rebound. He loved to snatch a rebound with one hand, smack it with the other, and take off. People said he couldn't shoot because they didn't see him do it too often; most of the time he would push the ball down the floor and go coast to coast. Clyde just wanted to get the rebound and run, that was his first choice: Just go.

I don't know how he did it but he positioned himself so that every time a shot was blocked it went right into his hands. The ball goes up, everybody fights for it, it gets grabbed by somebody. You wonder, Who's that? That's Clyde. When a ball gets swatted away and somebody saves it — What, who's that? That's Clyde. One day I sat in practice and watched him, just to find out how he did it.

He moved around. He moved with the ball on defense. You couldn't really box him out because he kept moving. When someone was driving to the basket he would see his big man coming in to block it *and he would step back.* Everybody thinks this guy is going to the basket, everybody on the court is going *in* . . . except Clyde. He moved *back.* He anticipated the block, he saw where it was likely to be swatted to, and he went right there. And when he got the ball he took off. He would terrorize his opponent, rushing down the court and converting the basket on the other end with a nice dunk. You didn't have to worry about finishing a fast break, Clyde would finish it. Clyde was also a team player, a terrific passer, and he passed the ball naturally.

Michael Young had been a high school All-America and he just loved to shoot. A sharpshooter. Shoot, shoot, shoot. He was a forward, he was strong and also loved to run, but the difference was that once he pulled up he did not see anything around him. It was him and the basket. Clyde was going to pass and score, an all-around player. Michael Young was a pure shooter. If he was on, he would kill you. He was an excellent offensive player, only an average defensive player.

Lynden Rose was the senior point guard. He set up the action and had the court sense. He had played for Coach Lewis for three years and was a smart ballplayer, pro material. He had been overshadowed by Rob Williams but he was a hard worker with great court awareness, a driver who also knew how to feed the post. He was honorable and perceptive, a valuable man on and off the court, and we became very good friends. I had great respect for his game and for him as a person.

Larry Micheaux's nickname was "Mr. Mean," and he lived up to it. He was the man in the middle and if he was limited in skills he made up for it by being a very physical, very solid power player. He was extremely strong, he could box out and rebound and do all the little things that needed to be done. He was also very aggressive. The first thing Micheaux wanted to do was elbow you — that was the way he played. He would grab the ball, cradle it in his arm, and put an elbow in your chest to knock you away. He was always up in your face, throwing elbows.

One of our guards, Reid Gettys, saw Micheaux in the locker room one day with a bump on his arm bigger than any bruise Reid had seen in his life. "Mean," he asked, "what in the world happened to you?"

"Buddy," Micheaux said, "somebody hit me with a crowbar."

"Someone hit you with a crowbar?"

"Yeah, buddy."

"Well, why?"

"I was driving by and he cussed at me."

"Did he have a crowbar in his hand?"

"Yeah."

"Did you see the crowbar?"

"Yeah."

"And you stopped?"

"Yeah, buddy."

That was Mr. Mean.

The red team's job was to get the white team ready for competition. There was me; forwards Benny Anders and Bryan Williams; guards Eric Davis, Reid Gettys, Rodney Parker, and Eric Dickens; and the Bunce brothers, David and Dan. Benny Anders was my roommate and was pretty wild and crazy. He was a 6'5" guard who could handle the ball and shoot and jump. He loved the alley-oop. He was too big for the little guards and quicker than Clyde and Michael Young. He had long arms and created a lot of trouble. You had to guard him because he was a pure shooter and would kill you if you didn't, but if you got too close he would just go right around you. He had all the offensive weapons, all the skills, so in practice he was a weapon. The white team didn't like to play against him.

The Bunce brothers. There was Big Bunce and Baby Bunce. They practiced hard but got no respect. Baby Bunce was 6'11". He had a very nice jump hook but very small hands, he couldn't control the ball; when he put the ball on the floor they waited for him. He was a very good half-court player, he could box out and shoot his hook; I could see him playing on an international level. If he was on he could kill you with that jump hook, but he had trouble running the floor. Once he went up and down the floor twice, he wasn't the same. Big Bunce was 7'2" and a sharpshooter, but very skinny. A very good practice player, he would never miss a shot. In the game he was not the same, he would miss wide-open shots that he never missed in practice.

But I respected them because they practiced hard and were good for the team. Micheaux was 6'9" and when he went up against Baby Bunce he had to fight to shoot over him. Micheaux always used his elbows and pounded and tried to intimidate them. The Bunce brothers used to get all bloody and go to the training room for stitches, but they kept coming back. People used to talk about how they couldn't play, why'd they even get scholarships, it's only because they were white. But they were tough, they weren't pushovers, and even though they were not used in the games they were a big part of getting the team ready to dominate.

I was out there to challenge every shot. My strength was my jumping ability, and no matter where the shot was I was going to try and block it. I especially liked to pin the ball on the glass like I did at home. All the guys would holler "Goaltending!" but I disagreed. If you pin it against the glass it's goaltending, if you *take it to the glass* it's a good block. Everybody who knows the game knows the difference; if the guy is shooting and you take the ball as soon as he releases it and pin it to the glass, that's a pin, not goaltending. They would scream at me, "This isn't international rules!" and at the end of the day I'd lose the argument. In international games, unlike in American college ball, you can slap the ball off the rim and block it on its way down. But that didn't stop me from pinning them the next time.

I just loved swatting away shots all over the place in practice. There was no shot anywhere near the basket that I would not challenge. One day Reid Gettys took a jumper from the top of the key and from a standing start at the bottom of the circle below the foul line I went straight up and took it out of the air. I handed it back to him. "Here is your shot." Reid was so mad. He started screaming, "Coach, he can't catch my shot! I don't know the exact rule but that can't be legal!"

Guys like Clyde and Michael were always looking for an opportunity to dunk on me. I blocked their shots so many times, that's how they got their satisfaction: they waited for their chance and then they went in and jammed strongly over me. They did it many, many times. Sometimes I would set traps for them, let them think I was out of position and then swoop over when they came to the basket. But I miscalculated; *they* were setting traps for *me,* they were ready and even more determined to put it in my face.

Coach Lewis didn't call fouls in practice, he let us play and the frustration and pounding always built up. He knew what he was doing. We had two or three fights each day in practice. There were fistfights every day. That's the way he liked it. Coach Lewis wanted a team of brave, tough people; he wanted players who were tough mentally and tough physically, and to survive with our team you had to be both or you were going to get chewed up. Coach Lewis felt if you were a man and you were going to be tough, you had to stand up to people. It didn't matter whether you could fight, it didn't matter whether you got beaten down or knocked out. What mattered was that you stood up. This was Coach Lewis's test. Some guys would mouth off, say, "I'm gonna kick your butt. Yeah, I'm gonna kick your butt," but never backed it up. Those were the guys who didn't get the coach's respect. He'd say, "All right, if you're not man enough to fight then let's practice."

I fought with everyone: Clyde, Micheaux, Lynden Rose, everybody. So did almost everybody else. After living through the Cougar practices, the games themselves were easy.

I worked on my offense in practice, but with all the scoring talent on the team when I was playing, I was the fifth option. I had my jump hook, I had a turnaround jump shot, and I was working on the shake-and-bake moves I had seen at Fonde. Upstairs in the intramurals I liked to bring the ball down the court.

But Coach Lewis hated when I put the ball on the floor. I did it anyway, I was always working on new ways to get some offense. Moses Malone did it against me all the time and it always worked. "How come a big man can't put the ball on the floor?" I wanted to know. To me, if you don't put the ball on the floor, you travel. You can't just turn around and shoot; I'm a shot blocker, I know if someone just turned around on me directly without making a move I would get a block.

Coach Lewis didn't want to discuss it. He didn't think I could shoot or handle the ball when I came from Nigeria and he didn't like what he called the "bad habits" I picked up at Fonde. College ball is all zone, they pack defenders in around the big man under the basket, and Coach Lewis believed there was no place to dribble. In practice he would run guards around me in the post to slap the ball away, just to prove his point. If it came close to being stolen he would stop practice and tell me in front of everybody, "Hakeem, if you put the ball on the floor again, you're heading up the stairs." I was stubborn, and I did it again. He snatched me out of the game. "Up the stairs." I'd have to run them.

Coach Lewis liked what he called the Guy Lewis Step: You get the ball, you fake, you take one step and shoot. I never felt comfortable with that move and I didn't use it. The coach and I disagreed the whole time I was in college.

We scrimmaged at eight o'clock on Saturday mornings. We had been practicing for so long — working on individual plays, stopping in the middle to go over positioning and passing — that a scrimmage, with real referees, was like an actual game. About a week before the 1981–82 season was scheduled to begin, Coach Lewis held a scrimmage to choose the starting five. Most of the positions were already established; the only one in any doubt was center. This scrimmage was very important. Here was a chance for everyone to make one last impression on the coaching staff.

Some players were nervous and they tried too hard to impress the coach. That's when I am at my best, when other people make mistakes. A player escapes his man and thinks he has a clear path to the basket — and he's thinking about how good he's going to look — and I come from the weak side and am waiting for him. I got a lot of blocks and rebounds, I threw the outlet pass and ran the floor, I looked for and found the opportunity to take off in traffic. When the other team made mistakes and gave up the ball around our basket, it was a dunk. I played both ends and I really dominated.

I was very happy. Back in our room Benny Anders and I were going, "Did you see that one? *Ooooh!*" Benny was competing with Clyde and Michael Young. He played well but didn't think he was going to start. I didn't know if I was or not but I was on top of the world.

I went to the gym the next day but I couldn't practice. I tried to stretch but the more I tried to relax my muscles, the tighter they became. My back froze up on me, everything just locked in a terrible back spasm.

I couldn't tell the coach. He was very businesslike, he didn't like excuses, he was a tough man. I told Coach T. Coach Lewis got the news through his assistant coach.

I tried to play in our first two games but I couldn't. I lasted two minutes against West Texas State and five minutes five days later against Seton Hall on national TV.

The day after that I couldn't even stand up straight. The pain was terrible. I sat in my room and started to cry.

The talk started going around campus almost immediately: Hakeem is scared to play, he doesn't want to play basketball; he's just a practice player. They'd been talking for a year now about this Nigerian guy who was going to be the greatest; now the time for me to play had come and people thought I was frightened. That hurt me. I was trying my best to convince people that I really was injured, that it was out of my control, but they didn't believe me. "How's your back?" they would ask me, but the question was not serious, they wanted to hear what I had to say so they could go back and criticize me.

I sat out four games. I didn't go to them; I couldn't walk. I had to move so delicately I couldn't even go to class. It was real bad.

The team took me to a doctor. He took an X-ray and said, "You have not been drinking water, you've been drinking a lot of soda. You have a problem with your kidneys."

He was right, I hadn't been drinking water. Athletes are supposed to drink at least eight glasses a day and I had been drinking soda instead. My back was in serious spasm. The doctor gave me muscle-relaxer pills but they made me weak and tired, so I slept a lot. And still my back wasn't loose. I wasn't getting any better.

Terence was doing everything he could think of. Finally someone told him to take me to an acupuncturist. I had never heard of acupuncture, but he took me to a little house where this Chinese guy put me on a table and stuck needles in me. He said there were pressure points and if he placed the needles properly I would feel better. I was ready for anything to get rid of the pain and get back on the court.

The acupuncturist put about a dozen needles in the instep of my feet and up and down both calves. I was nervous but he stuck them in quickly with a swift motion and all I felt was a pinprick. The needles lay there on their sides.

All of a sudden the needles stood straight up by themselves! They shook and vibrated and stood straight up! It was amazing to see. "How do you feel?" the acupuncturist asked me.

I looked at the needles hopefully and felt my back. It hurt just to sit there. "Still the same," I told him. I was disappointed. This was the last resort and it wasn't working.

"You don't feel anything?"

"No."

"That's all right. In a couple of days you will see the difference."

I hobbled back to my room. When Benny came back I asked him how was practice.

"We missed you, man."

When I had to go to the bathroom, Benny had to help me stand. When I came back and tried to get into bed I was walking like a robot.

The next day was the same. It was terrible. I went to sleep early because there was nothing else I could do.

When I woke up I got out of bed and went to the bathroom. Benny was in his bed on the other side of the room and I tried not to wake him. When I came back he was up. He looked at me and started smiling.

"Your back is okay."

"Yeah!" I had forgotten it until he mentioned it. I moved my back one way and then the other. Everything was back to normal.

I couldn't wait to go to practice. When I got there everybody was saying, "How's your back?" "Let's see your back." "Hey, your back's okay!" Some of them still didn't believe me, they had that kind of look but wouldn't say anything.

That weekend was a four-team tournament called the Kettle Classic, held at Hofheinz Pavilion, where we had our home games. The papers were saying I would play.

During warm-ups before the game I was jumping way up there so people could see how high I could go, so they could see I was ready. I wasn't on the starting five and the fans wanted to see me get in there; I could hear them yelling from the stands. Coach Lewis kept them waiting. He's that kind of a coach. Maybe he didn't have confidence in me, maybe he didn't know what I could do. I think he was trying to keep the pressure off me and let me develop naturally.

The starters played the whole game. With about three minutes left and the win safely in hand he called a time-out and put the whole second team in. The crowd screamed and we all ran to the scorer's table.

The other team put their bench in too, so we weren't playing against top competition, but I remember the first shot I blocked. Somebody made a good move to the basket and I socked that ball! I blocked it so hard, the crowd just went crazy. We took it and ran the fast break.

I blocked two or three shots in a row and when I got back again on defense I stood in the middle of the paint with my arms up, taking up space. Don't come in here! I was the center, I was the zone.

Three blocks in a minute was the talk of the tournament.

In the finals against Iowa, Larry Micheaux was battling with their two seven-footers, Michael Payne and Greg Stokes. We should have been winning easily but they were getting uncontested lay-ups. This time Coach Lewis didn't wait until the last few minutes to bring me in. He called down the bench. Coach Lewis didn't take his eyes off the game, but when he called you, you knew what you were supposed to do: "Take care of that."

I went in and blocked some shots, started the fast break. Most of the time the guy with the ball is going to dunk it — Clyde will dunk it — but sometimes he gets cut off and throws the ball up for someone on the wing to finish. I finished it once or twice. My game was always corrections: if someone got beat I went and helped by blocking the shot, if someone missed a lay-up I put it back in. Most of my points came from capitalizing on other people's mistakes, not from people passing me the ball so I could make my move.

I got called for goaltending and I was still jumping at everything, so Iowa began to give me head fakes. The coach told me, "Stay down!" but I kept jumping and quickly got into foul trouble. I had to learn to restrain myself. It was something I worked on the whole year.

The starting lineup was set so I spent my whole first year coming off the bench. I liked that very much. Larry Micheaux took the heat in the beginning of the game and I got to watch for a while before I went in and cleaned things up. The week after the Kettle Classic we played in the Sugar Bowl tournament at the Superdome in New Orleans and I won the MVP award coming off the bench. I scored twenty points in the final against Louisiana State, the only time all year I scored twenty. If I had three dunks a game, a lot of rebounds, a few blocked shots, and we won, I was very happy.

Somehow I had gotten the nickname "Jelly." I never liked it. I think it started with Lois Thorn, Coach Lewis's secretary, who was very friendly and always asking me questions and joking with me in the basketball office, making me feel at home. I would sometimes go to the office just to talk to her. She was an older woman and a big friend, and she began greeting me by saying "Hey, Hakeem, jellybean." She liked the way it sounded.

I didn't know what a jellybean was. Did I look like a jellybean? It didn't mean anything to me and I didn't really like it.

But people in the office heard Lois call me "Jellybean." The guys on the court shortened it to "Jelly." I didn't like that, either. I wasn't soft and sweet, I didn't jiggle.

I don't remember who it was who first called me "Hakeem the Dream." It might have been a reporter in one of the newspapers, it could have been someone on the sidelines talking, but I began hearing it around the gym and around campus. I would walk on the court or try to get into a pickup game and someone would say, "Hakeem! The Dream!" I liked that. They were talking about my game, they liked the way I played, and it seemed to me that this nickname was earned.

And it grew. Instead of calling me by my name, sometimes people simply shortened it to "Dream." "Hey, Dream." "What's happenin', Dream?" I liked it a lot when this caught on. My nickname was both rhyme and reputation.

My life was entirely on campus, life outside campus did not exist. From the time I woke up in the morning to when I went to sleep at night my day was established. I went to class, I went to practice, I ate my meals, I did my homework and studied, I went to sleep, and the next day it started all over again. Homework was a big task and when I finished I felt fulfilled, as if I had accomplished something. Doing well in school meant something to me. My grades were pretty good and I took a business law class that I particularly liked. On the weekends I went to the park in the daytime and partied at night. I started learning the American slang that everybody in Lagos was so excited about, and I started learning more about girls.

Benny Anders, my roommate, had a Pontiac Trans Am, so we were mobile. He and I did everything together. He was from Bernice, Louisiana, a small rural town, and once he hit the big city of Houston he got down and partied. I had partied in Lagos growing up, but it was mostly kids whose parents had traveled out of the country and left them alone in the house. They weren't supposed to, but they'd invite some friends and some girls from school. Parties at home were always basic.

At the University of Houston, fraternities would get a band or a disk jockey, a keg, and charge a couple of bucks at the door. Inside you could dance all night.

I was never much of a dancer. I was too self-conscious. You could never get me out on the dance floor; I was so tall that everybody would watch me and I'd be so awkward and nervous I wouldn't be able to move. A beautiful girl might ask me to dance, someone you could not turn down, but it didn't matter. I would politely decline and say, "I cannot go out there." Some of them were persistent. "Aw, come on, come on, dance with me." I'd be embarrassed because everyone was looking at us. I would draw them close so no one could hear and I'd let them in on the secret. "Look, you don't understand. *I cannot go out there!*"

I didn't like to be in the center in almost any situation. I liked to blend in with everybody. Unfortunately, there were times when I couldn't. Once attention fell on me I always felt uncomfortable.

There were some guys who liked hanging around with ballplayers because girls were always coming over to us, and if they weren't, these guys would use lines to get them over. They were crude, they'd go out of their way to impress girls, and if that didn't work, they would say bad things about them. That was the wrong approach and never attracted the kind of girls I was interested in. I was always standing half a step back and I was drawn to the quiet, shy girls who had the same nature. A lot of the guys treated girls badly; I was brought up to be respectful. This may have been exotic to some of the girls I met. It turned out they liked me, too.

The UH Cougars had an up-and-down season. We won ten in a row and were ranked number ten in the nation. Then we lost four tough

In Lagos, basketball was "the American game." They told me,
"You should go to America."

My family is very important to me. From left, here are Akinola; my mother, Akibe;
Tajudeen; my father, Salam; and Afis.

Phi Slama Jama in action: Reid Gettys (left), and Clyde Drexler (right).

The University of Houston coaching staff (from left): Coach T (Terence Kirkpatrick), Donnie Schverak, Coach Guy V. Lewis.

Richard Mackson

In the 1984 NCAA finals against Patrick Ewing and Georgetown, it wasn't personal.

Playing at Fonde against Moses Malone: "Be a man!"

Phil Huber

Ralph Sampson and I, the
Twin Towers, worked hard
and had mutual respect.

The Twin Towers had the
answer for the Lakers.

Larry Bird wouldn't even look at you. That was his game face.

D.H. (center) and the Rockets with our game faces on. We were joking! You intimidate with your game—how you play, not what you say.

John Incono

Coach Fitch was tough!

I formed the Dream
Foundation to improve
educational opportunities
for kids in Houston and
across the United States.

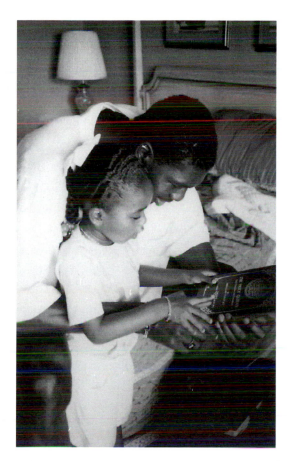

I am a hands-on father.
It is my responsibility to
raise my daughter, Abisola,
the best way I know how.
She is so important to me.

Although Lita and I have
separated, we join together
for a happy, healthy, and
strong Abisola.

John Kaplan

When I was re-introduced
to Islam, my life changed.
I finally found what I had
been looking for.

On my pilgrimage to Mecca,
understanding came over me
and my faith became very,
very strong.

Amin-Camerapix

games in a row by a total of seven points and dropped out of the rankings. Then we won nine straight, including beating our toughest rival, Arkansas. We lost four of our first five Southwest Conference games but came back and placed second in the Conference. Then we lost the SWC play-off championship game to Arkansas. We were unranked but we got an invitation to the NCAA tournament.

UH hadn't won an NCAA tournament game in ten years. Last year's team had lost in the first round to Villanova. But we got past Alcorn State and Tulsa and then had to play the University of Missouri. This was a big test for me; they had lost only three times all season and their center Steve Stipanovich was a senior All-America.

Nobody gave us much of a chance. We were unranked, Missouri was the number-five team in the country, and we were playing in St. Louis. Coach Lewis sat the team down and said, "Look, two weeks from now I'm going to New Orleans for the Final Four and it would be great if you guys could come with me." Everybody looked at each other, like, What is he talking about?

"To play," he said. "I've gone to the Final Four for the last fourteen years, since 1968 . . . by myself. I'd like to take the team with me this time." Until that time I don't think any of us really believed we had a chance to win.

I got in the game against Missouri and played Stipanovich tough. I was a freshman but I played within our system, getting rebounds and blocks, starting the fast break. We beat them by one point, on Coach Lewis's sixtieth birthday.

We beat Boston College when Rob Williams scored nineteen points in the second half and Reid Gettys hit ten straight free throws, the same number he'd taken all season, in the last few minutes. We were going to the Final Four.

Everybody was so excited. They were talking about Final Four, Final Four. On television, all they talked about was "the Road to the Final Four." Everything was Final Four. What was this Final Four? I had no idea. Until a few weeks before I had never even heard of the Final Four.

Until you are in the middle of the action you don't really understand what the Final Four is. In 1982 it was held in New Orleans, a perfect place for a party. Our hotel was in the French Quarter and the lobby

was swarming with people. The elevator door would open and there would be a lot of movement. Press from all over the world, people you don't know coming up to you all the time, talking to you and trying to make conversation or just staring. Coach T had family who lived in New Orleans so he showed me and Benny Anders around the Quarter, told us about the tradition, got us the best gumbo. There were kids in the street with bottle caps on the bottoms of their sneakers, tap-dancing in front of the hotel for spare change. I had never seen this. It was a different world.

The games were going to be played at the Superdome. We got there and the court was right out in the middle of what was usually a football stadium. It was huge. The court was at least thirty yards from the baskets to the stands in each direction. The place was so big it was like practicing in an open field.

The Superdome holds around sixty thousand people and there were about twenty thousand screaming fans inside for practice, twice as many as filled Hofheinz when it was sold out. Their cheers were loud and echoing in this big arena. I could hear the squeaks of our sneakers on the hardwood floor as we ran our fast-break drills in front of the constant roar of all these basketball fans. Practice was very active, almost hyper, like a game. I was so excited I got pumped up, then I got winded, tired. It was a wonderful experience.

The teams in the 1982 Final Four were Houston, Louisville, North Carolina, and Georgetown. We were going to play North Carolina in the semifinals but I was most interested in the center for Georgetown, Patrick Ewing.

Before the season started Lynden Rose had pulled me aside and said, "There's a TV special tonight about this guy, I want you to watch it." He and I watched it together in his room. It was a documentary about Patrick Ewing, who had just graduated from high school and been recruited by everyone and had decided to go to Georgetown University and play under Coach John Thompson. Lynden was interested in him because Ewing was from Jamaica, another island guy, "Look at him." Lynden knew about a lot of players down there, he was proud of the island guys.

I watched the footage of Ewing in high school. It was beautiful. He could catch the lob, dunk the ball, block shots, rebound and run,

dominate the game. Lynden said, "It isn't even showing him at his best."

If that's not his best. . . .

I had great respect for Patrick Ewing immediately. He was doing everything I did at home. The footage was identical to the way I'd played at the Stadium. It was the way I pictured myself; this was the first time I saw someone who was doing *everything*. I thought, This guy's better than I am.

On TV, the replays looked incredible. He looked like a natural, like he was on a different level.

And he was so much more well known. It was big news when Patrick Ewing decided to come to Georgetown. Here was this documentary all about it. During the pre-season and throughout the season they were writing articles in newspapers and magazines all over the country about Patrick Ewing, the best freshman basketball player in the country. Nobody knew I was coming, nobody cared. Nobody knew who I was except people in the Southwest Conference. He played in the Big East and they thought their whole conference was better than ours. My first national exposure was at the end of the season, in the NCAA play-offs against Missouri.

So when I saw him play I saw instantly that he was very talented. If I thought I might be the best freshman in the country, I knew very few people would agree with me. But when people wrote articles about me they often compared me with him, which made me feel comfortable. From what I saw, it was a compliment to be compared to Patrick Ewing.

In New Orleans I began to think, I might play this guy!

But first we had to play the University of North Carolina.

They were the number-one team in the country. They were supposed to win it all. Their main players were James Worthy, Sam Perkins, and Michael Jordan, and they were coached by Dean Smith, the foremost basketball coach in America, who had never won an NCAA tournament.

I knew from the films the coaches had played for us and from what I'd seen on TV that James Worthy was quick. He played small forward and had a first step that would blow right past his defenders, and usually those quick guys were lean but not too long. But when I passed him in the hallway on the way to the court at the Superdome, the first thing I noticed was that James Worthy was *big*. A definite 6′9″. I hadn't realized he was that big because of the way he played his game. Most of the time when you meet someone after having seen them play on TV, he seems smaller. A guy who's supposed to be 6′9″ turns out to be 6′7″. Not Worthy. He was a big guy, not much smaller than I was.

Worthy was the star of the UNC team. Sam Perkins got a lot of build-up, but he appeared to me to be a role player. Michael Jordan was just a freshman. Their whole team loved to run. So did we. They were older and more experienced, we were inexperienced but we were tough.

There were more than sixty-one thousand people in the Superdome for the semifinals, the largest crowd in Final Four history. The noise was intense: everybody was screaming. They screamed even more when North Carolina ran out and began scoring whenever they wanted to. They scored fourteen straight points before we could put the ball in the basket. In the first five minutes we were down 14–0.

James Worthy made the lasting impression on me. His game was outstanding, better than any other player's on the floor. He was twice as fast as I thought he'd be. I couldn't believe it; how could someone be so fast? Every time I looked he was waving the ball with one hand and on his way to dunking on the other end — with no one around him. We would be running down the court chasing him and he would already have scored and be coming back, *passing us on his way to play defense.* I said, "That isn't possible." I sat on the bench and studied him and I found out how he did it.

When one of us went up for a jump shot, he released. He would not go in for a rebound — he would let his teammates take care of that — he would take off. They would get the ball and swing it to a guard who hit him in full stride, only two steps from the basket. His hands were very large and he would catch the ball, wave it in the air like he was flying down the court showing off a prize, and jam it through the hoop. Then he would circle under the basket and hustle back while whoever was chasing him tried to catch his breath before inbounding.

And he did it all the time. Just up and down. His anticipation and quickness were incredible. He would run through the passing lane and take advantage of any mistake we made. A careless pass, a slow reaction coming to the ball, and he was gone and you couldn't catch him. Running through the passing lane was Clyde's strength, but James Worthy was playing on another level.

I didn't notice Michael Jordan much in that game. He scored eighteen points and played okay, he was competitive, but the man on the court that night was James Worthy.

Lynden Rose had a great game — a *great* game. He carried the team and we caught up and tied North Carolina right before the half. Unfortunately Rob Williams, our leading scorer, went 0 for 8 from the field and scored only two points the whole night. When I got on the court I played like a freshman. I tried hard but there was a time when I was struggling just to catch my wind. North Carolina beat us, 68–63.

Georgetown beat Louisville in the other semifinal. I didn't want to go to the NCAA finals and watch two other teams play, so I watched Georgetown against North Carolina on TV in my hotel room with some teammates.

Once again I watched James Worthy carefully. Just the way he ran the court, he was dangerous. He was best in open court, where he was completely unstoppable, and he was almost as good in the half-court offense, where he had a very quick move and first step to the basket.

Sam Perkins had scored a lot of points against us but in this game I mostly watched Patrick Ewing. I was impressed that Ewing, a freshman, was starting against a team that had beaten us. Even though he goaltended the first three shots North Carolina put up, he was a shot blocker, making people change their shots; he was very aggressive and although he wasn't really dominant, he played well. He was the key force in the middle. He seemed like a mirror of myself. He could do all the things I could do, only better. It wasn't often that you saw big men who could run the floor, fill the lane, and be the trailer in case the man with the ball missed the lay-up. Patrick did all of that.

They called goaltending on him a lot too; he would go up and block anything. You couldn't just turn around on him in the paint because he would block you. His turnaround jumper and his jump hook were the staples in the offensive pivot. He did everything I wanted to do.

Georgetown lost a tough one when, with five seconds to go and losing by one point, their guard Fred Brown threw the ball directly to Worthy, thinking he was a Georgetown teammate. It's the kind of mistake you hope the guy doesn't keep with him for the rest of his life.

8

THE BROTHERHOOD OF PHI SLAMA JAMA

BY SPRING 1982 I had moved off campus to a one-bedroom apartment in a complex near the Astrodome. It was nice to have my own place and be able to decorate it, to start getting furniture and a good stereo and plants. I love interior decorating and I slowly began to acquire things. It was exciting to be so independent. I had watched my mom in the kitchen all my life, and though I had never cooked at home, I tried to remember which spices she used as I cooked my own Nigerian stews.

But there were drawbacks to living off-campus. I began to realize that American life was not like the African life I was used to. Living alone, I had no sense of community around me. I didn't know my neighbors in the apartment complex, I didn't even know who lived next door. There was no field to go out on and find friends. After practice during the season, the day was over. I did my homework or whatever I had to do, and the rest was up to me. It was a very independent life but there was a lot of isolation.

I had a summer job at a gas and oil company owned by one of the alumni, and with the job came a leased company car. I couldn't wait to drive in America. I had learned how to drive in Lagos by borrowing my brother Yemi's car, but having transportation in Houston meant I could really get around. I drove to Fonde in the afternoon and hit the clubs at night.

Fonde in the summer of '82 was very competitive. There were street players on the court who were as good or better than anybody out there. We were a Final Four team now, and we were still young. The Rockets had been beaten in the first round of the NBA playoffs. We started beating them more often than before. Not all the time, but enough to make us feel strong. Now all the professionals wanted to play. They had Moses and Robert Reid, Major Jones, Alan Leavell; some European players came in. The crowds got bigger and the place got sweatier as the games got more competitive.

I competed against Moses at Fonde all summer again. He had been named the NBA's Most Valuable Player for the second time only a few weeks before. *"Be a man!"* Putting the ball on the floor; exploding to the basket; trying to block his shot; banging on the boards. I loved it, and because I was playing against the best player in the game, my game kept growing.

After the game guys would say, "Let's go to Frenchy's." Frenchy's was a take-out restaurant right by a park near the UH campus where they served the best chicken and fried food I had ever tasted. They had chicken with a spicy Louisiana seasoning that was just the best. So we'd all meet there.

But all these pros lived a very dangerous life. Before they left they bragged about who was going to get to Frenchy's first. They would run to their rides and you could see them hit the freeway, about fifteen shiny Porsches and Mercedeses and Cadillacs whizzing in and out of traffic, pro athletes going as fast as they could go. It was like a rally, like Le Mans, with the sunset kind of orange from the refineries, every early evening on the freeways of Houston.

Moses always won. Other guys may have had their hot cars but Moses drove a Maserati and some other fast machines and he was a good racer. He would always be finished eating and standing outside Frenchy's when everyone else finally pulled up, just talking to whoever was around. He would always joke about how slow the guys were. That would be the first twenty minutes of conversation each night at Frenchy's: Who won.

I never joined in that competition. By the time I pulled up guys would be spread out on the park grass, eating. Moses always bought the chicken. He would buy it by the bucket and leave it for everybody. All these ballplayers would be standing or lounging in the park, talking about Fonde and dipping into the bucket, eating great fried chicken. Eating and talking, talking and eating, as the sun went down. It was beautiful.

The second topic of conversation every evening, after the race to Frenchy's, was which club everyone was going to that night. There was an unofficial schedule: this club on Tuesdays, that one on Thursdays. You could leave town and come back and meet everyone on the same nights in the same clubs, nothing ever changed.

The same guys who hung out at the pickup games were the ones I saw hanging out at the clubs. Ballplayers and hangers-on. The legal drinking age in Texas was twenty-one but I was 6'11" and I walked in with the pros, so no one asked me for proof. I never really liked beer, I always preferred sweets.

Most of the pro ballplayers talked trash to women, trying to impress the other guys. They didn't show any respect or dignity and acted as if the women were supposed to recognize them. I started feeling uncomfortable around all this, and the pros didn't want college boys cramping their style anyway, so instead of standing at the bar with the rest of the gang Benny and I walked over and stood in our own corner somewhere. Benny was much more outgoing than I was and made contact more easily. Some girls would come around because they saw this group of ballplayers. A lot of them asked me my height. I met a lot of girls and I had some dates. I was still shy and still appreciated the quiet ones, not the loud partiers who just wanted to be around ballplayers. I met a lot of girls but I never had a steady girlfriend.

Rice University is a more intellectual hall of education than the University of Houston. To stay in school at Rice the students had to be serious, and it showed in their character. In Nigeria education is important so I admired the reputation of Rice and the people who went there.

I also admired the young woman who was walking across campus one evening that summer when I was at Rice to play in a pickup game. I was attracted to her immediately. She was not only pretty, she also had the very innocent look of a girl with serious academic ambition. She looked like she had a goal. She was in summer school at Rice, so she must be doubly devoted.

She walked by with her friends while I was standing outside with some basketball players. This was not a promising combination. I watched her go into a classroom building.

I had just finished playing and the guys were about to leave. "See you in a few minutes," I told them. I stayed outside her classroom building and when she came out I found I had the ability to talk to her.

"Excuse me."

She didn't stop.

"Can I speak to you for a second?"

Two of her friends went to their next class and she said she was going to her car.

"Where did you park?"

"Oh, I parked kind of far away." That was good; it would be a long walk. I just started talking. I told her I had heard good things about Rice academically. Is it as tough as people outside think it is? How are you finding classes? Are you in summer school or a full-time student?

She said she was full-time. I asked her, "What's your major?"

"I'm a double major: business and pre-law."

I was very impressed.

I think I caught her attention because I was interested in her goals and her work ethic not just her good looks. She didn't expect that from a person my size, still sweating from playing ball.

"Are you a student here?" she asked.

"No, I'm at the University of Houston." I was proud to tell her.

We talked for a while — it *was* a long walk. When she got to her car I tried to get her phone number but she wouldn't give it to me. I didn't press her about it; I wanted her to be comfortable.

"I'd like to talk to you again," I said. "How can we continue this conversation another time?"

"Well, I'm in summer school, I have class every day, maybe I'll see you here."

I waited for her outside the classroom building several times that week. The first two days she didn't know I was coming. After that I was expected. It became a way to enjoy my evening. I would play at Fonde, eat at Frenchy's, go back to my apartment and change, and go wait for this girl at Rice.

Her name was Lita Spencer, and she was a freshman. I didn't ask for her number again for a long time. I was content to visit her. It seemed like a pilgrimage worth making. Finally she agreed to go out with me, and slowly we became a couple. Very soon I loved her.

We spent all the time we could together and everything we did was natural. She was smart and devoted and she anticipated my needs. She was so pretty and all her attention was on me. It felt so good. She never made me feel worried or insecure, and I did the same for her. I knew she was the one for me. Our relationship was beautiful.

Every opportunity I had I drove over to Rice and picked her up. I brought her flowers. One time I was rushing so fast that a policeman chased me onto the Rice campus and gave me a ticket for speeding. I got pulled over and when some of her friends saw the patrolman standing over my car writing out the summons they went and got her. She was touched that I would go so far for her.

We spent a lot of time together at my apartment. We would cook together, read together; we had a home life. I was very content. Almost from the beginning it was like being married.

Lita and I created some controversy. Rice and UH were rivals; they were superior academically, we were better at sports. Everybody knew your business on both campuses and a lot of Cougar girls felt I was being snobby by going out with someone from Rice. "What's the matter, we're not good enough for you?" That kind of thing. Lita went through the same thing; I'd go to her campus and people would look at me with disdain. They got over it.

A lot of the ballplayers had three or four girlfriends, but I had only Lita and I was more than satisfied. We had a great time and it made my college life very special.

When the school year started we had a routine. I would call her and say, "What is the plan? Where do you have to be, what time will you finish? Can you do your homework here? If you can't stop by now, come over later. What time will you be free?" If she told me "Eight o'clock," I had the time between the end of practice and 8:00 to shower, eat, and do my homework or whatever I wanted.

I had less and less time to hang out with the guys and they started giving me a hard time about it. They'd say, "You coming tonight?" and I'd tell them, "I'm gonna meet a girl." They knew it was Lita and after a while, when they saw I wasn't coming to the clubs so often, they started playing mind games with me. The guys made it seem like I was on a leash, that she would not *let* me come to the clubs, that she was in control, that I wasn't a real man.

I didn't want to have to defend my girlfriend to the guys. I was happy with the way things were going; I had a wonderful girlfriend, I had a great team and fun friends, and I wanted it all to continue. When I went to a club with the guys I always ended up going back to see her later anyway.

But you can't hang out at the clubs if you bring your girlfriend, it's not right. There are too many guys hustling and you can't be with the team if you're with your girl. They would put me on the spot and say, "Oh, he's not gonna come, he's gonna stay home and be with his girl."

Sometimes, when I wanted to be with the guys, I'd step up and say, "No, I can come."

"You're just gonna bring your girl along."

"No, I can come, I'm not gonna bring her." It was like responding to a challenge. I couldn't back down.

"We'll see. We'll see."

So on those occasions when I did go to the clubs with the guys I didn't ask Lita to join me. She was disappointed that we weren't spending that time together, and finally she invited herself. "Can I go?"

I tried to explain the situation. I was completely honest with her. "I truly love you," I told her, "and I enjoy all the time I spend with you. You know how I feel, we have a beautiful relationship. It's not like I don't want to be with you, it's not like I don't want to take you out. I would rather spend this time with you, but all the guys are going after practice and if I take you it would not be appropriate; I would spend all my time with you and it's just the guys tonight."

She didn't understand.

I was disappointed and I began to get upset. I wanted Lita to trust my word and my judgment; if I said something it was important to me that she believe it was true. I wanted her to know inside that I would never lie to her and would never let her down. I wanted her to take that as one of the basic truths of life — because it was true. If I turned it around, it was what I believed about her. I wanted her to trust me the way I trusted her: completely. "I'm not looking outside," I told her. I wasn't going to meet anybody else, I wasn't even looking. But Lita always thought I was getting tired of her. I couldn't make her happy; the only way she would be happy was if I stayed home or took her.

I was very disappointed. For her to think I would lie to her showed a distrust that I found worrisome. It got to the point where I just went anyway.

Her friends didn't help. They would see me in a club just talking to another girl and they would report back to her and cause trouble. That was more friction. It was heartbreaking. Still, I loved Lita.

I was studying business administration. The coaches watched the players' schedules closely to make sure we all stayed eligible and from the beginning they had suggested courses I could take. But I didn't want to take just physical education courses. My favorite class was business law. The coaches were very worried that I was taking it; they thought I might fail. The class was very challenging and I got my best grade in it.

The campus was full of action and movement and people. Noon was primetime, everybody had just finished classes and was hanging out. In the middle of everything, University Center (UC) was packed with girls and fraternity boys called Q Dogs; you could tell them by their T-shirts. It was a meeting place for the entire university and I couldn't walk across it; it reminded me of high school, too many people watching me. I had a 1:00 class before practice and I had to walk by there three times a week to get to it, and *every time* I would go all the way around UC rather than walk through it. I only went through UC once, and that was with Benny Anders. Benny loved attention and as people recognized him his walk changed, he got smoother, he put the glide in his stride; mine just got all wacky.

I could not walk in front of people; I felt like they were watching me. My walk would get goofy and uncoordinated, I would trip over my feet, I would freeze up. I could play basketball in front of sixty thousand people I didn't know and it wouldn't bother me. But if I saw even one person I knew in the stands it would throw me off altogether and I couldn't perform. My run would become different, I would be totally out of sync. Some guys brought their girlfriends to Fonde and I don't know how they did that. Lita didn't come to the UH games for almost half a semester because I didn't think I could handle it.

Our practices at Hofheinz Pavilion were always full and I didn't mind that. Even when practice was supposed to be closed there were physical education classes held in the gym and it was always filled with students running around the track. But most of the time it was open to everybody and we would have as many as three or four hundred students and media people watching us.

We were a running team now. Rob Williams had entered the draft as an undergraduate and been taken on the first round by the Denver Nuggets. Lynden Rose had the misfortune to be drafted by the Los Angeles Lakers at a time when they had Magic Johnson, Norm Nixon, and Michael Cooper already in their backcourt. (Lynden didn't make it in the pros but did get his law degree and went on to become a successful Houston attorney.) We had Clyde Drexler, Michael Young, Larry Micheaux, and me, with most of the point-guard time split between Reid Gettys and Alvin Franklin.

Pre-season magazines were making all kinds of predictions about us: who was going to win the Conference, how far we were going to go in the NCAAs, who was going to be All-Conference, who was going to be All-America. Big honors. It was a lot to live up to, but we had grown from going to the Final Four and all our games had improved over the summer.

Practices were intense because everybody had incentive to play his best. Everyone believed he should be starting, we all wanted our playing time, and we had six or seven guys who truly had a legitimate chance to play in the NBA. Clyde had been chosen Honorable Mention All-America, I'd been named SWC Freshman and Newcomer of the Year, Micheaux was talking about leaving school early and had a chance to go high in the draft, Michael Young was expected to step into Rob Williams's scoring shoes, and Benny Anders was dying to step up.

The court at Hofheinz was not hardwood but some rubberized substance, and the team wore out several hundred pairs of sneakers that year running up and down it. Practices were tough and competitive and fun. We ran plays where all we did was press, and drills where people dunked on each other with both hands so hard the building would rattle. We'd had these ugly, badly padded old backboards that had been there probably since Hofheinz had been built, but that year the university installed new, modern, high-tech Hydra-rib goals, the kind that collapse like a jackknife for storage and were the latest in basketball technology. The man from the Hydra-rib company rolled them down the court, lined them up, and said, "Here you are." The coaches and everybody said, "Great!"

At our first practice — just our ordinary practice, nothing special, just the usual couple of hours of everybody jamming over everybody else — the base of these new goals moved around the floor so badly we had to use the ones on the sides of the court for shooting practice. They called the installer and he came in and said, "Well, what we're going to have to do is put two-hundred-pound weights on the back of each stanchion." The maintenance staff did that and he looked over the work. "There's no way you're going to move these around now," he said.

That lasted one day. We were dunking so ferociously that the goals were bobbing like buoys. Finally they had to call in the maintenance department to drill through the floor and bolt the goals to the concrete. The next year they got a new floor and had to start all over.

We opened the season by beating Arizona and Lamar in the Kettle Classic 104–63 and 106–72. After the first jump ball we looked for the first dunk and never slowed down. That's all we wanted to do. It didn't matter who was under the goal trying to stop us, he was just there to get some punishment. We weren't competing with the opponents — whoever they were, they were going to lose — we were competing for who had the best dunk. Once the barrage started there was no way to shut us down.

Someone in the newspaper came up with a name for our team. We had "Clyde the Glide" and "Hakeem the Dream" and "Mr. Mean." We were a fraternity, the brotherhood of Phi Slama Jama.

The name got us going even harder.

We won a couple more and then Auburn University came to Houston with its forward Charles Barkley. We didn't know much about him, just that he was a fat boy. He had the nickname "the Round Mound of Rebound."

Players are always trying to psych each other out before, during, and after games, and in the tunnel from the locker room to the court he looked at our team and just smiled. He was so confident. We were

Phi Slama Jama but he didn't show a sign of worry, no sign of worry at all.

When the game started, Barkley got the ball and drove on Micheaux. Larry Micheaux, Mr. Mean, is a strong guy. When Barkley hit Micheaux he threw him into Clyde and there was nothing Micheaux could do. Later in the game I was going from the weak side to help out on a drive, I jumped, and all of a sudden I was hit by something flying in the air. It was Michael Young, who had bounced off Barkley and plowed into me. Michael Young was 6'7" and strong, but Barkley would drive and just throw people off him. One time he was standing in the middle of the lane and everybody just got out of his way. *Boom,* he dunked and the rim was shaking and Clyde was just standing there underneath as he came down. Barkley turned around and pushed him out of the way and then barreled downcourt.

We beat them but Barkley was clearly outstanding. He was so physical and such a jumper, he was so big and still handled the ball with such skill, that he was in a class by himself. He would have fit in perfectly with our fraternity. From then on I followed his career. I was glad this guy wasn't in our Conference so we didn't have to play him twice a year; this guy was *tough.*

We lost at Syracuse on national TV and then went to Japan and got beaten by Virginia even though Ralph Sampson, their 7'4" center and the NCAA Player of the Year, was injured and out of the lineup.

Coach Lewis was very upset on the long flight home. He hated to lose. He would make us feel like boys, not men, like cowards. He wanted brave men on his team and if you didn't have that inside you, you couldn't play for him. He would never tell anyone he'd had a good game. He might go back and tell the alumni or the assistant coaches that one of his players had played well, but he would never tell him himself. I was close to Coach T so that's where I got my praise. It was not personal, but to get Coach Lewis's attention and impress him you had to play your best. Even the assistant coaches straightened up when they talked to Coach Lewis. He was a great guy but he kept us at a distance. I was so shy that I didn't see how we could talk anyhow. I knew he liked me, and I liked him.

Coach Lewis was a motivator, a leader, a tough, tough man. There was always somebody bleeding at practice, someone throwing elbows,

We won twenty-two in a row and went undefeated in the SWC. We knew there were great players out there because we played against them. We knew there were great teams because we read about them, but when it came time to play we dominated everybody. We kept waiting to meet our match. We would prepare for our next opponent, we would beat each other up in practice, and then we'd go on the court and find that they were not what we'd expected. Practice games between the red and white teams were much harder than the ones on our schedule. We kept waiting to meet a team that could dominate us.

We swept the SWC tournament and were back in the NCAAs. We beat Maryland, Memphis State, and Villanova, and we were in the Final Four for the second year in a row.

We were Phi Slama Jama, number one or two in the country depending on what you thought of Louisville's Doctors of Dunk. They were in the Final Four with us. We were looking forward to playing them in the semifinals, in Albuquerque, New Mexico.

The papers were calling it the Game of the Century. The only game bigger in UH history, maybe in basketball history, was the legendary game against UCLA in the Astrodome that I had been hearing about since I was in Africa with Christopher Pond. We and Louisville were very similar teams: we both loved to run, we loved to dunk, we were fast and quick and fearless. We both had cool nicknames. They were leapers; they didn't have great height but they could leap. Their starters were Scooter and Rodney McCray, Milt Wagner, Charles Jones, and Lancaster Gordon.

Albuquerque is up in the mountains and the first two days we practiced breathing the air. If we were going to run we had to have our wind. We held an open practice the day before the semifinal in the university arena, where the games would be played. The place was full — sixteen thousand screaming fans. The previous year we had practiced before even more but the Superdome had still been two thirds empty. Now we had fewer people but no empty seats, and the fans created an amazing wall of sound. We loved it; the louder it got, the faster we pushed the ball, the harder we dunked. When I wanted some peace and quiet to concentrate on my free throws I had to plug in my headphones and wear my Walkman at the foul line.

The game against Louisville was great fun. The pace was so fast everyone felt free and comfortable to create. There were a lot of nice moves, a lot of blocks, everybody was running down the floor — pass the ball, pass the ball, *dunk*. Take it out quickly, pass it, dunk on the other end. Up tempo all the way. It was like a game at Fonde.

As a shot blocker you cannot take getting dunked on personally; it's the price you pay for trying to stop every shot. In a zone defense I could control the area around the basket and never have to go very far. The way to beat the zone is to shoot over it and make the defense come out to guard the perimeter shooters, which opens up the middle for drives and post-up moves. Ricky Pierce of Rice and Scott Hastings could kill a zone. But Louisville was not interested in shooting over us, that wasn't their game. They were the Doctors of Dunk and they came right at us.

I was leading the nation in blocked shots and had a reputation, so when players drove into the lane and saw me they often changed their minds in midair, which gave me even more time and a better position to block them. But there were always some players who, when they saw they had no chance of shooting over me, decided that their only chance to score was to force everything, come in hard, and dunk. Those were the players I respected. Louisville had a lot of them.

Benny Anders had a highlight-reel game. He was running the floor, catching lobs, and dunking. All season long he came off the bench as instant offense for us, but he would have been starting for any other school in the country.

I scored twenty-one points and got twenty-two rebounds and we beat Louisville, 94–81.

We won the Game of the Century. We were the undisputed number-one team in the country. All we had to do was go to the finals and beat North Carolina State, which ten teams had done already that year. Everybody was saying we would kill them.

The final against North Carolina State presented us with some problems people weren't aware of at first. Their coach had them very pumped up. Instead of being overwhelmed by our reputation they came out after us. And they were united; every little thing any one of them did, the whole team shared. Simple things like making a lay-up would get them going on the court and on the bench, you could see how excited they were when they got back to play defense. They really fed off each other, they had terrific team spirit. They truly believed they could win.

We didn't think it would matter, but they were bigger than we were. Cozell McQueen was 6'11", Thurl Bailey was 6'11", and Lorenzo Charles was 6'7". They were a big team and when they got us in a zone and put their hands up the only way we were going to beat them was to run. That was fine with us, our game was speed and quickness, we had the best running game in the country, and we built up a lead. But late in the game, with a six-point lead and three minutes to go, we switched our strategy. Coach Lewis told us to spread things out, slow things down, work the clock. It didn't work out.

The flow of the game changed. When we were running they couldn't keep up, when we slowed down they were bigger and clogged the lanes. When we allowed them to get back on defense we played away from our strength and to theirs. Our team played best against structured teams; we could break them down with all our movement and they didn't know how to handle us. But the NC State guards, Sidney Lowe and Dereck Whittenberg, were more like street players. They were smart and they started to pick our guards' pockets. The lead went away.

Coach Lewis took all the blame for what happened but he didn't deserve it. Yes, he told us to go out there and slow things down, but he also told us, "Let's take advantage of what's out there. If the opportunity's there, you take it." We didn't. Several times when we had clear paths to the basket we hesitated and pulled the ball out, choosing to go by the book and run down the clock rather than go in for the score. I was under the basket all alone one time and whoever had the ball looked at me, dribbled toward me, and then dribbled out. Coach Lewis took too much blame; he told us to kill the clock but he never told us not to score. That was the doing of the guys on the floor.

NC State tied the game and had the ball with seventeen seconds left. We were confident of our defense and ready for overtime, when we knew we would run away and surely beat them. They swung the ball around, looking for a shot. Benny Anders, who was quick and fast, thought he had it timed. He jumped into the passing lane, stretched out his hand, and was all prepared to drive the rest of the court and jam the ball for the winning basket. I saw him go for it and took a step forward.

He missed it by a hair.

Their shooting guard Dereck Whittenberg got the ball and out of complete desperation put up a shot from twenty-seven feet away.

I could see it was going to be near the rim but short. The clock was running out and I thought, If I jump and catch this they're going to call goaltending. The ball was going to miss, we were going to overtime, we were going to win.

As soon as I dropped my hand their forward Lorenzo Charles grabbed the ball and dunked it in. The clock expired. The game was over. They won.

People rushed out, the place was bedlam. I collapsed on the floor. People were stepping on me.

The locker room was very quiet. What could you do? It was over. What could you say? There was just silence. We knew we were the better team, we knew if we played them again ten times we would win every game. We could tell ourselves that we were the best team in the country — and the alumni and our friends told us that all summer long. But no matter how much we denied it, the fact was we were not national champions. Maybe we were the best team never to win a national championship; all we knew for sure was that we didn't win the national championship, and that was devastating.

I was chosen the Final Four Most Outstanding Player but I would have traded the honor very quickly for the team championship.

Clyde was thinking seriously about leaving school a year early and declaring himself eligible for the NBA draft. All season the pro teams had been sending scouts to Houston to watch us play, and Clyde wasn't very pleased with what they were saying about him. They were saying he couldn't shoot. His jump shot was suspect because all they ever saw was him running the floor and jamming. He had a very good jump shot but no one knew it because he dunked all the time.

Ralph Sampson had been chosen College Player of the Year, he was a senior, and unless something very unusual happened he was definitely going to be the number-one pick in the draft. I was chosen Honorable Mention All-America and the scouts told me that if I entered the draft I would be the number-two pick behind Sampson. Wow! I didn't think I was ready; Coach Lewis was always telling me how far I still had to go. Number two in the whole draft! I couldn't believe it.

Clyde and I talked about declaring for the draft together. The Houston Rockets had the number one and three picks that year, 1983, and we talked about coming out as a package deal. The Rockets would get a center and a guard, a young nucleus to build a team around; we could be teammates, we could play right alongside each other and take Phi Slama Jama straight into the pros. So Clyde wanted to know, "Are you coming out?" I said, "That sounds like a very good idea."

That's when Coach T stepped in. "You know I will never stand in the way of your best interests," he told me. I knew that to be true. "You should stay another year," he said. "After that you can do anything you want. One more year will make all the difference." He knew I wasn't ready. "You will be the number-one pick in the draft next year, there won't be any doubt. You'll have experience, you'll have more exposure, you will definitely be number one."

All of a sudden the NCAA gave me a year of eligibility back. The year they had taken away from me for playing in one scrimmage in the fall of 1980 they decided to return in 1983. Instead of one year left, I had two.

It was all politics. The Phi Slama Jamas had drawn so much attention that we had given basketball and the NCAA a big public relations boost and they wanted to keep us. They knew I was trying to decide whether to stay in school, and I was not the only one. Many players were considering leaving after their junior year; if they had a bad year as seniors they would be drafted low and might lose a lot of money as a result. So I was a junior again.

I went back and forth for days: I was leaving school, I was staying. I was driving Lita crazy; we were having too good a time together and she didn't want me to leave. I would say, "I'm gone" — not "I'm going," but "I'm gone." Then I'd wake up in the morning and say, "What am I *doing?*"

Scouts called and asked the same question. The NCAA was very strict; if they felt a player had been tampered with he could immediately lose his college eligibility. So I just told them, "I don't know."

Clyde was nervous about the draft. Even though scouts were telling the newspapers how good we were, no team had said, "If you come out we will draft you." A lot of players come out and get drafted in the second or third round and never really make it. It's very different, being a second-round draft choice instead of a first-round pick. A first-rounder will make the team, he will get a lot of attention and money and a good chance to play; a second-rounder has less invested in him and gets less of a look, less of a chance. So the decision whether or not to enter the draft is important, it can affect the rest of your life; your entire future is being decided and if you make a mistake you can't jump back into school and start all over again.

It was scary.

Finally, I decided to stay.

I didn't go to the press conference when Clyde declared for the draft. I didn't want to have to answer all the media's questions, and after all it was Clyde's day. When Clyde got chosen in the first round by the Portland Trail Blazers I was very happy for him.

9

DRAFTED

WHEN I FIRST came to America and began watching NBA games on television I looked at the pros as if they were from another planet. They were big and fast and it seemed like they were playing a different game than we were. In Nigeria we thought they could close their eyes and still hit every shot, but by the time I was a junior and had been in the country for three years I felt like I could compete, I didn't feel the pros were so out of reach. I saw them make mistakes, miss open jump shots and blow lay-ups. They weren't perfect and that gave me comfort. It also occurred to me that all of them had gone to college and, rather than comparing myself to the men they had become, I should be measuring myself against the players they had been in college.

That summer, 1983, was a lot of fun. Lita was in summer school again, I played every day at Fonde, and we spent almost all of our free time together. My brother Akins had made his way from Lagos to Rhode Island and I sent him money for a plane ticket to Houston. He arrived and stayed on the couch in my apartment until he found his own place. I was so happy to see him! With Akins and Lita, two people who meant so much to me, I had a real home life for the first time in America.

Fonde was very competitive again that summer and I liked that. We Houston Cougars had our reputation and we played the pros even tougher. There was no pressure, only the desire every day to play my best against the best. Moses was there again and we always went at it.

By this time I knew my way around Houston, and wherever I went people seemed to know me. If some of the fellows and I walked into a club the DJ would make a big announcement: "Welcome to our own Phi Slama Jama Houston Cougars!" Everyone on the team was a big shot.

The city of Houston was still riding on the Phi Slama Jamas. Even though we had lost in the finals there was no question in any Houstonian's mind that we were the best team in the country and that next year we would win it all.

When practice came around in the fall it was clear that we were still the team to beat. We had made excellent appearances in the Final Four two years in a row, we were picked to win the Conference, and we were ranked high in the national pre-season polls. There were a lot of high expectations; everybody expected us to step up to another level.

We had lost Clyde and Micheaux to the pros but the basketball program had signed two new guys who could run up and down the floor and loved to dunk: Ricky Winslow and Greg "Cadillac" Anderson. Ricky Winslow was 6'8" and a real jumper. He came in and played the role Clyde had been playing, and he did it perfectly. He was like Clyde except taller. Ricky Winslow was an excellent ball handler and he loved alley-oops, loved to dunk. Running and catching lobs and dunking on people, coming from the weak side and blocking shots; you don't see freshmen jumping like that. We missed Clyde but this young guy wanted to be like Clyde and he was playing Clyde's game. In high school Ricky Winslow's dream had been to be part of the Phi Slama Jamas, and now his dream had come true. He added so much to the team, he could not have been any better.

From the start I felt the 1983–84 season was going to be my year. My first year the team focus had been on Rob Williams and Clyde; my sophomore year it had been on the Phi Slama Jamas, all of us. But with Clyde and Micheaux gone, Michael Young and I were made co-captains, and Michael Young was more of a role player — a scorer — so I became the focal point of this great team. It was fun!

We lost four games that season, including one to a tough Kentucky team with Sam Bowie, Melvin Turpin, and Kenny Walker, and once to Arkansas with Joe Kleine and Alvin Robertson. But when it counted we beat Arkansas by one point in the SWC finals, then we ran through

Louisiana Tech, Memphis State, and Wake Forest. We were in the Final Four for the third year in a row.

The 1984 Final Four was held in the Seattle Kingdome. Georgetown beat Kentucky in one semifinal and we played the University of Virginia. Ralph Sampson had graduated the year before but they still had a very good team. They had beaten us in Japan the previous season but we had won 74–65 this year. They had good guards, good forwards, and Olden Polynice at center, and they slowed the game down. We were used to running but in this game it seemed like everything went at a crawl. It took two overtimes before we beat them, 49–47.

I was finally going to get a chance to play against Patrick Ewing for a championship.

Of course, in college there are no real man-to-man match-ups because of the zone defense. I was going to check Patrick, and he would guard me, but both of us were going to get a lot of help inside. Even so, we would get a feeling of playing the other and I was excited to play against him.

We were basically the same player. Big, foreign-born, dominating inside, known more for defense than offense. Our statistics in scoring, rebounding, blocked shots, everything matched up evenly.

On the court before the game started we came out and shook hands. We didn't know each other aside from what we had read but I gave him respect and he gave it right back to me. We didn't say anything to each other the whole game, we didn't know each other that well. It was a championship game so the competition level was high. We were two top college centers going at each other. It wasn't personal; we were both working hard.

When the game began I contested his shot and he contested mine. Neither of us shied off that level of competition. When I went up I had to go up high; when I didn't feel comfortable I passed. He was not someone I would dominate and he would not dominate me.

Patrick and I matched up evenly all night but the guy who killed us was Georgetown's forward Michael Graham. He was a street guy, 6'9", left-handed, no offense but just dunks and catching lobs and throwing elbows. He was the one who really dominated us. Every time we tried to run, there was Michael Graham going in the opposite direction. He was right there on the outer edge of Georgetown coach John

Thompson's control. Some guys rise to the occasion, and Michael Graham wanted to win that game so badly he played as if his life depended on it.

The battle between Patrick Ewing and me that night was unresolved; Michael Graham was the one who really stood out. We Houston Cougars lost the war. Georgetown beat us 84–75 and Michael Graham was chosen the Final Four's Most Outstanding Player.

At the end of the game, while Georgetown was cutting down the nets and celebrating all over the court, I sat on our bench and cried. This one hurt much more than the last-second disaster against North Carolina State. I thought I took that one well; we should have won, but we lost. This one we just lost. I didn't know if Georgetown was the better team; I did know they out-played us and deserved to win.

There are games when you look back and see lots of opportunities where you could have done better, you see all the things you should have done. That's what I felt seconds after we had lost the national championship. I had rushed some shots because I didn't want Patrick to block them, and he hadn't even jumped. In the future I would learn from that experience. But that's not the way it is in college basketball. No second chance, one game, one chance to win, and we had lost. It was over and I knew I could do better, and that's what hurt.

I was also crying because I knew I was leaving school. In the silent locker room after the game, reporters hovered around me asking, "Are you going to stay? Are you going to declare for the draft?" But it was too early to say. The NCAA had given me a year back and I could stay at UH if I wanted, but the combination of the frustrating zone defense and my being ready to face the world made my decision pretty obvious.

Another factor that influenced me was the fact that in 1984, and 1984 only, I had a one-in-two chance of playing for the Houston Rockets.

I really wanted to stay in Houston. Houston was the only city I knew in America. The climate was great; I didn't want to live in the cold. All my friends, all the places I felt comfortable, everything I knew about the United States was in the city of Houston, and I liked living there.

In 1984 the Rockets and the Portland Trail Blazers would toss a coin to determine who had the first pick. Next year there was no telling who would choose first; the Rockets were one team among twenty-three, and I might play for anybody.

Most people don't think about this, but getting drafted into the NBA is one of the few times when someone who wants a job in his chosen profession has no choice as to where he's going to work. It's as if when MBAs got their degrees, employers stood at the graduation ceremony going, "You, Sacramento. You, Phoenix." You get drafted and you go where they tell you or you don't play in the NBA. So the fact that I had a very real chance to stay in a city and a community where I was comfortable made the decision that much easier.

I talked my choices over with Coach T. He had been my legal guardian and my friend, and I trusted his opinion more than anyone else's in America. He had been right, I was going to be the number-one pick in the draft. I was very honored. To be chosen first among all the excellent players in college basketball was a tremendous honor for me and I was excited that people had such confidence in my abilities. I was looking forward to playing in the pros.

A year before Coach T had told me he would always do what was in my best interests and I knew he had been sincere. Now I asked him again, "What should I do?"

Coach T said, "It's up to you. I would love for you to stay. If you stay I will be the happiest man, but whatever you do it's up to you." Almost any other coach, whose job is to win games for the school, would have pressured his All-America center to stay one more year. There were many buttons he could have pushed: how much UH had taught me and how much time they had invested in developing my talents; how they had given me a scholarship quickly and made my life on campus so comfortable and pleasant; how I had stayed with Coach T and his family and become like a son to him. There were many ways of presenting the question complete with preprogrammed "I'll stay" answers. But Coach T was an honorable man, and though we talked through the pros and cons of turning professional or staying in school he left the final decision up to me.

I didn't really have any doubts. I would have been staying in school just to play basketball, and I didn't like college basketball anymore. Double- and triple-teaming in heavy zones, guys grabbing on to your jersey, referees calling ticktack fouls . . . I had had enough. The coaches tried to teach me to be effective in the zone defense, keep my hands in the air, take up space, intimidate people, discourage anyone from coming near me. I was a fence. I didn't want to be a fence, I wanted to be a force. I wanted to be *active,* to sneak up on people and block their shots. I wanted to run and score, to put the ball on the floor and dribble and drive and shoot. The game I learned in Nigeria, the one I played at Fonde in the summer, one-on-one with room to move and put on moves — that was my game. I wanted to create.

I decided to enter the draft. I finished my classes and the semester was over.

Coach T got fired. He called and told me. The university had questioned him about why I had left; he was my friend and confidant, why hadn't he prevented me? Terence had told them, "The guy has a mind of his own," which is what an educational institution should prize above everything else. But they weren't interested in philosophy, they wanted me to play another season. Coach T couldn't have kept me in school. When he'd had the opportunity a year earlier he had presented good reasons and had influenced me to stay, but this time there was nothing anyone could have said that would have changed my mind.

They didn't believe him. They thought maybe he had encouraged me to leave, that he had been too loyal to me and not loyal enough to them. So they fired him.

There was also politics that went on between the coaches that I believe played a part in their letting Coach T go. Coach T was the only black assistant basketball coach at UH. There were a couple of white assistants and Coach Lewis, but Coach T was the one who related with all the players. He was the one who put all the players together. Most of the players were black and he could talk to black kids in ways the other coaches couldn't. Coach T had coached high school basketball in California and knew about all the high school kids in the nation: who was coming out, who was considering which schools. There was no question about it, he was the best recruiter. He knew how to talk to kids and their parents. And he was an honest guy. When he'd gotten his chance at the University of Houston he'd been living his dream. A *university* coach. He did all the work and somebody else got all the credit. Now it was over.

I was disappointed and shocked. I felt very bad for Terence.

There was nothing I could do. They suspected Coach T of influencing me, so anything I said was suspect. And I had left school; once you've left school you can't help anyone, your power is gone. Everyone wished me well but Coach T stayed fired.

Terence Kirkpatrick had a hard time of it after that. As good a coach and recruiter as he was, for one reason or another he found it difficult getting another job. He and I remained close but eventually he moved on. Coach T died on his forty-third birthday, in 1992.

I didn't want to go to the cold in Oregon but I had no control. As the day of the coin toss approached I got nervous. I had concentrated so hard on all the good things that would happen if I stayed in Houston that I hadn't paid any attention to the upheaval my life would go through if I had to move to Portland. The Trail Blazers had picked Clyde Drexler the year before so I would have one friend on the squad, and they had come in second in the Pacific Division behind the Los Angeles Lakers so they were a good team, but that's all I knew about them. Everyone I asked said Portland was nice but chilly. I had never lived anywhere cold, and on the road trips north we had taken over the past three years I hadn't seen any reason to change.

I had a summer job at a UH alumnus's gas and oil company and some reporters chased me down at work to tell me: Houston won the coin toss. I was *very* happy. I was going to stay in Houston! I was going to be a Rocket! Lita came over that afternoon and we had a celebration lunch. Everything was working out perfectly. We would stay together, my home and my family were going to be in Houston.

I had been pursued by many agents since sophomore year. I didn't talk to any of them until after I decided to turn pro, and then I had to make a decision. It wasn't easy. Both my parents knew how to do business and I grew up watching them. I was young and inexperienced in business matters but I was not without background. I knew that most of all I wanted to be represented by someone I could trust. Every agent had impressive clients in the pros and every agent had a story. One specialized in representing big men, another had a very select list of clients and promised me great personal attention. They all said they could make me a lot of money. I was very interested in the money but I was also interested in being careful.

Ultimately I selected a man who was not a sports agent at all. He was Mike McKenzie, the UH alumnus whose gas and oil business I had worked at for three consecutive summers. We'd had discussions while I was interviewing agents about what to look for in a representative, and when I looked at him, he was the man. First of all, Mr. McKenzie didn't need my money. There was something a little desperate about the agents who approached me, as if they needed me a little too much. With his gas and oil business, Mr. McKenzie was already rich. I liked the way he ran his business. For three years I had seen how efficiently he ran his office, and I liked him as a man. He was a straightshooter and a successful person and I was comfortable with him. Despite the fact that he wasn't a sports agent I asked Mr. McKenzie and his lawyer, Pat Ellis, to negotiate my contract for me.

I wanted my parents to be at the NBA draft with me. They were responsible for my coming to America, they had showed the faith to allow me to come, and I wanted to show my gratitude. But I didn't want simply to invite them, I wanted to go home and see my friends and then come back to the draft with my parents. Mr. McKenzie gave me an advance of $30,000 against what I knew was going to be a big salary so that I could bring my parents and my brother Tajudeen to America.

It had been almost four years since I'd left. I called and told my mother and father that I was coming home. They were very excited that they were going to see me but they said, "Don't think the country is the way you left it."

When I got there I saw that things had not gone well for Nigeria while I was gone. The roads, which had been so smooth, were full of potholes, and the government-financed houses in my neighborhood that had been so tidy and well kept were now getting rundown as everyone was fighting for more space. Courtyards that used to be clean and neat were full of fences and clutter. A beautiful neighborhood looked deformed.

Our house, which I remembered as very comfortable, now seemed small. I had to bend down to go inside. The living room where I had played all my life was so dark I had to squint to see. The field where I had grown up and learned soccer and played all day every day wasn't the huge run of land that I remembered it to be, it was boy-sized.

But the people were still the same, the lifestyle was the warm and friendly way of living that I remembered. My parents didn't tell anyone I was coming. It was a surprise, and as word got around the neighborhood, people began dropping by. My parents received congratulations from a lot of visitors — "Your son came home"; a tribute to the success of the family — and they were very busy entertaining the well-wishers. A lot of my friends from school heard the news and came by. Some had gone to far parts of the country and traveled back to see me. It was like a class reunion. Some were in the advanced level at school, some were at university, and it was a very good feeling to get together. We exchanged phone numbers. Most of them still wanted to come to America.

Ola had moved to another state but I saw Johnson. He was in his senior year as a physical education major at university. He was getting ready for finals but he came down and saw me. We reminisced and spent a lot of time together like in the old days. That was wonderful.

I asked many people about Joyce. We had exchanged letters for several months after I'd left but it wasn't like putting a note in a book and handing it to Johnson and then getting a reply. It was hard keeping contact between continents, and finally our letters had stopped. But I thought about her. She had been such a big part of my life.

Joyce had moved back to her home in the midwestern part of Nigeria. Someone told me she had gotten married, but that was all right, I expected such a wonderful girl to find a man. I still would have liked to talk to her but I couldn't find her. I missed her. She had brought joy to my life just by being who she was, without any effort, just by being herself, and I had not forgotten her.

Nigeria's president had put an embargo on importation of goods in an effort to make the country independent and self-sufficient, but all it had done was devalue the Nigerian currency on the international market. As a result, Nigeria, which had been a trading nation, began to be cut off from the rest of the world. The *naira,* which had been worth $1.70 when I left, was worth around thirty cents when I returned.

In better times my father had borrowed money and built a house as an investment, and he rented it out as apartments. He was very proud of this house and it gave him good income. Just that year my father, who was not a young man, had stopped working at his cement business.

He was tired and he'd stopped trading. With imports embargoed, the cement business had all but dried up. Now he took me aside and said, "I have a request to ask you. I will understand if you cannot do this for me, but I would not forgive myself if I didn't mention it now."

I got worried. My father was a man with a lot of pride; he had never asked me for anything.

"You know the money that I always showed you that I saved for the house?"

"Yes, I remember."

"The economy has been bad and I have gone into the capital. The papers for the house are in the bank and if I cannot pay them off I will lose the house."

I was scared. I wanted more than anything to be able to give him what he asked. It would be the worst thing in the world if the one time my father asked for my help, I could not give it.

"How much do you owe?"

"Twenty thousand."

I smiled. "Dollars?"

"Naira."

My mother said, "If you can do that, you should do it."

I smiled even bigger. "Well, you don't have to worry about that." I tried to be casual, keep talking. "Is everything else all right? What else?"

"I have nothing else."

Someone knocked on the door and began talking to my parents. I said, "Excuse me," and went to another room. When I came back I handed my father an envelope.

"What's this?"

"This is what we have talked about."

My father opened the envelope and there was the money. I gave him ten thousand American dollars in traveler's checks.

"What?" He couldn't believe it. *"Like that?"*

That night he couldn't sleep. In the morning he went and paid off the bank and got his house back. I gave him extra money for his pocket until we went to the United States. He was thankful and I was so pleased and proud to finally be able to do something of significance for my parents, who had prepared me all my life for that moment.

I stayed at home for three weeks and then we flew directly from Lagos to New York, where the draft was going to be held. I arranged visas for my mother and father and my brother Tajudeen. I was an All-America; I visited the embassy and was treated even better than I had been when I'd first applied. My mother was coming to visit, T.J. was coming to live.

My mother could not believe New York. She had been hearing "America, America, America" and now here she was. But when she walked from the hotel to the place where the draft was being held and saw all the movement, all the action, she did not like it. When I was growing up I'd heard that everyone in America carried a gun. I don't know if she believed that but she did not feel comfortable in New York. I had never spent time in the city but I had been in America four years and had gotten used to the pace of the country. My mother was very happy I didn't choose to go to school in New York.

I was honored to be the first player chosen and to have my mother and father there to see it. I introduced them to Mr. McKenzie, who told them their son was already a success. The day passed by in kind of a dream. I was already thinking of playing in Houston in the NBA.

Moses Malone had been signed as a free agent by the Philadelphia 76ers in 1982 and went on and won both the MVP award and the NBA championship for the 1982–83 season. The center for the Rockets when I entered the draft in 1984 was Ralph Sampson.

Portland wanted a big man. They had a good squad, with Jim Paxson and Kenny Carr at guards and Mychal Thompson and Kiki Vandeweghe at forwards and Clyde Drexler beginning his second year in the league. The Trail Blazers felt they needed a powerful center to make themselves a legitimate championship contender. They were very interested in me, and when they lost the coin toss they were extremely interested in working out a deal with Houston. The Rockets would now have two big men and Portland wanted one of them. Before the draft the Trail Blazers offered the Rockets this deal: Clyde Drexler and the number-two pick for either me or Ralph Sampson.

I was happy to play beside Ralph Sampson; he had been a great college player and had just been named NBA Rookie of the Year. Once a team has a young, dominant center they don't usually go looking for another one, but I was too notable to pass up and the Rockets were

considering playing us together and collecting every rebound that came off the boards. It was understandable that the Rockets would keep us both. They turned the deal down cold.

But consider if they hadn't: If they had traded Sampson for Clyde and the second pick in the draft they would have been able to take the first two players available: Michael Jordan and me. From 1984 until today the Rockets could have had a lineup with me, Clyde Drexler, and Michael Jordan, developing together, playing together, winning together.

But the Rockets never made the move. I knew I was going to play in Houston.

The year 1984 was a very strong draft year. After I was chosen, Portland decided they already had a young guard in Clyde and passed over Michael Jordan for another center, Sam Bowie of Kentucky. The Bulls took Jordan, then Sam Perkins went to Dallas and Charles Barkley was taken by the Philadelphia 76ers; Alvin Robertson was taken number seven by San Antonio, Otis Thorpe number nine by the Kansas City Kings, Kevin Willis number eleven by Atlanta, and John Stockton was the sixteenth player chosen, by Utah. My Phi Slama Jama teammate Michael Young was chosen twenty-fourth in the first round by the Boston Celtics.

The next morning my family and I flew to Houston.

Lita was scared to death to meet my parents. She thought they would talk me into marrying somebody else, somebody Nigerian. But I knew my parents just wanted me to be happy.

When my mother met Lita she was very, very impressed with her. From the first my mother was extremely affectionate toward this woman whom I loved; she loved her and treated her as one of her children. They had very good chemistry. By the time my parents went back to Lagos, Lita was like one of the family.

10

BUILDING THE TWIN TOWERS

THE FIRST THING the Rockets did was let me know I wasn't very important to them.

My agent, Mike McKenzie, was a straightshooter, as I said. It was his business style and it had worked for him in the past. He wanted to deal with the Rockets as gentlemen and work things out in a pleasant way with no problems. He told them how pleased we were to be staying in Houston and how much I liked living there. Unfortunately, being honorable and straightforward are not useful qualities in sports negotiations. Once the Rockets found out how happy I was to be staying in Houston they used that as a bargaining ploy to drive down my price.

It was not a friendly situation to begin with. The Rockets' owner, Charlie Thomas, whose main business was as a car dealer, met me and my representatives in Mr. McKenzie's office. They wanted to see what kind of person I was. I was happy to oblige.

Charlie Thomas was a pleasant man. But from the first moment, I didn't feel comfortable in the presence of Rockets general manager Ray Patterson. You know how there are some people you don't feel comfortable around? It was something about his personality. It was Patterson's job to negotiate with us and he didn't even have the courtesy to welcome me to the club or say how happy the team was that they had drafted me. From the start he was playing games. I was the number-one choice in the entire draft but he told us, "We already have Sampson. We don't really need a big man, we just drafted you to trade you." It was unpleasant to hear, and it was not a good way to come to a ball club.

My representatives were a little thrown. An experienced sports agent would have said, "Okay, trade him. If you don't want Hakeem, trade him to someone who does. Let's go where the best deal is." He would have forced a trade to Portland and gotten me a world of money. The Rockets had turned down the combination of Michael Jordan and Clyde Drexler for me, so somebody there must have thought I had some value.

The organization will deny it, but my source was in Portland's management and there's no doubt the offer was made and rejected. Portland desperately wanted a center and would have given me anything to join them. The Rockets wouldn't part with me.

But I had told Mr. McKenzie and Mr. Ellis that I wanted to stay in Houston, that I didn't want to go to Portland, so our leverage and bargaining power went way down. What should have been a warm welcome to the start of a long-term relationship was instead a lesson in cold power.

The Rockets took advantage of my inexperienced negotiators and my own desire to stay in Houston. Not only didn't I sign for more money than the previous year's number-one choice — a tradition in the NBA, as well as a practicality, given the cost-of-living differential which decreased the contract's actual value — but also the Rockets insisted on lengthening the deal. After a lot of haggling I signed a six-year contract. My salary was the same as Ralph Sampson's, but his contract ran only four years, after which he could renegotiate and catch up to market value. I was locked in for six years.

So from the beginning I was not happy. I didn't like management's style, I didn't like being threatened, I didn't like being strong-armed, I didn't like the way the contract was structured, and I especially didn't like feeling unwelcome.

But if I didn't like the business of basketball I loved the game. I was very excited to be playing in the NBA against the best players in the world. In college I had dominated but all of a sudden I was playing in a league full of talented and veteran players from the old school. There were legends to face almost every night: Kareem Abdul-Jabbar, Moses Malone, Artis Gilmore . . . very big, powerful men who were sound in their fundamentals, knew more about the game than I did, and had been playing it since before I was born. It was a thrill to wear the uniform of the Houston Rockets, number 34, and step into that history.

My introduction to the NBA came at the hands of Rockets coach Bill Fitch. Coach Fitch was tough. He didn't care if the players liked him — this was his team and we were going to play the game his way. At practice when he blew the whistle for everyone to gather at center court after warm-ups you didn't take another shot and wander over, you didn't rebound with your teammates for the ball, *you didn't dribble the ball at all* — you got to center court in a hurry, you shut up, and you listened. Coach Fitch was in control.

Bill Fitch had been voted NBA Coach of the Year twice and had won the NBA championship four years earlier as coach of the 1981 Boston Celtics, who had beaten the Rockets in the NBA finals. He knew how to win. He loved basketball. I could not see him doing anything else. The man watched game films day and night; it was his life; he was married to basketball. And he wanted to make us feel the same way. A day off? No way! He would call practices on our days off so we could watch film and shoot free throws. He would keep all the players in a state of readiness where we could think about nothing but the game.

Coach Fitch had just turned fifty years old and this was his second year as coach of the Rockets. The team had improved eight games in his first year and he insisted on doing better. He was always talking about the Celtics and the Los Angeles Lakers, two of the dominant teams of the day. "This is how we did it," he would say. "This is what it's going to take. This is how it can be done." We didn't play for only the Houston Rockets, we played for Bill Fitch. He was putting *his* team together and whoever didn't fit the system was dispensable.

You couldn't have an attitude around Coach Fitch. His business was, I want to win the championship and these are the players I have to coach. He knew everybody's strengths and he wanted every one of us to improve. You had to give your best or you didn't deserve to be on the floor. He only wanted players with desire, players who would pay attention on the court, not guys who would go off on their own. He had a system and he had proved that his system worked. Either you worked for him or you didn't work at all.

Players were making a lot of money then, but when you came to camp Coach Fitch was not interested in how much money you were making; he left that to management. Coach Fitch wouldn't talk about money, he'd talk about someone who played before us, someone we knew was great. "This is how *he* got there," Coach Fitch would tell us. So now a player looks at himself. He's made a big name for himself in college and he thinks he's proved himself. No. You don't play one or two years in the pros and get proven, you have to prove yourself in this league over time, you have to establish your position in this league in order to be thought of as great, to be accepted among these talents. That's what Coach Fitch would put in our minds.

I was very happy to come into the league and work under Coach Fitch. It helped me tremendously to have to establish myself under the demanding eye of such a tough and successful master. He was like a Guy Lewis continuation. Some rookies or players new to the team might think they knew it all, they might not take the time to learn the extra details that separate the good ballplayers from the great ones. Those guys wouldn't last long under Bill Fitch. He had coached the greatest players in the world. Larry Bird and Robert Parish and Kevin McHale and Tiny Archibald had all played for him. He had seen great basketball played and he knew what was great and what wasn't. I was just another player going through his system.

Coach Fitch loved to talk about Larry Bird. He would tell us about Bird's work ethic. "You're at home getting dressed, getting ready to come to the arena, Larry Bird is already there shooting." You could see an empty gym, hear the ball bouncing and the sound echoing and the net swishing as Bird kept putting up his shots, the ones he was going to beat you with because you were a second too slow and the ball was going in. You could never catch him; he was on the court, you weren't. He was right on time, you were late. It was an unsettling thought. "He's a superstar and by the time you get there he's been on the court for an hour making his shots. That's a superstar. That's a work ethic. That's what you have to be prepared to beat." Coach Fitch put that picture in our mind: no matter how much we thought we had prepared, we had to be basketball players all the time, twenty-four hours a day, just to *compete* with Larry Bird.

Coach Fitch kept the competition for jobs going until the day of the final cut. Rookies were looking to make an impression and create their future, veterans almost at the end of their careers wanted to stay with the team and still have a future. He kept everyone motivated, there was no security in his camp. Everyone had to work extra hard or they could just disappear, their life in the NBA would be over. Bill Fitch had that power and he didn't mind using it. When the season started he would bench players with big reputations if they didn't perform the way he wanted. He was always saying, "We can win without you." Guys tested him and he proved it over and over; he benched them and we won. His grasp of the game was fundamentally sound, he had a reason for everything, but you didn't dare ask him what it was, you just had to accept his authority and trust that it worked. Coach Fitch was in control.

Like Coach Lewis, Coach Fitch was never pleased. In practice I would never get a compliment and neither would anyone else. It got so that we didn't worry about our opponents anymore, we were more worried about Coach Fitch. A player always knows what he's doing wrong and we knew that Coach Fitch knew it too, that he was watching, that no mistake was acceptable and every mistake was there for everyone to see. It made me want to be perfect because nothing less was any good. After a while I began to recognize I was never going to please this guy. After that, it was up to me. I felt, I'm just going to do my best. Nothing less. And when he finally did let a player know he'd done something good — you would hear about it secondhand — it made you feel extra-specially good because the praise was so rare.

Coach Fitch's Rockets system was built around what they were calling the Twin Towers concept. I didn't know that the Twin Towers were at the World Trade Center in New York until I was told, or that the Knicks had already had their own Twin Towers with Bill Cartwright and Marvin Webster. In fact, I didn't know a lot of NBA history at all; my whole basketball life had begun only a few years earlier. Ralph and I were the only Twin Towers I knew: two young, active, mobile big men with one year of professional experience between us. Actually, Ralph dwarfed me. He stood 7'4"; I was 6'11". He was five inches taller than I was. When I first stood next to him I was amazed.

Coach Fitch's offensive game plan began with the center. The ball was always pounded into the post, into the big man's hands first. From there he could shoot, dish off, pass it back out. All plays began with the big man because a dominant big man would always draw two men to guard him, which meant that somewhere on the floor one of the other four players was open. It's simple arithmetic. The big man's job was to decide whether the shot was there or if it was one or two passes away. Basketball is a team game, not one man against another, and Coach Fitch knew he could begin all offensive schemes by going to the one man the opponents had to respect. If a center can be guarded one-on-one by the opposing center this plan does not work, but with a dominant big man the scheme will work every time.

The Rockets had drafted me mostly as a defensive player. At UH, with defenders all over me, my offense had not been established. The Rockets knew I could block shots, they knew I could rebound, they knew I was an athlete and could run the floor and finish the fast break. If that's all they saw when I got to the pros they would have been very happy. But when practice started I just started playing naturally, like I was at Fonde. It was the first time in a structured team situation that I wasn't playing against a zone. I could put the ball on the floor, I could make my moves, I was free!

When Coach Fitch saw I could play offense he put me and Ralph at double low post. Although I was smaller than Ralph and a lot of the centers around the league, my game was more of a big man's game than Ralph's. Part of this had to do with physique. Ralph was tall and very skillful but he was thin. His strength was his shooting touch, his height, and coordination. He had great moves. In college, where he had dominated and been one of the best college players in history, his game was throwing and catching lob passes. He had the ability to reach in and grab lobs and rebounds that never came down to smaller players, then turn around and put the ball in the hoop. He had a nice shooting touch from inside and outside.

But Ralph was so tall and light and his knees were so high he was vulnerable to bulkier, more muscular centers who would lean on him and push him away from the basket. Other centers were heavier and rougher than he was and his knees, very fragile and tender joints, would take a pounding, and his game would suffer.

People looked at Sampson, 7'4", and expected him to be a traditional center, to go down into the paint and post up and fight. When he chose to shoot jump shots instead, because that's the way he could be most successful, they criticized him and called him soft. That was unfair and untrue.

A lot of people have the misconception that basketball is not a team sport, and they put the whole responsibility for the Rockets on one player's shoulders. When the team won fifteen more games with Ralph than they had the year before without him but still finished in sixth place in the Midwest Division, people were disappointed in his lack of impact. People have these expectations and if you don't live up to them somehow you're not a man. Ralph tried his best but he couldn't fulfill those expectations. But that wasn't his game.

I thought he was doing the right thing. He *should* use his height advantage. If he spent all his time in the post he'd be fighting a losing battle, he wouldn't be playing to his strength. Ralph's game was finesse — he had been successful with it everywhere he had played — but it was taken away from him when they made him battle it out with men stronger than he was. Ralph wasn't soft, he was just not a power player, and they were trying to make him into one.

Coach Fitch was a very tough coach who did not take well to anyone contradicting him. He demanded hard work, hard work, and wanted to get the most out of Ralph. He realized right away that Ralph liked to shoot from outside but he wanted Ralph to not settle for easy shots, he wanted him to work for his points. Coach Fitch didn't like the fact that Ralph wasn't playing like a traditional big man in a system that needed a dominant inside big man to work. So the coach wasn't pleased. But that wasn't surprising; Coach Fitch wasn't pleased with anybody. Ralph was trying hard — he averaged twenty-one points and eleven rebounds a game and was voted NBA Rookie of the Year — but there was always tension between them.

Then I showed up and could play the post. I was solid enough to take the pounding, I was known as a shot blocker and rebounder, anything I contributed on offense was a bonus. This was a bonanza for Coach Fitch. Now he had two big men.

I was very happy to be playing with Ralph. He took half the load of expectations and pressure off my shoulders. He was a three-time All-America, a college basketball Player of the Year, he was bigger than I was, he was supposed to be better. I didn't think I'd have any problem fitting together on the team with him.

On the court we complemented each other well. His game made things very simple for me. Because he was such a good shooter his shots were always around the basket. Ralph made a high percentage of his shots and when he missed he was always close; he would lean and shoot off the glass and the ball would bounce off the rim and sit right up for me. I would go over my man and get a slam dunk. I got my best highlights on power put-backs of Ralph's missed shots. When we ran down the court afterward he would shake my hand for helping him out; it made his shots easier to take knowing I was there to rebound for him. He'd say, "Hey, Dream!" and we'd talk for a second and plot out a play. That's when I knew he generally liked me. I came to the team not to compete with him, not to take the team away from him, but to complement him. And when he said, "Let's do this" and sketched out a play, that motivated me. I didn't want to disappoint him. I said, "Let's do it!" I showed Ralph I was backing him. "I'm right there with you!" I wanted him to know that I had good intentions toward him, that anytime he said something like that it meant a lot and I was ready.

Sometimes he would call me aside during a time-out and we'd talk. If a particular player was giving me difficulty Ralph would say, "Don't worry about him, just turn around on him. Just make your move." He knew my game, he knew my strengths. He was very much a leader. I had watched him closely through college and I respected him. There was never any conflict between Ralph and me.

We had a good team, a combination of young players and veterans. Rodney McCray from Louisville's Doctors of Dunk team was at the other forward, along with Robert Reid; our guards were John Lucas, Lewis Lloyd, Mitchell Wiggins, and Lionel Hollins (they called him "the Train"). We could run, we could shoot, we could rebound, we had a plan.

Our first pre-season game was against the San Antonio Spurs and I had to go up against their center Artis Gilmore. This may have been a pre-season game to everyone else but to me it was my first test against real NBA men. You can practice all you want, but games are different. Coach Fitch prepared you to approach every game as if it was the championship and I wanted to make a good first impression on him and around the league.

Artis Gilmore was 7'2", left-handed, very mechanical. He wasn't graceful, he didn't have a lot of fancy post moves, he was just very strong. A lot stronger than I was. I couldn't move him. He got in the low post and reached up and dunked the ball with his wrist. Most of the time I thought I could block it but he was deceptively quick. He would back into me, bang into me, and before I could get up and jump he would reach up, cock his wrist, and put the ball through the hoop.

I didn't have an answer for that. If I had time I could knock the ball away, but he was knocking me away instead.

Wow! The first thing I wanted to know when I got back to the locker room was "Are all the other big men that strong?" If they were I was in trouble.

We went and played the Boston Celtics in Boston Garden. They were the defending NBA champions, they had just beaten Kareem Abdul-Jabbar, Magic Johnson, and the L.A. Lakers in seven games to take the title. And we beat them. At home! It was a tough game and they played well and we won. It was a fantastic feeling; everyone was excited. They had a championship front line and we had beaten them in their own gym. People could say whatever they wanted to about its being pre-season and the games not counting, but to us that victory meant the world. We were the Twin Towers team. People had been wondering whether the concept would work. Well, the verdict was in: It would!

Our first regular-season game was against the Dallas Mavericks, on national TV. Dallas was an up-and-coming team with Rolando Black-man and Derek Harper in the backcourt and Mark Aguirre, Dale Ellis, Jay Vincent, and Sam Perkins all young and on the way up. It was a competitive game but finally they didn't have the big men to hold us and we won, 121–111. Three days later we beat them by twenty-two. We won our first eight games and around the country people began talking about the Twin Towers and how our future was so bright.

Then we lost ten of our next fifteen games and reality started to set in. We were a club that was only beginning to develop. After that first winning streak we went 40–34 the rest of the season.

The league was full of talent, full of superstars. Julius Erving — Dr. J — was still going strong for the Philadelphia 76ers. Dr. J made an impression on me before I even saw him. I had heard stories about him in Nigeria, how he could take a dollar off the top of the backboard and leave change — people say they saw it. I thought he had the coolest nickname.

When I finally did get to see him play he was very graceful, a fantastic player. Even though his best years were behind him he still had his own style. He was one of a very few people who personally changed the game. Where other players held the ball with two hands or drove to the basket with the ball protected by their body, Dr. J started the style of palming the ball, waving it in the air as he went by as if he was showing off a prize. He would glide into traffic as if he was going to dunk it and the defenders would all go after the ball like dogs after a rabbit, but while everyone was jumping Dr. J with his big hands would pull it back down, go around us, and flip the ball in with a finger roll on the other side of the basket, or find a way to jam it over everyone. That was an original style. Kids would imitate him. When somebody at the playground or at Fonde made that move people in the crowd would go, "*The Doctor!*" They knew. He had put his own personal imprint on the game. I was thrilled to finally see him play.

Moses Malone was on the same 76er team with Dr. J. In 1983, two seasons before I came into the league, they had run through the play-offs and swept the Lakers for the title. When I finally got a chance to play him on an NBA court it was the same as at Fonde. Moses was very tough. He knew my game, he understood my moves. I was more of a man now than I had been three years before when we'd started competing, so I was comfortable playing against Moses but I couldn't dominate him. We played them twice that season — each of us won at home — and both times it was a battle. Moses was very physical, tough on the offensive boards. I couldn't tell any difference in the way he played in the pros from the way he played at Fonde. He always played to win.

Moses had obviously thought about how to play me. He respected my shot-blocking ability and knew I was going to jump for everything, so he wouldn't just go straight up, he faked a lot. When I stayed down he would jump into me and draw the foul. Moses was always at the foul line. He knew how to play me and stay in the game, or get two quick fouls on me so I couldn't jump anymore that half. The way he used his body I had to be very careful with him.

I was playing against legends. When I came in, Kareem was first-team All-NBA and Magic was at his peak. So was Larry Bird. Isiah Thomas was coming into his own. We had to learn how to play them all.

The Lakers and Celtics stood out from the rest of the NBA. Detroit was coming up and fighting for recognition, but those two were the best. Some teams gave you opportunities to win by playing loose, making errors in judgment, throwing bad passes or taking poor shots. Not the Lakers or Celtics. We were confident we could beat them — we had done it! — but we knew every mistake would cost us. Coach Fitch told us, and he was proved right again and again: They beat you with your own mistakes and the only way to win is to play close to perfectly. The Celtics and Lakers didn't just lose games, you had to beat them.

Because we were in the Midwest Division and they were in the Eastern, we only played the Celtics twice all season. We had beaten them when it didn't count and then they came to the Summit when it did. They were tough.

Larry Bird was the strength of Boston but the key to the Celtics was that they were a team. They came at you from all different angles. Kevin McHale, at forward, was one of the best low-post players ever to play the game. His body was long and kind of awkward and his style wasn't fluid but his basic moves were very strong, very fundamentally sound. When he posted up and I leaned on him I thought he was going to break, but he would get that ball and make his move — the fake, the drop step, the turnaround jumper, with his long arms extended way above his head — and I would jump every time. McHale was smart, he knew I liked to block everything, so when he turned around to shoot he jumped so high and shot the ball so straight up that even if I jumped my highest and managed to touch it, the ball went in anyway. I would jump all day and he'd seem to know exactly how high I could get, and then shoot over me. At crucial times, he would deliver the tough shots. I had to work very hard against him. When I was guarding the Celtics' center Robert Parish, "the Chief," I also wanted to help Ralph by coming from the weak side.

Larry Bird, shooting deep from the corner or driving and drawing fouls, was a constant threat. He was one of the all-time greats and we didn't have anybody who could stop him for any length of time. Nobody did.

Danny Ainge, sharpshooter. Dennis Johnson, floor leader. Robert Parish, the Chief; you know you're going to have your hands full. They beat us by ten in Houston early in the season and by fourteen near the end. We had a lot to learn.

Then there was the Lakers. We played them four times that season and every game I learned something new. Magic Johnson was pushing the ball and running the floor, controlling the whole game. You often hear about the point guard being the coach on the floor; well, Magic was exactly that. He knew when to run and when to walk and how to control his team's emotions as well as their plays.

When the noise gets loud that's when you make mistakes, and when the crowd starts roaring and stomping and kicking up a storm sometimes players get frantic; you can hardly hear the ball slap off the hardwood, it gets hard to handle, you lose it, and they go the other way. When you get the ball out of bounds again the noise is louder, the pressure is greater, the defense is right in your face, and the chance for another mistake is in front of you like a nightmare.

But that was when Magic was at his best. He would take the ball very coolly and tell his teammates to calm down. In a situation where some players panic, the Lakers got the message that everything was under control. Maybe he would penetrate for a shot or dish off for a quick score, maybe he would make the perfect pass to Kareem in the post or to a guard for a three-pointer. Somehow he would make something happen, get a key basket or a quick steal, that would quiet our crowd and rouse his team. It was just the opposite with a team that didn't have a strong point guard; they didn't have that leadership and they couldn't get that quick shot of confidence.

So you had Magic running the show, you had James Worthy filling the lane, still the big guy who had run us off the court at the Final Four and now a solid grown man and even faster and more of a star in his third year in the league. You had Byron Scott and Bob McAdoo hitting jump shots, you had Kurt Rambis and Mitch Kupchak banging away, you had Michael Cooper doing everything. This was a team.

And, of course, in the middle was Kareem.

I had heard about the sky hook for so long, and now I was on the court against it.

We were the Twin Towers, we were young, we were supposed to be the future of the game, we played to win. But there was a certain angle when Kareem went up with his shot — from the right side of the basket, halfway to the three-point line — it looked so simple, so effortless, I just couldn't help but stop to look at it. The sky hook was the perfect shot; I don't know how anyone ever stopped it.

Ralph guarded him since he was two inches taller than Kareem and at least had a chance to get in Kareem's way. My only chance was to come off my man and come from the weak side to try to get a piece of the ball from behind.

The sky hook began with the legs. Kareem had amazingly strong legs, an extremely strong base, and when he spread them it was very hard to get near him. You had to expect the hook so you tried to deny him the post, but he was agile and strong and a fighter and he usually got his position. He would get the ball and your troubles were just beginning. Of course the hook was his first option, so you had to play him close, get a body on him and try to make his take-off difficult. But Kareem was also smart and quick, and to keep his man honest he would often fake the hook and turn to the middle of the lane where he was about a foot from the basket and could lay the ball in with either hand if you let him. So you couldn't give him the middle, you had to beware of that move. Kareem also had good court sense and a great eye; when Magic or Byron Scott would cut to the basket he would drop them the ball for the lay-up, so you had to respect the pass.

You had to respect everything. You couldn't overcommit to the right, you were never going to touch the sky hook from the left, and if you bumped him in the middle you'd be called for the foul.

The sky hook itself was the best shot in the game and the most difficult to block. When Ralph went out I had to guard Kareem and it seemed that every time I looked around there was a ball coming down into the basket. Kareem would dribble, sort of rock to his right to both fake and clear you out, then turn away from you, and as you tried to jump with him he would lift off his left foot and hold his left arm parallel to the ground, the point of his elbow like a lead pipe in your chest. By the time I got to the league he had taken that shot so many times it was automatic.

Kareem was so quick with the hook he would be at the top of his jump and you'd be trying to figure out when exactly to lift off. Kareem had an answer for that, too. The secret to shot blocking is timing, but he would be up so high that you'd have to use all your strength just to get near the ball. Kareem used an arc, not a flat shot, which made it even more difficult to touch. And on top of all that he would freeze you. He would get to the top of his jump, balance the ball on his fingertips, cock his wrist, and pause — not for long, just long enough either to get you off the ground or keep you on it. That little moment with the wrist made the shot devastating. No — impossible. Either way, when I jumped at his shot it wasn't there. Kareem was three inches taller than I was and when I looked at where the ball was — on top of his arm held all the way straight up above his head and over his far shoulder — I got discouraged. I was a shot blocker but I knew I couldn't block that shot. It was up so high, all I could do was hope that he missed.

Mostly I'd try to bother Kareem's shot, make him work for position, make him jump higher than he usually would because I was sixteen years younger than he was and he'd know I was going to jump as high as I could. I used every edge I could get and I hoped that maybe by making him change his shooting arc even a little it might throw off his rhythm or perspective or stroke. I can't say I was very successful. But then, neither was anybody else. The sky hook was unstoppable.

We looked forward to playing the Lakers and the Celtics; they were the standard to test against and we would get up for them. We lost to the Lakers the first time they came to Houston that season, then we went to the Forum the next month and beat them in their own building. They beat us the next two times we played that season. Every game was tough, the kind of game where we knew we could beat them but we lost because of their experience and their smart play, the kind of game where it hurts when you lose. I would wake up the next morning and think about the game and get upset. I was young in the league and I hadn't learned how to block out the bad games, to let them go by and not worry about them. That kind of overview comes with age or with having lost enough games not to take it personally. You don't have that overview when you're twenty-two.

I didn't like to lose and it affected me. I'd wake up and I wouldn't feel good, I wouldn't want to go to practice, and when I got to practice I wouldn't want to be there. Coach Fitch made us watch game films, so I'd sit at practice and have to live the loss all over again. It would be there in front of us and I just didn't want to see it.

I was excited finally to be in the NBA. Instead of being stifled by college zones, now I could post up and take my jump hook and my turnaround jump shot, I could put the ball on the floor and show my moves. I was getting ready to play the big man's game.

When you see a big man posting up, his legs spread wide, his butt out to keep the defender as far away as possible from his hands and the ball, *this is a statement*. His posture says: I am at work. He is in no mood to wait, this man is ready. When he reaches up with his shooting hand, fingers outstretched, muscles tense as if he's leaning against a door trying to hold off invaders, this is a *call*. At that point he's no longer playing, he's serious. He's giving the point guard a target — not a suggestion, a *demand* — and the point guard had better get him the ball right away.

For a while I enjoyed playing the big man's position. It was what I had looked forward to. I was a shot blocker and that's one of the things the big man was supposed to do.

Shot blockers don't like to get their own shots blocked. We feel embarrassed; we are used to rejecting others, we don't know how to take rejection. So if you can reject someone's shot the first time you can get them thinking: Wow! This is how those other guys feel.

One of my favorite plays was to hide behind the guard and come from the weak side and block people's shots. I would literally hide, crouch down behind the man I was guarding. I would defense my man but keep an eye on the man with the ball, and when he got by his defender I would wait until he had committed himself and then go over and swat his shot away. He never even saw me coming. I could see the surprise on his face. "Where did he come from?" That was real fun.

But while I played the big man's position I also found out that I wasn't a classic big man. I was too small.

I was 6'11". The Rockets and the Cougars before them had all said I was seven-foot because it seemed more impressive, but when I was measured I actually stood 6'11", which in terms of NBA centers wasn't big at all. I was an in-between player. Everywhere we played teams would either put their center on me, in which case I was at a height disadvantage, or guard me with their power forward, who would play me physical. Every night I had to go up against men who were either several inches taller or many pounds heavier than I was, sometimes both. Before long it became clear to me that I had to make up for this with speed and quickness. I would take a pounding but I either could shoot over or go around the power forwards. It was the centers who presented the problem. That's when the fade-away jumper came into play. If I went straight up with my jump shot I would get it slapped back at me, but I found that if I stepped back and leaned away from these big men they couldn't touch it.

Unfortunately, coaches don't like the fade-away. Not Bill Fitch, not Guy Lewis, not any coach I played for. They always tell you that you're falling away from the basket and aren't in position to get the rebound. (People said the same thing about Kareem's sky hook.) They would rather I took the ball to the basket strong, not fade away. However, if the fade-away was working — and I practiced that shot so much I became confident of it — they wouldn't say anything.

As I went around the league I got tested. All the big men wanted to know what kind of player I was and whether they could dominate me. It was a constant physical power struggle. If a player can establish his superiority the first few times he plays, that relationship gets set in stone. If someone thinks he can take you, he will; he gains confidence and will push you and push you, and if you back down the first time and then the second, he will push you your entire career. It's like that on the playground, it was like that at Fonde, it was very much like that in the pros. Guys wanted to get the best of me and I wouldn't let them. That's why I got into so many fights my first year.

I had been fighting almost as long as I could remember. Where I come from, you don't trust anyone who is walking toward you. In America guys jaw at you, they walk up and get real close and talk trash. The face-to-face argument is part of the American way of settling disputes. At home they would be on the floor with blood on their face. In Nigeria the first person who hits is the winner; when you hit someone in the right place, you're done. I'd seen a guy knock someone down, get separated, go over, shake hands, and knock the other guy down again. You don't trust the enemy; he can do anything.

At home we give space to talk; we turn, we square up, and I back off. When the talk is settled, then I feel comfortable enough to get close. So when a guy walked toward me with an argument on the court I told him to back off. If he didn't stop and kept coming, I would attack.

That's what caused most of my fights. People didn't understand that I didn't trust anyone; if a guy didn't stop, I hit him. The way I played the game, either you talk at a distance or you fight. Once you get across that line there's no talking left to do. In my youth the guys who were talking as they came forward would get up close and then head-butt you — *boom.* I'd seen teeth on the floor!

I didn't start the fights but people got frustrated with me. My game is, if you box me out under the basket I'm going to go by your shoulder and get the tip dunk. I fake outside, my man tries to box me out there, I quickly slip in behind him for the dunk. My man gets upset. The next time down the court, as soon as we start jockeying he tries to trip me or he elbows my chest. A cheap shot. I won't take that.

I never play the game to hurt people. I try to intimidate players with my game. I work hard and will make you work because you have to keep up. On offense, if you let me get the ball I will test your skills. You have to stop me. On defense I will challenge your shot. If someone is being very physical with me, using his strength to his advantage, I respect that. This guy is strong! As long as they keep it clean and they're playing basketball, we will not get into a fight. But once you start hitting me you will know the result, and you'll get the same result every time — I will attack. Always. That's my attitude. So after a while, when a player starts something I tell him, "Don't even try it." He looks at me and he sees I'm serious. We both laugh. There's communication. Now it's just basketball.

As well as learning how to play the NBA game I was learning how to live the NBA life. Coach Fitch, as I said, was married to basketball. He wanted to win, not to party, and he wanted us to sleep nights. We had some street players and he tamed them. Wild guys became disciplined.

We would play games at night and then get up and take the first commercial flight out the next morning. The team flew first-class but I was 6'11" and not all the seats had great leg room. I liked the bulkhead seat on the aisle right behind first class, where you could stretch out. Sometimes I would ask the flight attendant to make the request but usually I would go to the man or woman who was sitting there myself and ask politely if they would like to trade seats and go to first class. Usually they would. Only one time did someone refuse. It was a woman who was upset with me when I said hello. She saw all these tall guys come on board and I could tell from the way she looked at me, even before I asked, that she didn't want to be up there with them. I offered her a first-class seat and she refused. But that was the only time.

So most of the time on the airplanes I was sitting not with a Rocket but with a regular traveler.

It was fun. Basketball teams travel in their own little worlds; you meet only fans in the locker rooms and arena hallways, you eat room service alone at the hotel, you party with people who are looking forward to meeting you. It takes work to meet regular people with normal lives. My teammates would be dozing up front and I would just strike up conversations.

The people I sat next to were always surprised. They would ask me questions about the team — basketball questions or things like "Don't you guys have your own flight?" — and I got a chance to meet all kinds of different people, maybe a businessman or a teacher, someone flying for work or pleasure or just coming home. Sometimes they wanted to come to the game. "I don't know anybody in that city," I'd say, "I'll leave you my tickets." That never failed to shock them. After the game they'd come back and thank me and introduce their family or friends. That seat became very interesting for me.

One of the guys I hung out with on the road was the Rockets' equipment manager, David "D.H." Nordstrom. I met him the first day I came to camp. He introduced himself and said, "Whatever you need, don't hesitate to tell me." And D.H. had everything. Socks, shoes, the right places to eat, the best clubs, tickets to anything, anywhere; whatever you needed D.H. could come up with. He was the one guy who really made the organization run.

I liked D.H. right away. He treated everybody very well and he was sincere. I could tell immediately that he was just a nice guy. He had begun selling programs at Houston Aeros hockey games as a sophomore in high school, got a job at the arena as a stick boy, and worked his way up in the organization. When that team disbanded he started working practices for the Rockets. He had started at the bottom and created a very important position for himself. There have been guys handling equipment for probably forty years on other teams in other cities, but D.H. expanded his job into the first traveling secretary/

purchasing agent/all-around do-everything-type equipment manager, and he became a good friend of mine.

D.H. enjoyed life. He worked hard — D.H. was always taking care of something for somebody on the team — but he enjoyed what he was doing so much he didn't look at his job as work. He could eat in nice restaurants without paying and get himself and his friends walked into cool clubs on the road because people liked him and he got things done. He was a good-hearted guy with a lot of contacts. Everybody knew D.H. and his position on the Rockets; if someone wanted something, D.H. was the man. He'd invite friends to games or get players' autographs when people asked for them, and they would find ways to reciprocate. When he went out to clubs he'd want to buy drinks for everybody. He didn't have a lot of money but he'd always fight to pick up the check. (Ballplayers, who do have a lot of money, are notoriously unwilling to spend it.) He was only five years older than I was. He carried himself like a young guy but it seemed like he'd been around forever. He was a great talker and had a whole encyclopedia of stories about people he'd met and scenes he'd seen from way before I came along.

A lot of times on the road, instead of going out with the guys on the team I'd go out with D.H. We used to have long philosophical discussions. He was surrounded by players making millions of dollars and he was concerned about money, which I understood. But I told him, "D.H., you are rich in life. You have friends, you have a good job that you are happy with, you love what you do, you're always smiling. You're rich that way." I think he felt better when he thought of his life from that perspective.

The Rockets won nineteen more games in 1984–85 than they had the year before, and thirty-four more than two years before. We finished second in the Midwest Division and were being recognized nationally as other teams realized you could actually play two big guys together and cause all kinds of problems for the opposition.

I had thought that getting out of the college zone defense would free me up, but I was mistaken. It had taken only a few pre-season games for teams to realize that I was an offensive threat and needed to be double-teamed. So did Ralph. On a bad day that left the opposition playing one-on-three. Bill Fitch's Twin Tower concept definitely worked. It changed the game of basketball.

We played the Utah Jazz in the first round of the playoffs and we were pretty confident. Although we had split the season series 3–3 we were the young team on the way up and we had home-court advantage in a best-of-five-game series. They beat us in the first game at the Summit but we came back and took the fourth in Utah to set up a deciding fifth game at home.

I was having a good game and the Jazz brought back-up center Billy Paultz in to guard me. Paultz's nickname was "the Whopper." He had averaged 1.3 points and less than six minutes a game playing time all season long. He wasn't part of their offense, all he was out there to do was get in my way. And he did. It was very irritating. He shadowed me, hung real close, and wouldn't give me any room to move. When I tried to get some space he would flop, fall back like I'd hit him with a brick, and the referee would call a foul on me.

I don't like flopping; it is not real basketball. Playing tight defense and taking a charge is one thing, but making believe you are fouled on every play is not defense, it's dishonest, it is tricking the referees, it is faking. For some reason, that night the referees were letting him get away with it. He would flop, I'd get a foul. Flop, foul. They called one where he hit the ground and I hadn't even touched him. He was a pest. I couldn't even shrug him off because once I moved so much as an elbow Paultz would go crashing to the floor and the referee would whistle me again.

The game was close and I was getting mad. He'd been flopping all day so I got ready for him. I said, "Well, if you're going to flop I might as well hit you for real." Ralph Sampson got a rebound and as soon as Paultz came over to cover me and flop, I hit him. I gave him a real good shot.

The referee didn't see it! The whole crowd saw me crack the Whopper, everybody on both teams saw me smack him, but for all the fouls he'd called on me that night the referee missed this one completely.

Ralph dunked the ball and the crowd went wild.

The league didn't miss it. They watched the videotapes and fined me several thousand dollars.

We lost to Utah, 104–97. It was a terrible loss. Terrible. Our season was over.

I wasn't ready to stop playing. We'd had our sights set higher than a first-round knockout, but that's basketball. It doesn't matter if you want to play some more, you're finished and it's a strange feeling to wake up the day after the season and have nothing to do. You get so used to the routine — wake up, get on a plane, get off the plane, check into the hotel, practice, lunch, nap, shoot around, game, locker room interviews, with the press asking you questions whenever they see you — that the day seems very quiet when it's gone. I had gone from Phi Slama Jama to the Twin Towers to this terrible silence. The team was pleased with its season and with the attention the Twin Towers had brought to us, but none of us liked the way it ended. We could do better. We had to wait until next year.

And when it came time to divide up the playoff money, D.H. got a full share just like all the starters.

11

TO THE FINALS, THEN . . . TEARING DOWN THE TWIN TOWERS

I WAS NEVER DRIVEN BY MONEY. From the time I was a boy my needs had been small, and I could always fill them. Now that I had money from my new contract I didn't feel the need to go out and spend it all at once, but once again, what I wanted I could have. I lived in an apartment for half of my first pro season and then I bought a house.

A house meant a lot to me. In Lagos the big companies like Exxon and Gulf Oil put their presidents and executives in villas. There were lots of trees, and the houses, mostly white, were way in the back behind gates and lawns, very different, very outstanding. When I was growing up we would ride past those neighborhoods and look at these streets — sometimes you couldn't even see the houses, they were so private — and say, "Wow! I wonder what kind of people live in there." I couldn't even picture myself having that kind of home. You just wondered which people were so privileged that they could live on those estates.

That's what I had in mind when I thought about owning my own home.

Unfortunately all the Realtors told me, "If you want that you'll have to build it." I didn't even know where to start. If I finally had the money, I didn't have the patience. Instead I bought a nice two-story, red-brick Colonial American–style house. It wasn't my dream house but it was in a nice neighborhood, a pretty subdivision to the north of Houston with a golf course, and it had a pool.

I was very happy to own a house. It meant a lot to me to be settled into Houston, to really live there now, to call it home.

The summer of 1985 was fantastic. I love decorating and I had a good time shopping for furniture and fabrics for my new house. It's hot in Houston, and during the day when the summer sun was at its worst I'd be inside playing ball at Fonde. You had to play at Fonde. Every summer. You had to play. Then I'd go home and lift weights and sit by the pool. It was a beautiful summer, very relaxing.

When my second NBA season began I met another important person in my life: Henri de Ybarrondo. He and I were introduced in the Boardroom, a lounge in the Summit, and we hit it off immediately. Henri had been a very successful trial lawyer who had retired and become an even more successful investor. He was about twenty-five years older than I was and he was cultured, sophisticated, and knowledgeable, a family man and a world traveler. He considered himself a "citizen of the world" and I gained tremendous respect for him. Henri became my personal lawyer, my business manager, and my friend. Our relationship has continued ever since. His advice has always been for my benefit and best interests.

Henri and I spent a lot of time discussing philosophy and theology. One of the main things Henri taught me was to be master of my own fate, to concentrate on what I do best, and to keep things simple. Henri made me understand the relationship between money and freedom. That's what financial security gives you, he told me: freedom. You see many people who make a lot of money and seem successful but they cannot take a vacation, they have to be at their jobs. And if they happen to take a vacation they can't stay away from the phone, they're not free. Henri told me, "After the hard work of winter, keep your summers free, enjoy travel, see the world."

Henri was also an art connoisseur. I had always loved art and design, and he helped me purchase museum-quality work for both enjoyment and investment. He and I liked a lot of the same things, so our friendship was wonderful.

Henri is a principled man and he taught me to live life the right way. His foundation was honesty, integrity, things of value, things that really count. I asked him, "How come you never deviate from your principles, never make an exception?" He told me that every time he compromised on what he believed, things went wrong. "Later in life," he told me, "you will see."

The 1985–86 Rockets were very much the same team as the year before, except more mature. We had been playing together for a year, and the Twin Towers concept didn't have to be learned anymore, just refined. Ralph's role and mine began to be reversed. Unlike my rookie year, Ralph pulled down more rebounds than I did that season and I out-scored him.

Coach Fitch really worked on us. He got us to believe we were the best. Our opponent didn't really matter, they had to beat us to win, we weren't going to beat ourselves. He got everyone to do his job the way it was supposed to be done.

John Lucas was our point guard and he was known for throwing lobs, perfect lobs. Ralph was trained to run and catch lobs; he would come all the time from his forward position and slam them through, so they worked together beautifully. With my back to the basket I'd get a lob every once in a while, but John Lucas really knew how to feed the big man.

Our shooting guard was Lewis Lloyd. They called him Black Magic. He was a driver; he gave me many dunks because he was an excellent player who could drive and dish off. Lewis Lloyd loved the fast break. He had such long strides he looked like he was moving in slow motion but you couldn't catch him. And he could shoot. Coach Fitch loved his game. He was explosive in short bursts, the best player in the league for twenty minutes. That's what they said: "Lewis Lloyd is the best player in the league for twenty minutes." He was a very important player for our team.

Rodney McCray was an all-around player. He coordinated everything: he passed the ball to Ralph, he scored every once in a while, he did all the little things that needed to be done.

The guy I played against every day in practice was Jim Petersen. He was a big, strong white guy, 6'10", drafted by the Rockets out of the University of Minnesota in the third round the same year they drafted me. Pete was a very nice guy, and he and I were good friends. We faced off every day in practice and we worked on the same moves together.

Pete knew all my moves and he would use them against me. He had no ego, didn't mind copying me or asking instructions. He'd say, "Do that again." I wouldn't know what I'd done but he would learn how to do it. The misdirection, the fake; you think he's turning left but he's turning right, you go after him but he freezes you. He got to be very good. Pete would use a move in practice and lose me completely. Wow, I thought, this is what people must think when I make my move. It was only then that I started to realize how hard it must be to guard me.

We played and played and played, and I learned in my second year in the league that if the coach and personnel stay constant, every NBA season is like the one before — except for the playoffs. You might have good individual games or plays or match-ups that you remember, but none of it is very important. What you remember from year to year are the playoffs.

Unfortunately, before the playoffs could begin we lost our point guard. John Lucas tested positive for drugs with seventeen games left in the season and was kicked off the team. Coach Fitch was very tough. Coach Fitch didn't rely on the NBA to check on his players, he did his own checking. When Coach Fitch found out that Lucas was doing drugs he buried him, he didn't let Lucas play. The NBA didn't know, but Coach Fitch knew. That's the kind of coach he was. He was a man of principle and I liked him for that. When the NBA finally found out, Lucas was banned from the league.

I thought John Lucas was wasting his life. It is so rare for someone to make a living as a professional athlete, and we are treated so well everywhere we go that to put all that at risk by doing drugs seemed to me to be criminal. If you throw away this life you dishonor yourself. You are destroying your own life and should be held accountable. You also harm the teammates who are counting on you and the organization that is paying you to win, and you disappoint the people who are looking to you for direction.

People say that parents should be the most important role models for their children — and they should be — but we cannot deny that kids look to athletes for ways to live their lives. And when an athlete throws his life away he is at the same time leading kids astray. Players forget that, but we are all in the public eye and kids never stop watching.

Losing John Lucas made things much more difficult for the Rockets.

We had worked for two years to develop a team where everyone knew his role, where every role was filled, where every teammate knew that if he just did what he was responsible for doing we would win. That had given us confidence, and now that confidence was shaken. We would have to adjust, move people from position to position. Robert Reid, bad knee and all, went from forward to point guard. He was 6'8" and playing against all these quick, quick guards and he did not have a point guard's mentality, but he was the man Coach Fitch picked for the job. It's not the kind of thing you want to do going into the playoffs.

We remembered very well how bad it had felt losing to Utah in the first round the year before, so this year we didn't want to mess around. Our first-round opponent was the Sacramento Kings — Reggie Theus, Larry Drew, Eddie Johnson, Otis Thorpe. We came out very focused; we wanted to establish right away that we were the better team. We beat them by twenty points in the first game and swept the series. Next was the Denver Nuggets.

Denver had finished four games behind us in the standings and we had split the season series 3–3. They were led by Alex English, Calvin Natt, and Fat Lever.

Alex English didn't seem to be putting in any effort until you realized that nobody could guard him. He had averaged a fraction less than thirty points a game that season and finished third in the league in scoring. He was very slim and he would kind of glide along and take this very unorthodox running jump shot. He was not a power player but his game was in the paint, around the basket, and nobody could block him.

Alex English's success was all in his footwork. A normal player will dribble the ball, take one step, bring his trailing foot even with his front foot, jump and shoot. Dribble, step, step, jump and fire. But instead of taking two steps, Alex English took one and a half. He would dribble, take one step, and while he was running release the ball. Dribble, step, fire. This was unusual; nobody else shot that way. I would be coming from the weak side for the block and before I got there he had already released the ball. I couldn't time him. He would take that same shot over and over again and I could not block it. The only way to stop it was to jump one count too early, but he always gave himself several options and sometimes he would fake and I would be up in the air with him going around me. Nobody could figure it out. And Alex English would not miss. His shot was automatic.

I didn't understand Alex English's game and it wasn't pretty, but it was effective. He created a lot of problems. We beat the Nuggets twice in Houston and they went back home and beat us twice in Denver. We played well enough to beat them but they won one game by one point and the other in overtime. What we thought would not be a difficult series was getting tough.

We beat them in Houston and went back to Denver one more time. We didn't want to go to a seventh game; you never know what's going to happen in a seventh game. Game six went to double-overtime, Alex English scored forty-two points, it was a great game, and we won.

We didn't even come home — we flew straight to Los Angeles where the Lakers were waiting for us.

We were celebrating, and we weren't even thinking about the Lakers because the Denver series had taken a lot out of us. But at our first practice Bill Fitch got us focused. "Forget about Denver," he told us. "Now we have a big job." We were up against the great Laker team: Magic, Kareem, Worthy, Michael Cooper, Byron Scott, Maurice Lucas, Kurt Rambis, Mitch Kupchak. The defending champions. They had beaten us four games out of five already this season. Everyone who knew anything about basketball was predicting another classic Laker-Celtic final.

Coach Fitch tried his best but it didn't work. It's natural: we were excited after a big victory, and we let down.

The Lakers jumped on us. We were not together and they beat us in the first game convincingly. They almost drove us out of the gym, running fast breaks, dunking. The game was kind of over in the first quarter. Magic ran, Worthy moved; Kareem, at age thirty-nine, scored thirty-one points.

Coach Fitch was not pleased. Two days before, we had been celebrating. Now everything had turned negative, they had beaten us badly.

The next day's practice was tough. Now we had to focus for real. We could not look back at Denver, that was two days and two hundred years ago. Coach Fitch made us watch films of the L.A. loss to rub our noses in what we'd done. We hadn't run back on defense, there was no pressure on the ball, and the Lakers were doing whatever they wanted, running up and down the floor, moving the ball in and out and over and around us. Everyone was very embarrassed.

We knew the Lakers were a great team but we were confident we could beat them. We had the ammunition. We were young and fast and if we all did what we were supposed to do we had the power. We could beat them, not by chance but by work. Instead of partying and doing L.A., we had to rest and focus.

Maybe the Lakers were comfortable. They had beaten us with such ease in game one, maybe they lost some of their edge. I don't know what it was but we came out in the second game and our team was ready. We were on top of them from the beginning, on the attack. In the first quarter I took the ball in for a powerful dunk — with *authority.* We were all playing with authority. "Block my shot? Put your hand there and I will break it!" That kind of authority. Ralph was getting every rebound. The Lakers would attack but they couldn't penetrate; our guards were pressing up front and Ralph and I challenged every ball that came into the lane. Every shot they took from outside would miss, and we would snatch it and go down and throw it into the post. They didn't have an answer for us.

Ralph was with Kareem and I was matched up against Maurice Lucas. Lucas had a great reputation; he was very strong, very physical, he could do everything but jump. He couldn't guard me, I jumped all over him. Finally the Lakers had to put Kareem on me and I was throwing in the jump hook, the fade-away. Kareem was 7'2", so I had to use the fade-away.

We worked Kareem on both ends. When he had the ball and beat Ralph, I was there over Kareem's shoulder every time. We were blocking the sky hook! Ralph denied him the middle and when Kareem turned to shoot I would come from the weak side and block him. Not once but *twice!* When I was guarding Kareem, Ralph would do the same thing. Kareem was thirty-nine, I was twenty-three. He had two big guys pushing him, putting hands on him. In the paper the next day Kareem was quoted: "It looked like these guys were dropping from the sky."

The Lakers started missing their shots and we began to dominate. We weren't doing anything we didn't ordinarily do, just throwing the ball into the middle and powering for the basket. When we went outside

Lewis Lloyd would drive or shoot. Lewis Lloyd was guarding Magic and did a good job. Magic was helpless, he was trying everything and nothing was working. He'd take it inside himself and get it blocked. What made us feel even better was that we weren't doing anything fancy, we were winning just by playing our game.

We won game two by ten points. This was a team that had run us out of the gym three days before and now the same team tried everything and nothing worked. Los Angeles was very quiet.

I could not believe how many people were at the Houston airport to greet us when we got home. Texas takes its sports seriously and the city of Houston had never won an NBA title, a World Series, a Super Bowl. The whole city was hungry for a championship. We had only tied the series and the place was so crowded it was scary just trying to drive out. People were yelling and clapping and shouting our names. When I got to my house I found the neighborhood kids had wrapped it in crepe paper. I didn't know anyone knew where I lived. There were streamers in the trees!

We had the Lakers exactly where we wanted them, tied one to one and at home. They had won sixty-two games and worked hard all season to be able to play the first two games in Los Angeles and then go on the road with a demoralizing 2–0 lead, and we had made their entire season meaningless. All that work for nothing. But these were the Lakers, we knew they were champions and would want to break back immediately and regain the home-court advantage, so we prepared for a tough, strong game three.

Game three at the Summit was packed with wild Rockets fans kicking up a tremendous roaring din. In the cinderblock hallway before we went on the court we heard the energy and noise gathering like we were inside an engine, and when we stepped on the court it was as if someone had stepped on the accelerator. We were jet-propelled.

It was a battle. They took us seriously now, they didn't back down, but we out-worked them. We didn't do anything fancy, just played our game and handled them. In fact, we overpowered them.

I felt so strong in the middle. The Lakers would double-team me, sometimes triple-team me, and I would just split the defense and go straight in and score. I was on the court against one of the great teams in the history of the NBA and I was doing anything I wanted to do out

there! Lewis Lloyd was driving and passing off, creating lots of opportunities for us. It was a big NBA game and we dominated. We beat the Lakers, 117–109.

Coach Fitch didn't let us celebrate. He was always looking ahead to the next task. Now we had a bigger job to do; it wasn't enough to lead the Lakers, being ahead wasn't satisfactory, we had to go for the knockout. We won game four, 105–95.

We went back to Los Angeles for game five. L.A. was stunned. They tried and tried but they could not come up with a solution for us. We worked Kareem mercilessly, we were bigger up front than they were, and we matched up well; we could handle them, but they couldn't handle us. Our defense was tenacious and didn't allow them to hit the three-point shots that would have forced our guards to go farther out on them and open up the middle for Kareem to work.

Still, they were the champs and Pat Riley was a very smart coach, and Bill Fitch didn't want to give them any time even to think about ways to beat us. We didn't want to go back to Houston for game six, let alone come here again to play one game for the Western Conference title.

Game five was tight. We all played well. The Lakers brought in Mitch Kupchak to play me and he was pushing and throwing elbows, and finally in the fourth quarter I retaliated. We had a fight. The referees kicked us both out. I was upset with Kupchak for playing me that way and with myself for getting thrown out of such an important game. I went to the locker room and watched the last few minutes on TV.

With the score tied at 112 and one second to play, Rodney McCray inbounded to Sampson. With Kareem in his face Ralph jumped in the air, caught the ball, and in one motion — there wasn't time for him to dribble; there wasn't even time for him to come down — he turned and put up an arcing jump shot that started at about his waist. The whole L.A. Forum seemed to suck in its breath. When the ball came down it was right in the net.

We had beaten the Lakers! No one outside of our own organization had given us a chance but we beat them four straight games because Coach Fitch had made us believe we could and had created a system that would win for us. (It is a tribute to the Lakers and their great championship spirit that they set about solving the problems we pre-

sented. Ralph and I had banged Kareem around all series long and he went home that summer and worked hard in the gym to build up his body. He came back the next year more fit and solid than he had been in ten years and he wouldn't be moved.) We had played great and kept our focus and our optimism and our enthusiasm high and not listened to anyone who said we would fail. We were young, we were the future, and the future was now.

Now we had to beat the Boston Celtics in the finals.

The Celtics played basketball as if they hated you. It was traditional NBA thinking in those days: Game face. You had to be intimidating on the court to play your game; you couldn't be nice to your opponent because he'd think you were scared of him and were trying to soften him up so he would go easy on you. *He'd* think *you* were intimidated and he would use that against you.

Larry Bird was the most traditional of these traditional thinkers. He didn't even want to shake your hand. When I made an effort to shake his hand on the court before the tip-off he was not friendly, he wouldn't even look at me. That was his game face. You were the enemy. He didn't care about you, he didn't want to be your friend, he didn't want to know you. He just wanted to play the game to win, he wanted to beat you and leave you totally defeated and leave it there.

I didn't like that kind of arrogance. I didn't think it was sportsman-like conduct and I didn't think it was necessary.

An NBA player is a warrior and over the course of a season, or many seasons, he plays against so many tough opponents and goes through so many different battles that he develops a warrior's tough skin. But the game is still basketball. If it's basketball you're going to compete in, there's nothing new. How can he intimidate someone by growling?

I can understand developing a strong hatred for someone who is making your life miserable while the game is going on, I can see the point then — winning is the goal and anything in the way is the enemy. But a player should be professional enough to differentiate between the opponent on the court and the man off it, and not let being friendly affect his performance. I can understand psyching yourself up. But the Celtics carried it too far. They were supposed to have the confidence of champions, but real confidence comes with being able to smile and

say hello and shake hands like a decent human being and then still beat your man all over the court. Kevin McHale said it was him and his teammates, and everybody else is the enemy. You wear a different uniform, he doesn't like you. I think that's all wrong.

In fact, I think it's kind of funny. When I've done my game routine — had my rest, eaten my meals, felt my surge in energy during warm-ups — I can smile because I know I can do whatever I want to do out there. Once I have that, the game is play. If some guy comes up to me all grim and angry, trying to intimidate me, I laugh and treat him extra nice. Who knows what he goes away thinking. He's growling; I'm laughing. Who do you think feels better when the game begins? I think you should always be friendly. That's not weakness, that is strength.

Larry Bird and the Celtics didn't see it that way. Neither did Coach Fitch. Anytime during the season, if a player on the other team fell and you tried to be a nice guy and pick him up, you'd never hear the end of it. He would make an example of you at every practice for a month. No. Coach Fitch was very Old School.

But he was right about one thing: Larry Bird never quit. He was already on the court when I got to the Boston Garden. Bird had a ballboy rebounding for him and he was practicing his shot, sweating.

Larry Bird loved the game. He wasn't graceful but he was smart, he knew his limitations, he worked hard and maximized his talent and stuck to basics, and it worked for him almost every time.

People didn't see how Larry Bird got things done. I really didn't know until I played against him. This guy was big. He was *wide* and he would box out and fight for every rebound. Bird used everything he had for that team. He couldn't jump but he was 6'9" and heavy. He was a forward and many times when I picked off my man and was getting in position for the rebound he would see me coming and box me out before I could get there. He was strong and always pushing and grabbing, and as quick and young as I was I couldn't get around him.

Back then people were saying he didn't have any talent; he's a basketball player but not an athlete. Because Bird made it look so easy by hitting all his open shots and grabbing balls without jumping, people didn't see how hard he worked. I had played only four games against him in two years in the league, and the Celtics had won all four. It wasn't until this series that I really understood how good he was, and then I saw what Coach Fitch had been saying about his hard work and I developed an even deeper respect for his game.

At the same time, Bird talked a lot of trash on the court. It was part of the way he played the game. Everything was a challenge for Bird and it was up to him to see that you lost. The ball would be swung out from the post to a guard and then to Bird, open at the top of the key. As the defender flew toward him with no chance to block it, Bird, in midshot, would say, "Stay down, fool." He knew he had already beaten you, you couldn't get there no matter how tall you were. You tried to distract him but he was so confident he could rub it in your face. You looked like a fool for real, trying to save something that couldn't be saved, but you couldn't let that disturb you; if you didn't come after him he would step up the next time and make an even easier shot. All you could do was swallow the insult as the shot went in. And, of course, he would not miss. That's what he was practicing two hours before the game. That was his shot.

There was another Bird trick: Boston would move the ball, work it around, everybody moving. All of a sudden Bird would pop behind the line for a three and they would find him. The guy checking him would go *"Oh!"* So the defender is running to block the shot, Bird fakes, the guy jumps, Bird is still on the ground, and as the defender is in the air Bird slaps him on the butt with the ball. The defender flies out of bounds. *Bird threw him out of bounds!* Bird shoots. And of course the shot goes in.

He had to practice that. He knew the height at which the defender would come at him, he knew the angle. He didn't just want to fake out his guy, he wanted to embarrass him, humiliate him and fire the crowd. And he'd be talking while he was shooting. "No, not this one!"

Everybody's got tricks. What made Bird so amazing was that he would do this with the game on the line. This wasn't a stunt he would pull when they were up by twenty points with a few minutes to play. No. He would do this at a crucial time when the game was serious!

That whole Boston team was made up of a bunch of mature hard-working men. The 1986 NBA championships was men versus boys. We had young guys with a lot of energy, they had older guys with years of experience. They wouldn't lose; if we were going to win we'd have to beat them. We'd have to show them we were much better than they were.

It was a tough series that opened at Boston Garden. When we had played there during the regular season Ralph had taken a hard fall. Someone had undercut him, and ever since he hadn't had a good game in Boston. We had a chance in the first game but lost it and then got blown out in the second. We came back to Houston and won game three. Game four at the Summit was the turning point.

It was close. At the very end of regulation I went for a block and the shooter missed. Bill Walton — who had starred while winning a championship with the Portland Trail Blazers and then gotten injured and now, nine years later, was coming off the bench for the Celtics — got the ball. Walton was a true big man. He didn't put the ball on the floor, he kept everything up by his chest with his elbows out like railroad ties, just like his coaches had taught him. UCLA coach John Wooden had done a very good job with a very good student; Bill Walton was fundamentally sound. Coach Lewis would have loved him. When our coaches showed us Walton's form I said, "That's impossible. How can he do it like that?" I didn't believe it until I saw him do it myself. With the ball at his chest Walton could snap a pass or go up for a dunk or shoot the jump hook. Bill Walton had the best jump hook in the league that year, that was his strength.

So with a few seconds left Walton faked the shot. I almost went for it but I recovered. Right then I saw there was no way he could shoot over me. I had him. When he went up to shoot I went straight up with him.

But Walton had a very quick release. I touched the ball. *I touched it!* The ball barely glanced off the glass and went in.

That was the backbreaker. A crucial basket, the turning point.

I had him, I knew I had him. I had my legs under me, I was in good position, I went for it, *I touched the ball!* Nine times out of ten I block that shot, but he shot over me.

We lost 106–103 and were down three games to one. We could have begun congratulating ourselves for beating the Lakers and simply getting to the finals, but Coach Fitch wouldn't let us. He told us we had to win the next one at home. He was a hardworking tough guy who made sure everyone believed we could still win it.

In game five at the Summit, 7′4″ Ralph Sampson fought 6′1″ Celtic Jerry Sichting. Some dirty play must have started it but it was amazing to see. This was a real fight, both men swinging, punches being thrown and landed. Sichting ducked under Ralph's arms and put a shoulder in his stomach and tried to pick him up and body-slam him. Teams jumped in on both sides. Even Coach Fitch tackled someone.

Whatever caused it, the fight made the crowd at the Summit crazy. Their energy churned to another level and we caught it. We beat the Celtics by fifteen points and went back to Boston for game six.

It seemed like all of Boston was at the airport to jeer at us. They were already making fun of Ralph for not picking on someone his own size. Inside Boston Garden the sound was much worse. They booed us so much that it boosted the Celtics and was hard for us to beat. We played hard but the Celtics won, 114–97. They were champions, we were runners-up.

But back in Houston the city was very proud of us. We had surpassed all expectations, we had given the Celtics a fight, and the future looked bright for us. The only other superpower in the west was the Lakers and we had proved we had the players, talent, and system to beat them. This Boston team had beaten us by capitalizing on some of our mistakes and game errors. It wasn't like we hadn't had a chance to win. I was convinced that we would get there. I felt it would be the same as it had been in college when we had gone to the Final Four each year. I looked at our team and thought, We can win this.

Things didn't work out as I'd planned. In the middle of the 1986–87 season our frontcourt, Lewis Lloyd and Mitchell Wiggins, tested positive for drugs and were banned from the league. John Lucas had been banned the year before. Drugs in the NBA were a real problem. We never recovered.

Worse, a little more than a third of the way into the season Ralph Sampson went down.

Ralph was a big man who could play like a guard and he liked to do it. He could dribble the length of the court, he had one-on-one moves that were unusual for a man his size, he was fast and graceful and agile — and fragile. Not soft, just breakable. Ralph was so tall and had such long legs that his knees, which supported his weight and were called upon to do more twisting and turning than they were designed for, were always vulnerable. His knee finally gave way. His injury was a real tragedy.

Ralph had surgery and went directly into physical therapy and rehabilitation but he was never the same after that. His game relied on his quickness and mobility, his ability to change direction in an instant, and with bad knees that was no longer possible. I felt very sad for him. Before the injury he had been under constant pressure to be consistently great. Afterward it was a constant struggle just to play at all. Maybe because he had performed so effortlessly, Ralph got the reputation of being lazy. But I was there and I saw, from the inside, that he was just the opposite. He stretched, he trained, he would stay after practice and work out with weights. People said he was weak and lazy. No. He was a very hard worker. His problem was that his body betrayed him. It never came back.

With Ralph gone for most of the season and our backcourt decimated, we were in trouble. We needed players all over the court and we needed someone in management to look forward and begin putting together the Rockets of the future. Only six months before, the future had looked bright. Now it was clouded with questions.

That's when I began to disagree publicly with the Rockets' management over the direction of the team. The Rockets' front office did very little to improve us. As important as they had been to us, these players were gone — they were each responsible for their own actions and they weren't coming back — but all the front office did was moan over the loss. The Rockets' front office looking backward meant that no one in charge was looking out for our future. I got so sick of people coming up with excuses about why they couldn't get one player or another. The Phoenix Suns had half their team caught with drugs and suspended, and those guys were all traded to different teams as the Suns rebuilt their program. All we got from the Rockets' front office was a superficial repair job, not an overhaul. And when they did acquire new bodies they got players who were on their way out of the league. For the next few years it seemed like the Rockets were the place all players went to exit the NBA. We were the dying gasp.

We went 42–40 that season and got by Portland in the first round of the playoffs before losing to Seattle in six games. After starting with such high hopes and plans, our season was over much too early.

In the locker room after the final playoff game, a television sports reporter from a local Houston station asked me what I thought it would take to get us back to the championship level we had been at a year earlier. It was a legitimate question, we all wanted to look to the future and see the team being successful, and I gave an answer I thought was serious and considered, but also obvious to everyone.

"Well, definitely we have to have a point guard," I told them. John Lucas, old as he was, was the best guard we had. When he was suspended we lost our floor leadership and he had not been replaced by someone of equal stature. "Lewis Lloyd was a small forward or 'two guard,' we have to have a player of that caliber again. And we need a young small forward." Anyone looking at our team who knew about basketball could see that.

What I didn't know was that the same reporter would go directly to my teammates who were playing those positions and tell them I had blamed them for our losing.

The next day all over the media I was accused of criticizing my teammates. Several of them took it as a personal attack. That was the last thing I'd meant to do. I was giving an honest assessment of the team, and in the way they wrote their pieces the press turned it around and made it seem as if I was saying I was better than everybody else, as if I was trying to say it wasn't my fault we lost.

First of all, you win as a team and you lose as a team. *We* didn't play well. I would never blame individual teammates; I held the entire squad — including myself — responsible for our mediocre season.

I had been in the league for three years and I had seen how the press operates. I had talked to reporters about their job. Sometimes I would say, "This must be very tough, because if there's nothing to write one day you still have to write something. This is a full-time job, you have to create something." I had seen them waiting for a window of opportunity to create a controversy, something that sells. I asked Tim Melton, a TV reporter, "How come when something good happens you never report that, but when something bad happens you're all over it?" I could ask him because we had a good relationship and made jokes together. He said, "Okay, I'll be frank with you. Nobody, not the public or the press, cares about something good. If it's real, real, *real* good then *maybe* they might be interested. But if it's bad everybody wants it!"

A good reporter could build a reputation based on his own style and writing and principles, that's where he can be creative. But reporters are all trying to come up with exclusives, a story that nobody else has, to establish their uniqueness. And the best way to make a name for yourself on the sports page, they think, is to write something controversial.

More often than not the press doesn't come into the locker room to get the story, they come in with their story already in mind and look for quotes to confirm their own ideas. Reporters don't give athletes enough respect for having minds of their own; they don't think athletes have anything significant to say. They don't really care to know us as people and report what they learn; they listen until they get what they think they want and then they're gone. Some reporters are subtle, some reporters you can see their angle coming a mile away. They try to trap you with leading questions to create some tension between teammates, and most of the time you can cut them off.

But this time he had asked me a legitimate question and turned the answer into scandal.

I got the label *selfish* and it was hard to shake off.

When the next season began I wouldn't talk to the press at all. For the first three months I had no comment to anyone. But not all reporters played dirty, so after a while I just picked and chose the people I would respond to. Over the years you get to know the ones who cause trouble for a living. In the locker room I saw the reporter who had created all the problems. "I don't have to talk to you," I told him, "and I'm not going to. I don't want to give you any story." He had distorted his reporting and I wasn't going to let that happen again.

Nineteen games into the 1987–88 season the Rockets traded Ralph Sampson. We could almost see it coming. Ralph's knee was not perfect and when games got to crunch time Coach Fitch began playing Jim Petersen in his place.

Ralph and guard Steve Harris were traded to the Golden State Warriors for center Joe Barry Carroll, guard Eric "Sleepy" Floyd, and cash.

The Rockets' organization didn't do it gracefully. We had just come back from a road game in Chicago when an older gentleman from the front office came to the airport and told Coach Fitch. They didn't show Ralph the courtesy of telling him in private. He had been the Rookie of the Year, the All-Star Game MVP, an All-NBA performer for the team, and they gave him no respect. Rather than doing it in a proper setting where he could react to this upsetting news privately, they pulled Ralph aside in the airport lounge where everyone could see and told him he had been traded. I thought that was very cold.

Ralph's whole career was undermined by expectations that he shouldn't have had to live up to. Ralph was even more fragile after knee surgery; he certainly wasn't going to go inside and bang with the power forwards and he had lost some of the mobility that made him such an unusually quick and gifted big man. And still people wanted him to perform miracles. He should never have been asked to be a post-up center; he wasn't built for it. He and I complemented each other, and even though we didn't have a close personal relationship I enjoyed playing with him and we played well together. People who had been on his case from the beginning — media and some fans — called him lazy, didn't appreciate the things Ralph could do, and instead wanted him to do things he couldn't. He left Houston without people truly understanding what a good player they had been seeing.

Now I had a new teammate in the frontcourt. I had always liked Joe Barry Carroll's game. He came the closest of anyone I ever saw to recreating Kareem's sky hook. Joe Barry was a nice guy, not really an athletic guy, more of an intellectual player. He was very intelligent and well-spoken and he loved the lifestyle of fine dining in good restaurants. But if someone said, "Let's go work out," he would not enjoy that. He didn't have fun running the floor. He played hard but he had his own ideas about what was good enough shape to maximize his play.

Because he had interests other than basketball he developed the reputation of someone who "plays just for the money," not for the love of the game. He didn't deny that he was playing for the money, but that didn't mean it was bad. Most people work at their jobs for the paycheck; it is unusual when someone can earn a living doing something that is fun for him. But because people saw him playing a game they had played when they were children and wished they could still play instead of working, they felt he wasn't respectful enough of the opportunity he'd been given. I didn't have a problem with Joe Barry Carroll's motivation but Coach Fitch had some concerns about his work ethic. Joe Barry played for the Rockets only that one year.

We came in fourth in the Midwest that season and were knocked out of the playoffs in the first round by the Dallas Mavericks.

The Rockets fired Bill Fitch. After going to the finals two years before, we had been sliding backward, and getting knocked out in the first round was the final blow. We had lost our backcourt to drugs and one Twin Tower to injury, which definitely affected the way the team played, but management needed to fire somebody and they put all the blame on Coach Fitch.

There were rumors that I got Coach Fitch fired, but I liked Coach Fitch, and Coach Fitch knew I liked him; we had a good relationship and I liked his system. Coach Fitch thought of the team first, himself second. You could have a one-on-one confrontation with the coach and that was okay, he didn't care if you or anyone else liked him. But if you did something that hurt the team he would take you apart. His discipline was firm but he let you know in the beginning that he expected to be obeyed. Just do your job and you had no problem. There were no surprises with Coach Fitch. I thought his values were very strong.

Coach Fitch knew I liked him. At the end of our playoffs he came up and told me, "I'm proud of you. And I deserve a lot of the credit." He did! He is a proud man and he helped me tremendously by drilling into my mind the work ethic necessary for me to establish myself in the league. I had come in as a number-one draft choice, the first pick in the draft; another coach might have let me coast or might have settled for less than my best. That would have been a disaster; if a new player learns he can do just enough to get by he will never achieve the full power of his potential. That was not going to happen with Coach Fitch, he was going to wring every last drop of ability out of me. I will always appreciate him for that.

My house was quite a ways out of Houston and in 1984 I had bought a townhouse five minutes from the UH campus for Lita to live in while she was going to law school. We had been living there together now for about four years. We were basically married. In fact, under Texas common law, if two people live together for six months they are married. I felt married to her.

When Lita got pregnant we had a big celebration. We were married under common law but now she wanted it official. I could not blame her; it was the socially acceptable thing to do. She began to pressure me to get officially married. I bought her a ring and we got engaged.

But as the baby's birth came nearer and nearer I found I didn't have a clear vision of the future, of what kind of life I wanted to lead, and when it got to the point where I had to make the final step I could not marry Lita because I knew something was not right. Something was missing in my life, I couldn't find it, and I didn't know what it was. I didn't have a clear direction, I couldn't make a decision for the future. There was something I needed to *feel* in order to get officially married that I wasn't feeling.

This had been developing for some time and it had to do with the way Lita and I treated each other. She was constantly demanding that I prove my love to her while I wanted her to take my love on faith. It was a basic difference between us and she would not budge. Lita was not a person who compromised easily and as the official marriage approached I felt that she would rule our lives without consideration for me.

Still, Lita was pregnant and we wanted the baby.

We went to Lamaze classes together, we made up a baby's room at the townhouse, we planned the child's wardrobe and began to think of this new life. I was never the kind of person who looked far into the future, I had always taken things one step at a time, but bringing a baby into the world meant that I had to consider exactly what my future would hold while I was holding my child. I didn't know the answer for Lita and me but I was excited.

Our baby was born on July 6, 1988. I was in the delivery room during the birth and I've never felt anything like I felt the first time I saw my child. It was as if all the miracles of the world had come to me. She was a wonderful, beautiful, healthy baby girl. My parents and Lita's were both in Houston to be with us, and my mother chose the baby's name: Abisola. Allah is the joy of the world, and *Abisola* means "born in joy for all."

Lita was joyful to have our child but she wanted everything official. She wanted to be officially married. Even though I was right there every day, committed to her and married by Texas law and in our minds, proud to be with her and proud to be the father of our child, she was unhappy. If she had let things happen naturally, I am sure, no question, we would have gotten married. But the more she pressured me the more I became concerned. She couldn't talk about anything but official marriage and when we had the same old conflict she started crying.

We had been so happy together for so long, why was she doubting me now?

She could talk about nothing else and we couldn't talk about that. It got so bad I could not spend any time with her. We didn't have a relationship anymore. Everything we had that used to be so beautiful was gone.

I tried to find a reason to put aside my doubts and marry her. It would have made Lita so happy, it would have calmed her parents and made things smooth for a while. But I knew in my heart that I would be making a mistake. I hadn't known until it was too late, but we were too different.

Lita stayed in the hospital for a few days and then came home to the townhouse. The first few days after a baby is born are hard for a new mother, and Lita's mother was in charge of all the details. Feeding, cooking, making sure the baby was getting everything she needed and Lita was getting her rest — Lita's mother took care of it all. I was there, but it was hard talking to Lita and there was little for me to do except hold the baby when she was awake and sit around feeling both ecstatic and unhappy. One afternoon a few days after Lita came home from the hospital, I went to play at Fonde.

I told Lita I was going. She said, "Go." I knew she didn't want me to, she wanted me to get her some food and prove to her that I loved her. Lita didn't say it — she didn't have to — but she was accusing me of feeling that the pickup game at Fonde was more important than she and our child. That was absurd, of course, but I knew that's what she was thinking. I went anyway. I would not be held hostage to her fears. *I* knew it wasn't true.

When I got back that afternoon Lita's mother said, "Lita wants to talk to you." I'd had a very close relationship with Lita's parents ever since college; we had gotten along terrifically, like family. Now Lita's mother did not look happy. I went to Lita's room.

I had never seen her so serious. There was a look in her eyes I had never seen before.

"Hakeem," she told me, "in order for us to stay together here under this roof we have to be officially married."

"We have been through this many times," I said.

"I have to draw the line," she told me. "I want you to leave."

I could not believe what I was hearing. I had a five-day-old daughter and she was being taken away from me. Lita wanted me to move out? I didn't try to argue with her. What was the use? I turned around and walked out of the room.

I went and found Lita's mother downstairs. "I think Lita has made a big mistake," I said. "I don't know why or what she's saying. She just got out of the hospital, maybe she doesn't mean it. But all this talk about drawing the line is the wrong approach."

I wanted to be around the baby — she was my daughter and I loved her — so I would visit the townhouse every day. I held Abisola when she was awake and waited around while she slept so I could get another chance to hold her. Things went on that way for about a month.

Lita's mother was going back to Port Angeles, in Washington State, where they lived. Lita told me she was taking the baby and going there with her. The mistake was getting worse, but I thought wherever she went she would be back.

I was terribly worried about not being able to see my daughter. I had great love for this little girl, but I didn't see anything I could do. The only option Lita left me was to say, "Okay, come back and I'll marry you." But if I married her that way it was not going to last. If she drew the line here this time and threatened to take the baby, she could draw it anywhere next time and the threat would be the same.

As much as I had loved Lita, she and I never got back together. Everything that she wanted about marriage was right. I'm not trying to justify what I did. Morally, we should not have been living together or had a child if we weren't married. I was wrong. What we did was wrong from the beginning. What she wanted, socially and morally, was absolutely right. Unfortunately, the person she was and the person I was looking for in a wife were different.

I supported Lita and Abisola when they moved away, and Lita established herself in a new city and a new job. It is my responsibility as a father to raise my daughter the best way I know how, to teach her what is important to me and to the world. I take that responsibility seriously. I am very involved in raising Abisola. I see her, I make decisions for her schooling and upbringing, I am a hands-on father, which is very important in a family where the parents have separated. Lita is doing a fantastic job as well. We cooperate toward the goal of a happy and healthy and strong Abisola and we have an understanding that works well — no restrictions on my seeing her, only the best for our daughter so she can feel secure in both places, with her mom and with her dad.

Abisola is so important to me and she needs to know that her daddy loves her. And I do.

12

ONE-ON-ONE WITH MICHAEL JORDAN

A GUY INTRODUCED HIMSELF after practice at the Summit early in the 1988–89 season. Many people shake players' hands in the locker room and hallways and try to get our attention. I try to be courteous to each one. He asked me, "Are you a Muslim?"

"Yes," I said. "How did you know?"

"Somebody told me. At the mosque."

I had never even heard that there was a mosque in Houston.

"At the mosque?"

"Yes," he said. "It's right here, around the corner."

"Around the corner from the Summit? No way." Then I got suspicious. "What kind of mosque is it?"

I had had several conversations with people from the Nation of Islam who wanted to talk about their religion and their organization. I had listened, I wanted to understand their concept. But what I heard was not Islamic teaching. They presented Islam as the black man's religion and their organization as the black man's organization.

Once I heard that, I had eased myself politely away. I did not want to offend them, and they didn't know I was a Muslim, but that kind of division and isolation is totally against everything Islam stands for. From the time I was first taught the religion it was made clear to me that Islam is for all people. That's the beauty of Islam, it cuts through race and culture and presents the word of Allah to everyone no matter his or her color or race or tribe or nationality.

Less than 10 percent of the Muslims in the world are black. I had not studied Islam a lot when I was growing up but one of the basic tenets I did remember was that the Qur'an was the word of Allah as revealed to the Prophet Muhammad, PBUH, that it presented the word of Allah in its perfect form, and that anyone who introduced *any* new elements into the religion was to be totally rejected. Allah says religion is for Allah only. Regardless of your color or race, you submit to his power. The Qur'an is the foundation of Islam and its final authority, it overrides all opinion. The Prophet, PBUH, said Islam was for all the peoples of the world, not just the black man or the Arab.

But this was a legitimate Islamic mosque I was being introduced to. I was happy to hear that. The guy said, "Would you like to come worship with us?"

"Sure!"

"When?"

"Friday." All devout Muslims pray five times each day, but at home in Nigeria I only really prayed on Fridays, the *Jumma*. I figured I would do as I did at home. "Do you have Friday prayers?"

"Oh, sure."

"We'll go."

That Friday when the guy arrived after practice I was still on the court shooting around. I had forgotten. I jumped in the shower, put on some clothes, and followed him in my car.

The mosque really was a couple of turns from the Summit, just a modest building, two minutes away. I had been here for years and not known about it. I parked outside. There was a mat on the pavement by the door so people could take off their shoes before they walked in.

I looked around and saw people of all different colors and backgrounds and nationalities — Arabs, Asians, Africans, white Americans, black Americans. I was happy immediately. Everything looked right. People were standing and talking. They were all friendly to each other, and when I walked in they were friendly to me too. In Islam you make your ablutions before praying so you are purified in the presence of Allah, and we all washed before we entered the mosque.

Then it was time for the Call, the *azaan*.

The Call is very powerful, very beautiful. It beckons you to the mosque to prayer. There is one man in each mosque, the *mo'azzin*, who makes the Call. That's his specialty: his long breath, his voice. When you hear the Call you stop speaking and repeat it yourself in a low voice.

The room hummed from about three hundred men reciting the Call in unison, each in his own state of communion with Allah.

I felt goosebumps all over my body. Everything I had known growing up came back to me in that instant: the feeling of my knees on the floor of the mosque, the sound of the words of Allah as they washed over me. I remembered walking to school on Friday mornings and hearing the Call on every radio, as if I was being shepherded. It was the most beautiful sound I had ever heard.

This was what had been missing. Missing for years. I was so comfortable, so excited. The Call usually goes on for three or four minutes but I got lost in it and to me it seemed endless. Sitting on the floor listening to that Call, these were the happiest moments of my life.

Islam had not been my major concern. Before Islam is called "the dark ages," I didn't understand my responsibilities. I was living according to my own understanding, but Islam isn't just a religion; it is a way of life. I asked, "What are my responsibilities as a Muslim?" There are books of the lawful and the prohibited. For example, Muslims are prohibited from drinking alcohol; we can neither earn nor receive interest on our money, we eat no pork, we fast during the month of Ramadan. I used to drink beer, my diet was healthy but not restricted, and I was not at all observant of the holidays. That's where my changes began. I made a commitment and I kept to it. I made that commitment with joy, and I began to grow.

I would arrive at the mosque after practice each day and I would pray and study, and before I knew it, it was eight at night. Then I would go to the home of one of my fellow Muslims where his wife would put out tea and plenty of food and we would study some more. I was trying to memorize some of the chapters and verses of the Qur'an in the beautiful rhythmic tone in which it is recited properly. My time became very valuable to me, there weren't enough hours in the day to read. I had found a community, and I felt completely at home.

Back at the Summit the Rockets had traded Rodney McCray and my friend Jim Petersen for rebounding forward Otis Thorpe, and had hired Don Chaney as coach. This was a big change.

Everybody had been complaining about Bill Fitch's system and they wanted to bring in somebody who was just the opposite. Don Chaney was the other side of Bill Fitch. Don Chaney was a nice guy. Nice guys, as they say, finish last.

Don Chaney had been a guard on Coach Lewis's great University of Houston teams of the late sixties. He came in and tried to please everybody. It didn't work. He just couldn't take charge and make the men do what we were supposed to do. Where it would cost someone money if he so much as dribbled the ball after Coach Fitch blew the whistle, the guys tested Chaney and he didn't stand up to them. We went from strict to loose, we lost our discipline. Coach Chaney didn't like confrontation and the guys knew it. From January 1 to the end of the season we played .500 ball. We came in second in the Midwest but were seeded fifth in the Western Conference playoffs and were eliminated in the first round by the Seattle Supersonics. I was disappointed but I wasn't surprised.

This was the first of the Detroit Piston "Bad Boy" championships.

One key to that Piston team was Isiah Thomas. He was a little guy, listed at 6'1" but maybe not that tall, and he was the best guard in the league at shooting over big men. He had studied all of us and his shot went straight up and dropped. He wasn't afraid to come into the paint and challenge us — in fact, he came in with confidence — because he had a shot we couldn't touch. He would come directly at me, I would leap, and he would put it straight up over me and into the basket. I was always just missing. I would think it was luck, that he could not do it again, but every time he came inside he would get the same result. And the higher I jumped, the higher he would shoot it. It was discouraging.

They had a lot of talent on that team — Isiah and Joe Dumars and Vinnie "Microwave" Johnson, John Salley and Dennis Rodman. Their coach, Chuck Daly, was an authoritarian from the same school as Bill Fitch or Pat Riley who could get the most out of his players. He was very good. I respected the Pistons' skills but there were two players on the squad who were way out of line.

Bill Laimbeer and Rick Mahorn were very dirty players. They tripped you when you were running and fouled you hard when you were coming down the lane just to hurt you, which is not basketball. They played dirty. They didn't even pretend to be reasonable. They promoted the image of bad boys as if that was something to be proud of. Laimbeer, in particular, was dirty, but he could not fight. But if you heard that Bill Laimbeer was in a fight you didn't have to ask who caused it; you knew it was Laimbeer.

The Rockets did not play well in the 1989–90 season. We went 41–41 and lost again in the first round of the playoffs to the Lakers. It was the Chicago Bulls' year. Michael Jordan won his first NBA championship.

Michael Jordan and I came into the NBA at the same time. It didn't take long for me to realize that this was the greatest player I had ever seen. There may have been greater players before him in the history of the league but I never witnessed them; when I saw Michael Jordan I saw a player strong in all areas.

When I analyze an opponent — or a teammate, for that matter — I try to see their weaknesses. You can break down most players that way. No matter how strong a player is in one area, if he is weak in another you can neutralize him by forcing him to go there again and again. It doesn't take long to find out. Usually, if one is a good shooter he doesn't like to drive; if he's a good driver he can't shoot. You use that knowledge. If a player is a weak foul shooter, foul him; if he can't hit jump shots in the fourth quarter, dare him to beat you by playing loose late in the game; if he is soft to his right, don't let him go left. If you take away all options except the one a player is weak at you have taken away his game.

But none of that worked with Michael Jordan. Whatever you gave him, he would take it. If you backed off, he would shoot. He would make his shot most of the time, and if he missed it was only because he was human. If you came too close he would go around you. If you gave him the right or the left he would go either way. If there was nothing there, he would create. He could rebound, he played good defense, he was quick with steals. He was strong in all areas; if you let him do anything at all he would beat you. Players liked to play against him because it was a challenge to go up against the best. I gave him the ultimate respect because he was a complete player.

Michael Jordan is a natural athlete. His form is perfect, he has strong basketball basics and fundamentals, and his game is all footwork. At 6'6" he is an in-between player. Most 6'6" ballplayers are small forwards; he is a natural guard. That's why he creates problems — Michael Jordan is a big guard. He does everything guards can do, and much more, with size. He's as quick as other guards but bigger, so he takes advantage by shooting over them. When he plays bigger guys he's quicker than they are and has great ball-handling skills, so he beats his man easily, makes the shot and gets fouled. He also has very big hands — big man's hands. When he shakes your hand you don't think he's a guard. He could palm the ball like Dr. J, which made his ball control even greater.

Playing against Michael Jordan is an all-day challenge. The first thing he does is get you off balance. His fakes are so sharp and real you have to go for them. That's the difference between Michael Jordan and everybody else: You don't know what is real and what's a fake. He can seem to be driving and then pop up for the jumper, or he can seem to be about to shoot and then go right around you for the score. When he fakes, you have to go for it, you can't lay off him because he can follow through on everything he threatens to do and he can make just about any shot. And he's so smart that just when you think you've got him figured out and he's faking all the time, all of a sudden he will keep you honest and just explode on you in one motion like you're not even there.

You have to honor his fakes and respect everything. Other players, you don't take them seriously. A driver faking a shot, who's going to go for that? A jump shooter who's faking to drive, you know this is a fake so you stay with him. And if he does drive you can catch up with him because this is not his game. But Michael Jordan does it all. First, he's a driver. That's his first option: to drive. He will flash by you in a moment, so to prevent an easy lay-up you have to try to cut him off when he moves. However, if you are quick enough to get in his lane he will pull up and shoot, he has that option. You will be low and off balance, you'll have used up all your mobility just to get to your spot, and you'll just have to watch him stop and put the ball up because you can't move. You have to be balanced to jump and he has gotten you off balance. And he will get a lot of points off you because his shot doesn't miss often.

Michael Jordan is a very creative player; you cannot predict what he is going to do. Even when you think you've got his shot blocked, at the last minute he will change it. You can never think, Well, I've cornered him, I've trapped him, there's nothing there this time. I have forced him into many difficult situations over the years and he has come out of them. Once he's under the basket, there's no way for a 6'6" guard to shoot over a man five inches taller than he is. We wait for these kinds of opportunities! But Michael Jordan would come inside and hang in the air. I knew I had him blocked — I could feel the basketball — but he would just hang there. Where most other players would try to force it over me, Jordan would realize there was nowhere to go and *on his way down* take the ball back and pass off — maybe to his man behind the three-point line. I'm coming down, he's coming down, and he still makes something happen. I thought I had a block, now they've got three points.

If a player like Michael Jordan catches me one-on-one outside, I will back off. I'll give him the jumper rather than have him go by me for an easy inside slam. When I see that he has truly taken off for his jump shot, *then* I will contest it. Even though I don't have a chance to block it I will run at him just to distract him.

But on top of being physically gifted, Michael Jordan is smart. He won't settle for an open jumper. Most players will, they like taking open shots. But Michael Jordan is a very intelligent player and he wants better than I'm giving him, so he dribbles toward me. It's unusual for a guard to dribble *toward* a big man if he wants to shoot a jumper. But this is Michael Jordan. If I'm going to let him shoot I back off some more, and some more, until he's even closer to the basket and has an even easier shot. I can't keep giving ground, and with every step backward I'm more off balance. Sooner or later I'll have to come to him, at which point he can either shoot before I get there or drive around me. It's a very subtle, very impressive set of decisions he makes.

I understood his game very well because if I were an outside player these are the decisions I would make, the moves I would use. I'm an in-between player too. When I play against a guy who is almost my size I just post him up; when I play big guys I go outside, make a move, use my fakes, and come at them. I know I can't do it in the paint but on the outside I have room. I stay on the attack, I don't let the defender make my decisions for me, I make my own decisions.

One time when Jordan was posting up I even saw him do the Dream Shake. That's my move, where you fake left in deep toward the basket, shake your man, take a step back, and turn around quickly for a fade-away jumper. I was watching on TV and Jordan got the ball and made the move and it looked so natural that I really couldn't claim it, he took what the defensive man gave him and used it perfectly. How could I say that was mine? That came naturally out of Michael Jordan.

When he came into the league Michael Jordan was criticized for being selfish. People used to complain all the time that he was shooting too much, twenty-eight times a game, and not getting his teammates involved. I never bought into that premise. Michael Jordan is a team player, he plays to win. When he takes his shot it's because he thinks he can score. And he can! He was just taking the first responsibility of the offense — creating opportunities. When he gets the ball he can pass or score or finish the play. Early in his career he was doing the work of two or three people, first in bringing the ball downcourt, then either shooting or passing; he was controlling the tempo of the game. And he still does. Inside, outside, he plays guard, he plays forward, he plays center — and he always does damage. I've seen big men not even try to stop him, they get out of his way; he explodes on them and they don't want to get dunked on.

When I look at basketball sometimes I think of animals. Michael Jordan is like a big cat hopping up on a rock; as soon as he lands he goes straight up. People think he's going to a spot on the floor but really the court is just a stepping stone. He gets the ball, hops to a space, and leaps. Against a big, solid seven-footer like Dikembe Mutombo I can play a cat's game, he doesn't understand it. Mutombo has to play a big man's game to be effective, and he usually is. But when the Rockets use our quickness, move up the court, dribble, shoot, he can't keep up.

When I've had success against Michael Jordan it's been by coming from the weak side and surprising him. I hide behind the Bulls' center and try not to let Jordan see me. Because I am usually smaller than the opposing center I can get away with this, I can literally hide. Some shot blockers, like Mutombo, want you to see them; they stand tall and large in the paint and turn drivers away with their size. Guards don't like shot blockers; once they sense you're around they don't come in. But I'm not that big, my shot blocking is all timing, not size. I stand behind the center but I'm watching the play on the other side of the court, and as soon as Jordan beats his man I come over. You can't be too eager, I've tried that and it doesn't work. If I get there too soon he changes hands or alters his shot or dishes off. If I get there too late the shot is gone already. I have to get there at exactly the right time. I study Michael Jordan's moves to learn when the right time is: it's when the move is finished and the ball is just being released. *As he is releasing it.* And when I get him — he's just seen me but it's too late and he knows I've got him; he tries to change the shot but he can't change this one, he changes it right into my hand — he gets upset.

Michael Jordan's game is very flashy, but not flashy for show; he's fun to watch but he's also very effective. And he is always playing this game to win. He's a man. A lot of people think he's just gifted, but he is also very tough mentally. He accepts challenges. If you challenge him you give him a bigger task and he will rise above the competition to complete it. If you surprise him he comes back stronger. In a series or in individual games he always takes things to a higher level as the play continues. When I see him go on a tear in the first quarter I always think, Okay, this is going to be tough. You think maybe he will slow down, but no, he will always take his game and raise it. In the fourth quarter, as tired as he might be from having played hard all night, he's even more intense than when the game began.

Most superstars, if they match up against each other at the same position, neutralize each other. When you put together your game plan you figure that unless someone has an outstanding night, this is a stand-off, the game will be won by the other teammates. But Michael Jordan isn't neutralized. He's different. Michael Jordan dominates superstars.

If he were an animal in the jungle Michael Jordan could lie out on the biggest rock and no one would disturb him, no one would attack him. He wouldn't have to watch his back. All the other animals would wait fearfully; they'd be scared even while he slept. He would stalk his prey and take down anything he wanted. Afterward he would prowl around, full, quiet, peaceful, his tail swinging. In the NBA, Michael Jordan walks around the jungle freely.

13

TO MECCA

IN THE 1990–91 season the Rockets finally decided not to be the place where old NBA veterans took their careers to die. We got some new blood.

Kenny Smith, a good shooting guard, arrived from the Atlanta Hawks in a trade for John Lucas and Tim McCormick. I was sorry to see Tim go — he played a good fundamental game, he knew where to go on the court, he rebounded and played hard. But Kenny was a spark we needed.

The year 1990 was the year Vernon Maxwell stepped into the Rockets' starting lineup full-time. He had come to the team the winter before when the Rockets had bought his contract from the San Antonio Spurs for cash. Vernon was young and wild but he was a player. He put up more than five hundred three-point shots and set an NBA record by making one hundred seventy-two of them. He also had a thirty-point *quarter* in a game against Cleveland. Thirty points is a very healthy *game* total. Our team had felt old and dull for several years, but now we were coming to life. With Otis Thorpe and Buck Johnson at forwards and Larry Smith and Sleepy Floyd coming off the bench, we could play.

We took some time getting going, playing near .500 ball until the first of the year. Then, against the Bulls at the Summit, I took a big elbow from their center Bill Cartwright and broke all kinds of bones around my eye. I was out for twenty-five games. Fortunately, Larry

Smith took over as center and the team came together and went 15–10 while I was on the injured list.

We lost the first game when I came back but then went on a thirteen-game winning streak that included beating Michael Jordan and the Bulls at Chicago Stadium. We finished the season twenty-two games over .500 and beat the Bulls both times we played them. We were looking strong for the playoffs but unfortunately ran into the Lakers, who swept us. It was the fourth year in a row we were knocked out in the first round. That was discouraging but at least the Rockets' future was looking brighter than it had in several years.

After I started practicing Islam in the mosque a lot of my friends asked me about my name. Before they knew me they thought it was an Islamic name, but they hadn't been sure. In Nigeria it's spelled many different ways: Hakim, Akim, Akeem, and Hakeem. They're all the same. In school back home, on papers and tests I spelled it Akeem. It was the way my parents spelled it, the way I'd always spelled it. Some of the more traditional teachers would put the *H* back on for me. I would get tests back and I'd see the spelling of my own name corrected in red pen. I didn't pay them a lot of attention and when I went to the University of Houston I spelled it the way I had always spelled it: Akeem.

In Arabic the proper spelling is Hakeem. Now that I was more serious about my religion I decided to make sure my name was spelled the proper Arabic way. One day after a game in March 1991 at the Summit I told the Rockets' P.R. person, Jay Goldberg, to tell the press. If my name was going to appear in the papers, it might as well be spelled correctly. It seemed like a simple thing; I didn't think much of it.

There was a rush to my locker after the game. I came out of the shower and was surprised at the frenzy around my stall. There were twice as many cameras as usual and the questions didn't stop coming. Apparently I had created big news. Lew Alcindor had changed his name to Kareem Abdul-Jabbar, Keith Wilkes had become Jamaal Wilkes; they had been Americans with English names and the changes had had meaning beyond just spelling. The press knew I had changed my life when I rededicated myself to Islam and they immediately took this as a symbol of that change. I told the reporters, "I'm not changing the spelling of my name, I'm correcting it." If they were looking for a meaning, that was it. It was kind of what I had done with my life — I hadn't changed it fundamentally, I had corrected it to where it should have been all along, all praise and thanks be to Allah.

I studied the Qur'an every day. At home, at the mosque, on the road . . . I would read it in airplanes, in my hotel room, before games and after them. I was soaking up the faith and learning new meanings each time I turned a page. I didn't dabble in the religion, I gave myself over to it.

There are five Pillars of Islam, the foundations upon which faith is built: The belief in the oneness of Allah without any association, and the messengership of Allah and the Prophet Muhammad as the seal of the prophets; the establishment of regular prayer, *salah,* five times a day; the fast during the month of Ramadan, when the Qur'an was revealed to Muhammad by Allah through the angel Gabriel; the cleansing of one's assets, *Zakat,* to pay the poor due; and the pilgrimage to Mecca and Ka'abah, the first place of worship of one God, built by the Prophet Abraham and his son Ishmael, and the birthplace of the Prophet. This pilgrimage is called the *Hajj* and it takes place in a single four-day period each year. Every Muslim, if he or she is able to and can afford it, at one time or another must make a *Hajj* and go to Mecca.

When I was growing up in Lagos, at a certain time of the year I would see the whole country preparing to go on this journey. It was *the* destination before you died. In Islam, the Prophet says, God knows your intention, so if you sincerely made the effort but were not able to go and you die without going, you would be rewarded as if you had been there. But people would save money all their lives in order to afford this pilgrimage and if they did not accomplish this goal they felt like they had not fulfilled one of the most important obligations as a Muslim.

My father saved his money and went. My mother raised her own money and went later. Both were treated with tremendous respect when they returned. When someone comes back from Mecca his level of practice of the faith is supposed to be different, elevated, and because of that he has earned the title *Hajji,* or *Hajja* for women. My parents were devout and earned their titles. My father became known as Hajji Salam Olajuwon. My mother became Hajja Abike. Often people didn't even use their names and called them only Hajji or Hajja. My brothers and sister took pride that our parents had made the *Hajj,* but going to Mecca was not our goal. The older generation dreamed of going to Mecca, our generation dreamed of going to England or America.

I was going to do both.

By the summer of 1991 I had been studying the Qur'an intensively for almost three years and my teacher, Hasan, the man at the mosque who helped me most, was from Mecca.

I was qualified, I was extremely interested, I had the obligation and the financial resources, and I wanted to go. Hasan said, "Our house is five minutes away from Ka'abah. If you go I will go with you. You can stay with me."

Millions of people each year make the *Hajj,* but Hasan's brother worked in the *Hajj* ministry and would make things more comfortable. The *Hajj* is scheduled according to the Islamic calendar, which changes in relation to the western calendar by about fifteen days each year. In 1991 it fell in the summertime, during the NBA off-season. It could not have been easier. All I had to do was say yes.

I was so excited. I was very fortunate to have such a knowledgeable and generous guide. There are many rules and regulations concerning the prayers to be said in Mecca and I took many classes to learn in more depth the purpose and practice of the *Hajj* so that I would be prepared and devout and appreciative when I arrived. I had not even considered making this kind of journey a couple of years before and now I could step up my devotion and fulfill a new life's dream.

Finally it was time to go.

The airplane to Saudi Arabia was filled with people making the pilgrimage. The flight took eighteen hours and you could hear people reciting the Qur'an, making their *salahs,* or specific prayers, in their seats as the times for prayer came and went.

When we finally approached Saudi Arabia the flight attendants made an announcement: "For those of you who are going to the *Hajj,* it is time to make your change of clothing."

It is forbidden in Mecca for pilgrims to wear shirts and slacks or anything sewn. You wear a length of light cotton, like a big towel, which you wrap around yourself. I had spent quite a lot of time practicing how to do this properly and I stood on line outside the little airplane bathroom as one by one almost all the passengers on the entire plane changed. Finally I got inside and struggled my 6'11" body out of my western clothes and into my wrap. We were getting closer. I sat back down in my seat and continued my prayers.

The plane arrived in Jedda, Saudi Arabia. When we touched down my Saudi friend went to the residents' terminal where he had arranged for people to meet us. But I was dressed for *Hajj* and was not allowed to follow him. Instead I was ushered into a terminal built for pilgrims only. I stepped inside.

What a revelation. The room was humming, filled with people from all over the world. There was no differentiation between nationalities, no simple way of separating people by country or even by continent. There was no differentiation between rich and poor. We were all dressed in robes, all there for the same purpose. All the same.

The room was designed specially for the *Hajj*. It was huge and open and had a big canvas top. This wasn't like any airline terminal I had ever seen. Houston International might hold a couple of thousand in any one area. Here, *tens* of thousands of people walked or sat or talked to each other. There were pockets of English and French and African dialects being spoken. There were languages I had never heard and faces that were sometimes familiar and often completely new to me. Some people were reading quietly, others were talking to friends, some were sleeping on the floor. I didn't know anybody there but everywhere I looked was a Muslim brother or sister.

I was overwhelmed. To be here, in prayer, with so many Muslims was incredible. I felt as if I had a warm international family with me.

After I got my bags I waited for Hasan's family to find me. I roamed around another great hall. People tended to stay in their groups because the place was so large and the dress so similar that once you got lost you might not find your companions again. There was little to do except read, talk, and pray, and over the course of the hours as I saw groups of worshippers discussing the Qur'an I would join them. I was traveling by myself and everyone was welcoming; I was comfortable right away. Nobody recognized me as a basketball player, they just saw this tall guy moving around.

Finally I heard my name over the loudspeaker. Hasan's family was there to pick me up. At first I'd been worried that I would never hook up with them but then it occurred to me: What was I rushing to? I'm here. This is part of it. That's something else the *Hajj* teaches you: tolerance and patience. I thought my *Hajj* would begin when I entered the city of Mecca but it began much earlier. I read and talked and learned almost from the moment I arrived.

I had scheduled my arrival for three days before the *Hajj* started. I wanted to get acclimated and be able to look around.

Hasan's brother lived only a ten-minute walk from Ka'abah, maybe three quarters of a mile uphill, and he and his family made me very comfortable. On the streets of Mecca the minarets of the mosque tower over everything. I strolled around. Already a million people had come to the city in preparation for the *Hajj*. I had never seen so many people and I didn't even consider that planes were coming in every hour bringing more. People came by sea, land, and air. Before the *Hajj* was over there would be three million pilgrims in the city and it seemed we were all in the street looking at the sights, soaking up the sense that we were walking where the Prophet had walked.

I began truly to appreciate my life at that moment. I looked at people who had saved money their entire lives just to afford to come here and saw how blessed I really was. They had nothing and spent everything to come and reveal their devotion to Allah. Once you are in Mecca for the *Hajj* you put aside your wallet; everyone is dressed alike, you pay a single fee, and food and water are distributed to everyone, rich and poor alike. Your money does you no good on a *Hajj,* everyone is equal in Allah's eyes.

Some people had very different ideas of personal hygiene than I did, but during a *Hajj* you learn tolerance of things you are not accustomed to. You humble yourself, so it's not a big deal. The bathroom is an unholy place in Islam, they would not build a bathroom in Ka'abah. I asked where one was. You had to walk a mile to get there and when I found the place I could not believe what I saw. I had never seen a bathroom that huge! It was built to service a million people and it was always full. There were people cleaning it twenty-four hours a day, shutting down one entire section and opening another.

Ka'abah is the center of the Muslim world. It is the mother of the city, it dominates Mecca, from its size to the fact that it is always the center of attention. When it is time for prayer, loudspeakers broadcast the Call and you can hear it everywhere. I wasn't being serenaded by a street full of radios, like in Lagos; everywhere I walked the Call filled the air. You could almost breathe it. I went to Ka'abah and prayed and made a special set of prayers and actions called an *umrah*.

I woke up in the morning and heard the Call for morning prayer. There are six minarets around the al-Harum, the sanctuary surrounding Ka'abah, and to hear the Call coming from them is the ultimate. I walked to Ka'abah and prayed. The mosque was air-conditioned and I found people sleeping on the floor. I stayed an extra while and read a little bit of the Qur'an. What an amazing experience, reading the words of Allah in the exact place where Muhammad, PBUH, had worshipped. Afterward I walked home and ate breakfast. I thought I would go out and explore Mecca some more but I hadn't counted on the heat.

I was from Nigeria, I liked warm weather, I had never had any problem being out in the sun. But the heat of the desert was different from anything I had ever felt. I was a professional athlete, I made my living with my body, I was strong and young and I wanted to get around. But I couldn't. I couldn't go out, the desert heat made me tired just sitting. Instead of seeing more of Mecca in the sunlight I went to sleep. Even then I wasn't rested; in the desert you get tired while you sleep! The house where I stayed was air-conditioned, but even so, getting up to make *salah* in the afternoon I felt like I was waking up too early in the morning. You feel that way. Tired.

So I slept in the afternoon. In the evening I got up, read, ate dinner with Hasan's family, said prayers, and discussed the faith. Then I had energy. The sun was down, the breeze, while not exactly cool, did not seem to be whipping me with a hot wire brush. This was my opportunity. My faith was strong, I was in Mecca, I wanted to do more. So I read the Qur'an, studied, did everything I could think of to immerse myself in my religion. Before I knew it, it was 5:30 A.M. and I heard the morning call. You have to train for a *Hajj*.

I had been in Mecca three days when the *Hajj* finally began. The first day you go to Arafat, a huge mosque between two mountains that is open only one day each year. It was not a long distance, perhaps a fifteen- to twenty-minute drive when there is no *Hajj*, but three million people were trying to make their way there that day. In order to make a *Hajj* you have to be in Arafat at sunset on the ninth day of the twelfth month of the lunar calendar. As soon as the sun sets you can leave. You then make your way to the mosque in Moozdalifah, where you pray before sunrise. After sunrise you may leave for the city of Muna, then back to Mecca.

The twenty-minute drive from Mecca to Arafat took four hours. When we finally reached the mosque we went directly to the air-conditioned house next door used by people who worked there. We had this great privilege and connection because Hasan's brother Saud worked there. After some time I went outside to wash for the afternoon prayer. I stepped outside and ran back in. The heat was ferocious. But I knew I had to perform my ablutions according to ceremony, so I went out again. Performing according to the Qur'an meant the difference between paradise and hellfire, but that was also the difference between air-conditioning and the desert in the afternoon. I could not believe people stood there all day, but they did, because they wanted to be there. Then I remembered one of the *ahadeeth,* or sayings and teachings of the Prophet Muhammad, PBUH. In it the Prophet, PBUH, says, "On the Day of Judgment the sun will be closer to our heads and you will see people drown in their own sweat. This will be a terrible day."

Understanding came over me like a cool wave. It is one thing to read the Qur'an and appreciate it intellectually; it is very much another to stand where Muhammad, PBUH, stood and feel the meaning. The entire idea of the heat of the Day of Judgment was singed into me. In that moment I witnessed the Qur'an.

In another famous *hadeeth* the Prophet, PBUH, talks about seven groups of people whom he favors, people who will escape hellfire and go to paradise. Among them are people who love each other for no other reason than for the sake of Allah. Not for personal gain, not for money, not for physical attraction or faithful admiration; they love their brothers and sisters simply because they are all servants of God. These people, say the *hadeeth,* are "under the shade of Allah."

Now I understood! How important, in this desert where the Prophet lived and wrote, was the shade of Allah. How strong must the creator be to protect the faithful from this burning.

This was what the *Hajj* was supposed to be. A time and place, in

In game six John Starks had no conscience; he was going to end the series. I deflected the ball! It took luck, experience, and destiny for me to make that play.

In the 1994 NBA finals, the New York Knicks' Patrick Ewing and I matched up evenly. I like him and have tremendous respect for his game. He's a true big man.

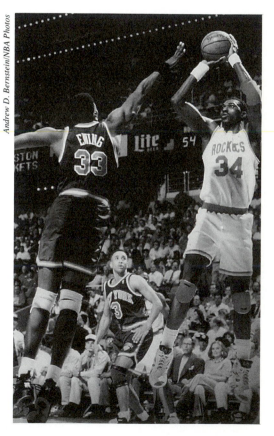

I was honored to be chosen the NBA's 1994 MVP, but I didn't want to accept the trophy by myself because I hadn't won it by myself. To show my gratitude to my teammates, I asked them to come onto the floor and accept the trophy with me.

Andrew D. Bernstein/NBA Photos

Champions! The team concept demands unselfishness. It needs guys like
Scott Brooks, guys who play hard when they're in there and understand their role
when they're not. It needs the starters to pull for the bench.

John W. McDonough

Clutch City! With Otis Thorpe, Larry Robinson, Commissioner David Stern,
and Kenny Smith. We celebrated with the entire Rockets family.

Clyde Drexler and I had talked about playing together for years.
This was too good to be true!

Rockets' coach Rudy Tomjanovich is a
great coach and a wonderful guy. He
treated everyone with respect and did a
fantastic job of creating team spirit and
team unity.

Vernon Maxwell is a very intense and
excitable player, but at heart he wanted to
do the right thing.

Playing against Michael Jordan is an all-day challenge.
You have to honor his fakes and respect everything.

John W. McDonough

In the 1995 Western Conference finals, David Robinson made me work
for every shot; if I made a mistake he was going to block it. He pushed me to
a higher level.

On the attack against the Orlando Magic and Shaq. To play with finesse you must have power. You must make the opponent respect your game.

The Rockets won back-to-back NBA championships, and the whole city of Houston loved us.

Believe it again!

14

"TRADE ME!"

WHEN I RETURNED HOME no one, not even my close friends, had any idea what I had been through. Few at the mosque had made their *Hajj* yet and although I tried to explain what had happened I don't think I did it justice. It is an experience each person has to have for himself.

Everything was back to normal, but for me "normal" had changed. When I read the Qur'an I saw different things than I had when I'd left, and each day I saw things differently in my life.

I had been taught patience and tolerance on my *Hajj* and I began to see the result. I began to look at life as a journey and asked Allah always to guide me so I could stay fast and firm in the faith. In the past when someone said something that really upset me, I exploded and fought them. Now I felt sorry for this person and prayed and asked Allah to guide him because he didn't know any better; if he did he would have made a better decision. Instead of falling into the old trap that would lead to an argument or a fight, I backed off. Not because I was weak but because I understood I could not make this person understand in any other way. Even driving on the freeway I was not in a hurry; I knew where I was going and I knew, God willing, I was going to get there.

But even in my new tolerance I was not going to be rolled over. Christianity teaches you to turn the other cheek, and when people found I had made my pilgrimage and was more serious than ever about my the heightened presence of your own faith, when you learn new meanings and experience things you have never in your whole life experienced before. I marveled at my good fortune to have come so far and learned so much so quickly.

Then I ran inside.

My *Hajj* made my faith very, very strong. I was totally convinced and blessed to be able to witness the history of Islam and fulfill my duty to it. The things I had read in the Qur'an had become real to me. When you are surrounded by lush, green nature, you imagine the Gardens of Paradise one way. In the desert it is quite another, much more simple and pure and rewarding. I came home with some sense of the physical reality of the Qur'an and the Prophet, PBUH, and what it meant to be a Muslim. I was determined to put that to practice in my day-to-day life.

religion they thought it might make me soft on the court. There was no chance of that. In Islam you can be as aggressive as you want as long as you play fair. You can never be the aggressor, you can't trip or elbow people, but I never played like that anyhow. I rely on hard work, skills, and competition. I wouldn't curse or use foul language anymore, that was out, but Islam is different from what people think. In Islam if someone slaps you, you have two choices: you can slap back as hard, but not harder, than you were slapped, or you can — and this is recommended — leave it for Allah to consider.

Allah says, "Be merciful toward the believers and very firm against unbelievers." To good-doers be kind because you know their intentions are good, but to others be firm against them, very hard. That's Islam. It teaches you principle and tells you to stay strong. On the court my issues remained the same: play fair, do not abuse me or I will deal with you firmly.

My changes were more noticeable in my social life. There is a *hadeeth* that says, "In a circle where Allah's name cannot be mentioned, you should not sit with them." That couldn't be more clear. If I had ever hung out with guys who did things outside the bounds of good behavior or even good taste, I was not permitted to do so now. I had to become a good Muslim.

I knew people looked up to NBA stars, that we were role models. Parents should be their children's first and best role models, but of course kids and some adults look to sports figures for ways to act and live their lives. I'd be kidding myself to think otherwise and I accepted the responsibility. But I could not in good conscience advise people to live a healthy and righteous life if I wasn't living up to my own counsel. The company you keep is important and I found I wanted to be friends only with people who were sincere. They didn't have to be Muslims — I would never limit my friendships to people of one faith — but they had to have the characteristics of believers: sincerity, honesty, trust-worthiness. They had to be God-conscious.

You should be able to trust believers; if they betray that trust they betray Allah. If someone is God-fearing, even if no one is looking he will try to do the right thing in the eyes of Allah. You will be comfortable if he advises you because it will be sincere, in your own best interest and not his own. My friends know where I stand, they know I will be honest and truthful with them; if I like something, I will tell them; if I don't like something, they will know. If they ask me my opinion they have to be open to hear it. If they don't want to hear what I think is the truth, they shouldn't ask me.

On the court, basketball became play. I had always enjoyed the game but in recent years people had begun to take the emphasis away from the game itself and onto the championship. I would hear it all over: If you don't win a championship you are a failure, your career is not complete. If you don't win a championship you're not a winner.

When I came back from Mecca I examined the whole question. I came to the conclusion that whoever said winning was the only thing was wrong and that whoever believed it was ungrateful. It is enough that you are able to play the game and enjoy it. There are so many people with physical handicaps that if you can run and jump and play well, that should fill you with happiness. Who am I to complain that my career is not complete when I make a living, have a comfortable lifestyle, and am blessed to be able to have it? How can I complain? Those things are said by people who don't understand. "You have to do this to be remembered as a great player." I want to be remembered as a great person; not the greatest player in the world but a person who was honest and gracious and honorable, a man who did his best, a good Muslim. That's as good as I can be.

That's the challenge: Be the best you can be. My work ethic is very important. It is up to me to maximize my talent. I take responsibility and I guarantee I will be accountable. In the court of Allah I will be asked: "This talent was given to you, what did you do with it and how did you use it?" I have been given something by Allah that may be used to benefit people. They enjoy watching me play, how can I destroy that talent by not working hard or by abusing drugs or by letting my success turn me into an arrogant person? I won't compete with other players over who has more money or more commercials or more championship rings. If they have more, so be it. I am happy and satisfied and content and grateful for what I do have. The real value of your talent is how you use it to do good and to encourage others, for the pleasure of Allah. With that I feel rich, not in material things but for what I have inside myself. The richness of the soul.

I drove to practice and enjoyed the beautiful day even before I got to the gym. On the court I felt alive every moment. Running up and down the court was a joy. If I won the championship I'd be happy. If I didn't win I would be happy as well. I just enjoyed the journey. I prepared to win, but win or lose it was not going to change my life. I prayed hard to win but all victory comes from Allah and Allah gives it to whomever He chooses. That's the Islamic way of looking at victory. It's not "I'm so good" or even "We're so good, we won the championship." As long as you know that you did your best you are blessed in Allah's eyes. And if you win you thank Allah for the victory.

But victory is not out of your control. You prepare yourself for victory, you think and plan and train and sweat and work as hard as you can to reach your goal. And you go out and perform at your absolute best because that's the only way to play. You will not win without that. You do your job, you do the best you can, but the actual victory — that's Allah's plan.

We had high hopes for the 1991–92 season but the team never really clicked. Finally, after fifty-two games of mediocre, .500 basketball, Don Chaney was replaced as coach by Rudy Tomjanovich.

Rudy T was a former Rocket, an assistant coach since the Bill Fitch years. He knew how players felt and acted, and he was right in there between the Bill Fitch I-don't-care-if-you-like-me-or-not school of coaching and the Don Chaney I-want-to-be-everybody's-friend school. He knew his basketball and he let us play it. Even though we didn't do much better in the last third of the season than we had in the first two thirds, and we didn't make the playoffs, having Rudy in charge was a change for the better and a good sign for the Rockets' future.

Unfortunately, when I looked at my future I didn't see the kind of respect from management I thought I ought to have. The whole league had grown to another level and when I looked at my contract it had become outdated. I felt it needed to be restructured.

Charlie Thomas and I had developed the best player-owner relationship in the league. I had gone over to his house for dinner, he had thrown a party for me with his friends in California, and he had flown me on his private plane. We had spent weeks together every summer. I expected my contract to be taken care of by management because I took care of them on the court. But when it came to business Charlie was a different person.

Instead of paying me market value the Rockets offered a contract extension. Contract extensions are usually a bad idea, since all they do is set your future salary at today's market value. You're always playing catch-up. Salaries had been skyrocketing, and by the time I got to the extension years my contract would be out of date again. I would still not be paid my worth. But I had no leverage, I was signed for four more years, so I took what was available.

I played for another several years and despite the fact that I was first team All-NBA, starting center in the All-Star game, leading the league in several categories, and widely acknowledged as a premier player, I was not paid my actual value. Not even close. As a businessman I needed to deal with this. I went back to Thomas and said, "This contract that I'm on now, it's not worthy of conversation. You know this is not fair so let's sit down as gentlemen and talk about how to accomplish this fairly." He knew that what I was saying was the truth.

I recognized that I was under contract, and I was willing to take less than market value, but he had to give me something close to what I was worth. Other teams had restructured their players' contracts to reflect market value and Charlie said he would, but he didn't.

It all came to a head in March 1992. I approached Charlie Thomas once again to take him up on his promise to do something about my contract, and he told me to call him at work.

I called twice and he didn't return either of my calls. I called one more time and left a message with his secretary that I wouldn't be calling back.

He returned that call quickly. He said, "Talk to Steve. We'll work something out."

Steve Patterson had taken over for his father, Ray, as general manager. He was the kind of guy who was not pleased at all these young players making a lot of money. He told me, "You're making more money than anybody on the team." I told him, "That's not saying much."

While this new negotiation was going on I strained a hamstring on the court. A strained hamstring doesn't show up on X-rays or in MRIs, it doesn't turn black and blue, all it does is hurt so much you can't run. You can't play with a strained hamstring, you go sit down and get treatment. So I was in the trainer's room getting worked on when Steve Patterson showed up at the Summit to watch practice. He wanted to know, "Where's Hakeem?" He didn't even come into the locker room, he called down to the trainer's room to see what the problem was. They told him the hamstring wasn't serious, that it would last a couple of days.

I could tell he was angry by the questions he asked everybody. "What is this all about? What's going on here?"

The next day I came to shoot around and couldn't run. My leg was very sore. Now Patterson came to me. He told the trainer to leave the room.

"Look," he said, "cut all this out."

"What are you talking about?" I knew exactly what he was talking about but I wanted to hear him accuse me of being a liar to my face.

"I know what you're doing and this isn't going to work. I've talked to Charlie and he said to play and we will work out the contract this summer. You have his and my word on that. We'll put it in writing."

I said, "I know you're not saying what I think you're saying. You can't be serious thinking I'm using this injury to get a new contract. I'm going to use my skills on the floor to get my contract. You know what I'm worth and you should pay it. I have hurt my hamstring and you say I'm lying?"

That's exactly what he was saying. "This will get into the papers, you know," he said darkly. "We will go public with this."

For everyone else, if they have an injury they dress in street clothes and sit on the bench. The Rockets didn't allow me to do that. They demanded that I play. I wasn't going to risk my career for these people; if I got seriously hurt out there they would not support my career, they were not loyal. I said, "I told you I can't play with this injury." I was very upset. "I don't want to continue this discussion with you."

Just as he had threatened to do, Steve Patterson called the press and accused me of faking the injury. He told the Houston reporters, "If we have a whole team of doctors looking at him and they find nothing wrong and if he threatens to sit out because he wants a new contract, it's not hard to put two and two together."

I was furious. First, I never threatened to sit out. Second, I was injured. "He's a liar," I told reporters. "For him to question my integrity shows no class. They are trying to use a power play on me, but it won't work. Nobody wants to play more than me, but I'm not going out there and risk my career when I'm not healthy. In this organization they try to force you to play hurt. When I'm able to run properly, then I'll play. Not before."

My teammates supported me. Kenny Smith said, "When you are injured only you know for sure how you feel. It's got to be hurting him because we all know how much Hakeem enjoys playing. I've had hamstring problems before and nobody can tell you when you're ready to play."

Otis Thorpe said, "It's got to be sore or Hakeem would be out there."

I appreciated their belief in me.

The Rockets' doctors had no such belief. They pronounced me fit to play. But I wasn't. I got a second opinion from a Houston orthopedic surgeon, who said my hamstring was injured and advised me not to play, and I refused to suit up.

The Rockets suspended me. My work ethic is second to none, I play my hardest all game every game, and they suspended me without pay for failure to render services under the terms of my contract. They tried to turn the media and the fans against me. They told everyone they were docking my salary.

But, of course, they couldn't do any such thing. The NBA Players' Association has a clause in the basic agreement with the league that says no team or owner can suspend a player without pay unless it goes to arbitration. Of course we filed a grievance, so they couldn't take a penny of my salary. The hearing was set for sometime after the season. They wouldn't be taking a cent from me. Patterson and Thomas didn't tell that to the media, they wanted to seem like they were playing hardball.

The Rockets lost five straight games while I was out injured. When I came back I told them and the press that I wanted to be traded. "I would not like to play for the Rockets next season," I said. "It's obvious. Would you like to work for management after they said all those terrible things about you? A lot of players have had to leave Houston. I love this city. And it's not about my teammates or the fans. It's about management. The damage has been done. I would prefer to start fresh somewhere else."

I'd had enough of Charlie Thomas and Steve Patterson and even the thought that someone would believe I was a liar. I had come back from an eye injury the year before, and this year I'd already been in the hospital for treatment for an irregular heartbeat. If I'd wanted to take both years off, I could have. If I'd wanted to use those injuries in a contract negotiation I could have, but that's not the way I work. For them to question my character and my professionalism and my heart was a huge insult. They had tried their best to damage me in front of the fans and the people of Houston and the nation. I wanted nothing more to do with them.

The trade rumor mill cranked up quickly. I was going to the Los Angeles Clippers for Danny Manning and Charles Smith. I was going to the Miami Heat for Ronny Seikaly and Steve Smith and Harold Miner. The Rockets, Clippers, New York Knicks and Orlando Magic were shuffling me and Manning and Sleepy Floyd and Charles Oakley and Mark Jackson and Gerald Wilkins and Loy Vaught and Stanley Roberts and a pack of draft picks. Whatever happened, happened.

Because of the losing streak we missed the play-offs by one game. I planned to travel all summer. When I left I said to management, "Just call and tell me where I'll be playing next year. Trade me." I was very certain I wasn't coming back to play in Houston.

I traveled all that summer, 1992. What better way to leave all the hurt and anger of that season behind than by going to Mecca? I made another *Hajj*. This time I took my brothers, Akins, Tajudeen and Afis. I was happy to provide them with the opportunity to make the pilgrimage. I believe they were as inspired as I was and it was great to travel and spend time all together again.

After the grueling four days of the *Hajj* we went to the town of Medina. Medina is the City of the Prophet, PBUH. Where Mecca is hustling and bustling with people and business, Medina is a calm center of Islamic studies. The Prophet Muhammad, PBUH, was born in Mecca but driven out when his revelation of Islam created divisions within the city's tribes and families and they planned his murder. The people of Medina openly accepted him and his followers and Islam. They built a community and an army, which in time Muhammad, PBUH, led on an invasion that conquered Mecca without force.

In Medina they built a mosque where the Prophet prayed and lectured. It is called the Prophet's Mosque and a visit there is a chance to walk in the Prophet's footsteps. In fact there is one specific spot in the mosque where the Prophet is said to have stood and prayed and reflected on the faith. That spot is one of the holiest places on earth and everyone who is aware of it wants to pray there.

It is traditional that you say two *rak'ah,* or prayers, on that spot. You must choose the opening chapter of the Qur'an and then any other to recite. When I arrived I saw a line of about a hundred people waiting for that opportunity.

But the line wasn't moving. The number of people waiting dwindled as time went on and they left rather than wait even longer. It was very important to me to stand in the Prophet's footsteps so I stood my ground. After standing in one place for almost half an hour I found myself third in line. Now there was a long line of people behind me.

Kneeling in the sacred place was a man praying. I asked the pilgrim in front of me whether the man on the ground was on his first or second prayer. He said the second. I didn't know how long this man had been praying — I had been there at least thirty minutes and he had not moved — but I did know he was being very inconsiderate.

This was a mosque so everything had to be done with the best manners, but I was upset.

You are not permitted to touch someone while he is praying. That is forbidden in the faith. I had to tolerate this. Perhaps this was part of the *Hajj*'s lesson of patience. There was nothing I could do but stand and wait for the man to finish.

Finally he sat up. The line of people sighed. We would get our chance now. Then he was about to start all over again.

I had to make a decision. People had come from all over the earth to pray here and the usual time allotted to these prayers is about five minutes. He was exhibiting extremely poor and un–Islamic behavior by disregarding his fellow worshippers and thinking only of himself. I had to do something. This man was using the trappings of the faith to act in a way that was against everything the faith stood for.

I picked the man up by his shoulders and physically moved him. It was that or leave.

The man didn't want to move. He put up a little resistance but I was strong in my body and my mind. If I wanted to move him he would be moved.

I placed this selfish man to one side. I didn't interrupt his prayers;

if he wanted to continue praying he could, he just couldn't do it in the sacred spot with a hundred people waiting. My knowledge of the *din,* or the faith, told me to be very considerate of others. Everybody shares. He was not practicing the faith properly, he was not taking care of the rest of the people—that was why I felt justified in moving him.

The man ahead of me thought I was going to step in and pray next. I told him to go ahead.

This kind of selfish behavior was, unfortunately, not uncommon. There are selfish Muslims as there are selfish members of every other faith on earth. There is another favored place to pray in the Prophet's Mosque, a place where Muhammad, PBUH, gave a lecture, and one man monopolized it for four hours. Almost everyone who prayed at Medina that day was denied the opportunity to pray there. I moved the first man; he struggled but he moved. They called the army on this second guy and still he wouldn't move. He was praying and crying.

I understand that people make it their mission in life to visit Mecca and Medina, and once they are there they are overcome with the strength of the faith. This is what they have been waiting for. This is their whole life. But you are acting contrary to what Allah dictated and Muhammad, PBUH, taught when you act so selfishly.

When I got back from Mecca I began training. I expected to be on a new team and I wanted to come to camp and establish myself right away. I might be playing under a different system but I knew my strengths and I built on them. I didn't want to have to make an adjustment or build up gradually, I was going to come in and play. It was the same league, the same players, the same floor. I would be wearing a different uniform but I'd be playing my game, and as long as I was on top of my game I had great confidence I would fit in anywhere.

I went to California to be with my daughter, Abisola. I was staying at Abisola's grandmother's, Lita's mother's, townhouse and it was beautiful. I would get up and pray and Grandmother would fix me breakfast early each morning, then I would go work out.

I worked hard that summer. I hired a trainer named Charles who helped with my program, and each morning Charles would pick me up and I would run on the beach. I didn't like running in the sand, it was tough on me, but it was worthwhile, building up endurance. I would eat a light lunch and in the afternoon I would lift weights. In the evenings Charles and I would go to a local high school and shoot baskets and work on my moves.

Charles also took me to Gold's Gym. He told me it was the weight trainer's Mecca. I had been to Mecca, all my life Mecca to me had meant the city in Saudi Arabia, the center of Islam. I didn't know that Mecca also meant the ultimate center, an ultimate place to go, but when I walked into Gold's Gym I understood exactly what he meant.

These people were like animals. Enormous animals. Even the women. Everyone there was pumped up and full of muscle and I looked so skinny. There were women much thicker than I was and everybody was intense. I said, "This is a place for the devoted. If you're not serious you shouldn't even be walking in here."

When I'd gotten to the University of Houston they'd taken me into the weight room the first day and I hadn't been able to lift the bar off my chest. The bar, by itself. I didn't have the technique and I wasn't very strong. I had put on a little strength since then but I said to Charles, "This is not my game." He understood clearly.

I started building by using light weights scaled to my abilities. At first it was strange. I had to get used to the technique and the concentration. But the more I worked with these weights the more I relaxed. In three days I really grew to like it.

I also realized I was getting immediate benefit from these workouts. When I took my shot or worked on my moves all the pain that I usually had in my knees and ankles went away. I was used to having my back ache and my muscles be tight and sore after a good session on the court — if you don't really work out you can't do the moves — but now everything seemed so relaxed and easy. Still, I would go to sleep *tired* at night and be sore in the morning. I knew if it was just me I would feel so tired I wouldn't go work out the next day, but Charles really pushed me and I would warm up and be surprised to feel my body respond and recover quickly.

Charles had arranged for some high school students to rebound for me, so all I did on the court was work on individual moves.

I had never worked on my moves before. During the summers at Fonde I just played and competed, and whatever I wanted to try I tried in game competition. I had never stood off to one side and worked on footwork or leaping or any technique at all, I had worked on learning what worked, I had worked on winning. This was very different.

There was music in the background, a tape of pop music, and it made me creative. I had a lot of energy. I would shoot my jumper and see how high I could go and release the ball. In my mind I saw myself making each move and I felt like it was art. I would fake right, fake left, spin to the baseline. There was a rhythm, like I was dancing to the music. I felt like I was dancing on the court.

My jump hook had extra spring. Everything was sharp. I would make a jump hook, get tossed the rebound, take one bounce, and *go!* I could tell I was on top of my game. In athletics everything is control, you don't do anything in a lazy way. I had energy and my breathing was easy because I was in condition.

I would shoot twenty-five jump hooks from the right side. Not just ordinary jump hooks, we were talking about preparing at a certain angle and jump hooks of a certain height. You did it right or you did it over. I stopped thinking about the jump hook and just shot it.

Then we worked on shooting jumpers from behind a pick. Sometimes in the past I would get the ball and realize I didn't want to shoot it. Now I began thinking like a guard, like the in-between player I was. I would work on making my inside foot, the one closest to the basket, hit the floor just as I got the ball so when I jumped to shoot I was already squared up, shoulders facing the basket. It's all in the footwork. Inside foot, outside foot, spring. If your feet are underneath you and your shoulders are not spinning to catch up, you will be balanced, your elevation will be better, you will jump higher and straighter and will have more time to take a good look at the basket. I saw how high I was jumping and that I was getting a good release. My shot was falling very softly. I was even hanging for a while and I had time, if I didn't like the shot I was taking, to make different choices. I could pass in front of me; I had time to find an open man on the perimeter. I was in control.

All of a sudden basketball became new again! I pictured myself shooting from the outside. My game had been all spinning moves for a couple of years; every game I was going up against men bigger than I was but not as mobile, and I could spin in the paint and lose them.

Now I began to bring those moves outside. If you can handle the ball a little bit outside you can spin and shoot the jumper, which makes your game much more dangerous because now they have to come get you and you can go right around them. When I pictured that I really got motivated!

I was being represented at the time by the Los Angeles–based agent Leonard Armato and one day he brought one of his new clients to the high school gym, this guy just out of Louisiana State University, Shaquille O'Neal.

I had spent entire summers going up against Moses Malone so I had some idea of what Shaquille might be thinking when he met me on the gym floor. "*Be a man!*" But Armato had told me Shaquille had said some very complimentary things about me, and, of course, I had heard about the number-one pick in the 1992 draft. I was having such a good time getting into condition and working on my moves that I invited Shaquille to work with me. This was not a game and we were not competing, this was going to be very pleasant. We trained together that day.

The first thing I noticed about Shaquille was that he was a lot bigger than I was. I was 6'11" and weighed about 250 pounds, he was 7'2" and up around 300 — and still growing! He had the perfect big man's body; once he got in the paint there was nothing anybody was going to be able to do with him.

We practiced moves together, big man's moves. He tossed me the ball and I put up a jump hook. I tossed him the ball and he did exactly what I did. We did that a couple of times. Then, as a courtesy, I said, "You do something and I'll follow you." He put up a turnaround jumper and I did the same thing.

To show him how to fake the turnaround and use it as a threat to make the jump hook more effective, I told him, "Okay, you guard me."

He didn't know whether I was going to shoot the jumper or the jump hook. The players I had gone up against in the league or in practice had consistently fallen for the fake. I got the ball with my back to the basket and faked to my right. He bought the fake. I turned hard to my left, and shot the jump hook. At that moment he was lost; that move was sharp and new to him.

But the next time I tried it Shaquille straightened out. That's when

I realized how quick Shaquille was. In the league when they go for the fakes they never recover. But that's what was different about Shaquille, he recovered and was there for the block. Shaquille wanted to block everything. I remembered how that felt.

Then I gave Shaquille the ball and showed him the basics of the Dream Shake. I showed him the moves and the footwork. Why would I do that when I knew we were going to play against each other for the next ten or fifteen years? I like sharing moves. If you're scared about competition you shouldn't even be in this league. I take joy in watching a skillful big man use his skills and I knew that if he wanted to, Shaquille would use the Dream Shake well.

Then I guarded him.

Shaquille was a fast learner. I had showed my moves to people before, and very often I'd had to instruct them over and over, something would be wrong. Not Shaquille. If he saw it he could do it. Show him, give him the ball, and he'll do it exactly. I saw how high he jumped, how he released the ball far out of my reach. He was bigger and stronger than I was and he was taking my shot at a higher level. I was there to block him if he tried only half-heartedly, but he found right away that if the move was *sharp* he could beat me. That, in a single lesson, is the bottom line of the NBA: Play hard, if people respect your move they will back off and you can beat them. And Shaquille got it.

Shaquille showed me some moves of his own. He had power and energy and he was young. He did not really shoot a hook shot, he threw it down. I would finish a move with a jump hook a few feet from the basket, he would finish with a hook *dunk* with his hand inside the rim! He also had a nice touch on his turnaround jump shot, which was unusual for a man as big as he was. The jumper was natural, nice touch, particularly from the baseline. He was so big I didn't have time to see if he was faking, I had to go up with him in order to have any chance to block him. One time he faked, I went up and he went under me. He made a nice move on me. I had tremendous respect for his ability.

In the league we would hear about kids in college who were going to come out and be a force, but we never knew what was hype and what was truth. College reputations are fine for college players, but in the pros you make your name all over again. Some guys start from scratch, some come from nowhere, some guys surpass expectations,

The Rockets' owner had stayed in the background during the public confrontation between me and Steve Patterson. Now he sat in the seat next to me and after a few awkward moments we began to talk.

"Why do you say something to me if you don't mean what you say?" I asked him.

"The media has blown this whole thing out of proportion," he told me. "I told you we would work something out and I'm still ready to do that."

"It's too late for that," I told him. "I don't want anything worked out, I just want to be traded."

"I tried to trade you but I can't get a good offer."

Leonard Armato had told me some of the offers other teams had made for me and I knew the Rockets were holding out for more; Charlie Thomas was still working the corners. He didn't want to pay me but he wanted to get a lot for me. If I was worth so much in a trade why wouldn't they pay me even half of what I was worth in a salary? He wasn't anywhere close. It had been a battle to get my worth from day one, it had never been pleasant.

"Just trade me. All the other teams are looking for big men, they would pay anything to have a big man. You've got a big man and you don't want to pay him. I can get much more elsewhere without going through all this, and they'd be happy to do it. If I play for you I have to fight you all the time, then you want me to do my best for you. What kind of situation is that? You know my value to the team, you know I produce for you, at least pay me at a level where I'm comfortable. Let's be reasonable, let's be businessmen.

"Look at Patrick, look at David." This was the same year the Knicks offered Ewing a tremendous amount of money and he still turned it down. David Robinson had just had his contract restructured by the San Antonio Spurs to reflect his place in the big man's market. "I'm not asking for what Patrick Ewing is making. Patrick is in New York, that's a bigger market, it's reasonable that he get a bigger contract, I understand that. But let's play in the same arena."

Charlie Thomas and I both knew that the seats at the Summit were empty, that the Rockets weren't selling season tickets, and that the season looked like a financial disaster about to happen. This controversy was keeping people away. But Charlie was the kind of person you had to force into a corner. Our conversation went on for a long time. I told him I wanted to be traded because of two issues: I wanted a contract that reflected my skills and I refused to have my integrity assaulted in the press. Maybe they thought everyone would fake an injury to get what he wants, but I was offended. Charlie told me he wouldn't trade me unless he got a good deal. I told him *I* wanted a good deal. Finally he said, "Okay, have Armato call me when we get back and we'll work something out."

Charlie had made that promise before but the press was aware that we had talked on the flight, and when we arrived in Japan we both acknowledged our progress toward a contract settlement. "There's no way to gain anything by us being enemies," Charlie told reporters. "We're absolutely good friends. We've always been good friends. We just haven't seen each other since it all happened. He's a businessman, I'm a businessman."

"I don't know if it is possible to rebuild what we once had," I told them. "But it made sense to at least talk about it. Talking is good. It is the way for two gentlemen to solve problems. Besides, when you're on a plane you can run but you can't hide. You can't get off, and fourteen hours is too long to spend locked in the bathroom."

It took another five months to finalize but I finally got a new Rockets contract.

15

RUDY T TAKES OVER

THE 1992–93 SEASON was Rudy Tomjanovich's first full year as the Rockets' coach. Rudy T was a former Rocket, a five-time NBA All-Star forward. His number, forty-five, had been retired ten years earlier and you could see it every night hanging on a banner from the ceiling of the Summit. He had been with the Rockets twenty-three consecutive years, beginning as a player as the number-two pick in the 1970 draft, then as a scout, then as assistant coach under Bill Fitch and Don Chaney.

He was also a regular guy, a wonderful guy.

Rudy ruled not by fear or friendship, he ruled by reason. Rudy presented a style of play that, he said, wasn't *his* system, it was *our* system. He was very strong in that: The whole team takes responsibility. He did a fantastic job of creating team spirit, team unity. It's *our* team and *our* system, he emphasized — the coaches, the players, all of us — and we should all care about the *team* and do everything each of us could do to win. "This is what you guys deserve," he told us, "and this is what I want you guys to have." He treated everyone like a man and he expected the same kind of behavior in return.

From the beginning he treated everybody with respect. Rudy had been a player, he knew what was right and what wasn't. He wasn't an intimidator, he wasn't interested in playing politics by fining players who weren't giving their best, he wasn't interested in punishment for getting into the hotel late, he wasn't going to play the guys who were his favorites; he was going to get as many people as possible into the games and get us all ready to win. He was going to be fair and he was going to be competitive.

Some coaches try to embarrass players into giving their best, they criticize them in practice or during the game or in the press. Rudy T did none of that. He knew when things weren't being done right but instead of calling out one player he would criticize the team: "*We're* not getting back on defense," "*We're* taking too many bad shots," "*We're* not working the ball." Everybody knew who he was talking about but no one was publicly embarrassed or made defensive. I thought this was a very good way to get the guys going.

Rudy T said all the right things and the best part about him was that he was sincere. When a coach is concerned for all the players, they have to take it to heart. We had to be sure we did the best we could for the sake of the team.

Rudy was a happy-go-lucky guy. He loved his work and he enjoyed life. He did not invade the privacy of the players, he just wanted to do his job and make sure everything was working fine.

The coaching staff in general was very good. Carroll Dawson, who had been a Rockets assistant coach since 1980, helped me tremendously by working with me one-on-one on my jump hooks and turnaround jumpers. He was fundamentally sound and was very helpful in reading the double-team. We had a lot of discussions about different moves and he could look at my shot and tell me why I was missing. He was very specific and he knew how to correct my game.

Coach Dawson was always prepared. If we lost a game it would not be because we didn't know what to expect. He was thorough, examining each player, his strengths and his weaknesses. After each game he and the other coaches would watch videotape on the plane and then go and put it together that night and have it ready for us to study the next morning. He loved the game, he loved his work. Coach Dawson was also a great guy.

Bill Berry had been scouting for the Rockets and was made an assistant coach a week after Rudy moved up. He was a good technical coach who worked on the opponents and their weaknesses. We had a great coaching staff with good chemistry.

Rudy's offensive system was very much the same as the one Coach Fitch had run before him. It all began with the ball being tossed in to the big man in the post. That is the only system for a team that has a good center. All good things flow from there. Any big man who requires a double- or triple-team should automatically be the first option. The coach can put in plays, we can run them in practice, but when the plays break down you can go back to the big man. That's your foundation. If you don't have a foundation your whole building will collapse.

It's very simple. When you establish your inside game it's easier to win. A dominant center who can score anytime you get him the ball will attract a crowd. If I can score over my opponent one-on-one, he will need help guarding me. That help has to come from somewhere, which means that one of my teammates is now open. I have two choices: I can try to shoot over both of the men guarding me or I can pass the ball out and we as a team can whip the ball around and find the open man for an open shot.

In order for our entire offense to be effective I must show the opponents that I'm going to score if they let me. I have to be a threat, otherwise they won't double-team me. So I have to prove I can score, and I have to do it immediately. I don't want to give the opposition time to run someone at me or to develop a rotation so my teammates will be covered. I want to damage them early. So I shoot. Over the course of my career I have proved I can score if I'm being guarded by only one man.

At the same time our coach is watching their rotation. Who moves to double-team me? How does the rest of the team react, what shifts are made to cover our other players on the floor? The opponents will, of course, have spent a lot of time developing a system to stop me and to cut down the options for the rest of my team. My coach will design a game plan to counter their game plan. For instance, when the Rockets' guard throws the ball into the pivot Rudy will see if the defense is coming from the baseline or from another angle to guard me, and he will use that knowledge to put our guys in the best position to receive a pass and score. If they collapse on me I can toss the ball inside to one of my men cutting to the basket or outside to a guard for a three-point shot. If a man runs at the shooter he can pass it around the perimeter until an open man gets it or he can step inside the defender and shoot. There are thousands of options and they all change each time someone handles the ball. It's chess with big guys.

*　　　*　　　*

People were telling me they saw a change in the way I acted on the court after my pilgrimages. I didn't see it at all. I think I was totally consistent before and after.

The public wants athletes to be role models, to be people worthy of being looked up to and admired — and we want that as well. When I meet someone I respect, someone who is a truly good person, I want to be his friend. I want to demonstrate my goodness to him, so he knows me, so he'll be comfortable. I try my best when I see somebody who has established that goodness for himself. And if someone treats me with a lot of respect I give him more respect. Someone who respects others respects himself; if you lack respect for others, you do not respect yourself. I don't feel pressure from playing basketball; that's just work and fun. I like it. I feel pressure from people who trust me. The pressure is to not betray that trust, to not let them down.

You see it all the time, at games and then on the news later that night, and over and over on NBA *Fan-tastic!* spots on TV: A guy gets the rebound or slam dunks over someone from another team and then screams in his face, or steps right over an opponent when he is on the floor. If the fans want to see that they should go to the wrestling matches. It's a low, low mentality. The guys who do that come into the league feeling insecure to start with. They come from the background of basketball in the park, in the street, where they're not playing for fun, they're playing to show off. They use street language that is not proper in the league's environment. It's not professional, it's not sportsmanlike, it's not right, it's an embarrassment. I suppose they're trying to be intimidating.

But you don't have to push someone down and step on him to be intimidating. You don't need to do that if you depend on your skills. Let your game speak for you. Your *game* should intimidate them; the way you play, not what you say.

You are intimidating when your man tries to shoot the ball over you and you contest it and your skills make him change. He shoots it higher and you still go get it. He says, "Wow, this guy's going to block it every time." So now he comes into the paint and wants to shoot and he sees you're going to block him, so he passes it out. You're intimidating with your skills, not with your mouth.

Basketball is a game of timing and opportunities and possession, like life in general. Sometimes you catch somebody at their weakest point, when they're off balance, or you have a step on them — and you explode. You are in a position of strength and he is in a position of weakness, you have the upper hand at that particular time and you can use it to your advantage. But even if you are beaten you deserve respect. You can't always have the upper hand, there will be give and take — it might be the next possession. The league is full of people dunking on each other; we have great dunkers and great shot blockers. I can get dunked on and turn around and dunk on somebody else. But you don't have to come around every time you score over somebody and embarrass him, that's showing arrogance; you've embarrassed him enough already just by dunking on him. Trash talking denies respect.

For the players, trash talking is a combination of arrogance and ignorance and insecurity. It shows no class. They want to get attention any way they can and they will do foolish things to get it. Good attention or bad attention, they just want to be in those *Fan-tastic!* spots, they just want to be in the spotlight.

How you play your game on the court is a reflection of your character in life. If you are selfish and arrogant on the court you are very likely selfish and arrogant off the court. The way you play with your teammates will be the way you are with your family and friends. If you have confidence in your abilities and your game, when you do something spectacular *you know.* Everybody has seen the move. If it's as spectacular as it seemed, let it speak for itself. When people compliment you about it you take the compliment with humility. It is most revealing when the man who has created this thing of beauty stays humble; that is the ultimate respect.

You can tell a true winner by how he handles adversity. When someone does something spectacular against him he is not afraid to give that man a compliment. "Good move." Showing mutual respect does not affect the competitive nature of the game.

The league and the media should be talking about professional conduct and a friendly image so that when a rookie comes into the league he already has the right behavior set in his mind.

The word *professional* has been misused and neglected. If you're from the Old School, *professional* means having standards; there's a level you don't go below because you're a *professional.* But in the NBA today, anybody who gets paid to do this work is called a professional. Professional athlete. It's a very shallow definition. All they're doing is making money; there are no standards. The crazier they act, the more attention they will attract. The more attention they get, the more endorsements, the more dollars. The more dollars, the higher a professional. It's that kind of thinking that encourages some of the players to act stupid and talk trash.

People forget what sports are all about, why sports cut across racial, language, cultural, and national boundaries and promote peace. A sport is friendly and educational, it has rules and regulations that everyone must follow, and its code must be reinforced. It does not take away from the competitiveness of sport to be friendly. Play clean. Sports are what countries use to compete against each other instead of war.

You don't have to be friends with everyone you play against but at least maintain your own standards. I'm impressed by a player who runs into an opponent and, when time is called, gives him a hand and helps him up. If you fall I'm going to pick you up. That doesn't mean that if you come near the basket I'm not going to try to block your shot, I'm still going to do my job the best way I know how. Being sportsmanlike does not make you less competitive.

The player who lends a hand is usually the one who has consistency, who does community work and sets an example for future stars to take responsibility as role models.

People who admire the sport of basketball automatically admire the players for their talent, so when a player enters the league he becomes a role model whether he likes it or not. I don't think of that as a burden; it is very satisfying to be a good example. Not to be a good example only in public and then lead a different lifestyle in private — no. To have character, to humble yourself, all the time.

To humble yourself does not mean you are weak. It has taken me some time but I have found that out. If you humble yourself people take it as a sign of weakness, but it's a sign of strength because you know yourself, you know what you can do, you don't have to wake up each morning and prove it to other people a hundred times over; in your heart you know your own strength, you know who you are, and that's all that matters.

It seems to me that what the NBA needs to stress is professional conduct, good home training.

It is professional to expect that the game be played and officiated properly, and the Rockets had a reputation for arguing with the officials. Before or after my *Hajj* I *always* complained to the referees. I hadn't changed in that, either.

I get fouled almost every time I take a shot. Most of the guys in the league know that if I call for the ball and get it where I want it, down low in the paint near the basket, most likely I will score. I have worked very hard for many years in practice, in training, in games, to develop the skills to do this. It's their job to stop me. That's basketball.

But basketball has rules. I don't shuffle my feet before taking a lay-up, I don't knock players down on the way to the basket, I don't bang people out of the way when I'm getting a rebound. I know the rules and I play within them. Players defending me, however, seem to think they don't have to play by those rules. They put their fists in my side and their knees in my back, they lean their bodies — most of which are bigger than mine — into me and try to push me out of my position. None of this is legal.

Of course, NBA basketball has developed its own set of rules over the years. Many people don't understand that, they think pro basketball is the same game they played in high school, and it's not. You can hear fans screaming in outrage every night when they see the steps that get taken on drives or the kind of physical banging that goes on with no whistle, particularly if it's happening against their team. You're allowed an extra bump, a knee in the back, contact under the boards. But what happens to me is way outside even this new set of rules. I take a pounding. The referees are right there, they see it. And when I try to hold my position or fend off these attacks by shooting my elbow back at the defender, they call the foul on me! That cliché about the second foul usually being the one that's called is very true.

On my fade-away jumper particularly, whoever is defending me usually can't get near the ball so he hits the bottom of my forearm right above my elbow. Not a big swipe, they give me a slap, just enough to throw off my aim. Try it and see if it doesn't mess with your shooting touch to have someone knock your elbow every time. The referee is standing right there, he sees it. I should be at the foul line every time

I take that shot, but if I take twenty shots a game I go to the line four times at most. Referees tell me, "You should make that shot anyway."

One thing I found that did help me with the referees was showing them my moves before I used them. During warm-ups before a game or at the half I will go over to the refs and discuss the technicalities of the game. Maybe they have called traveling on me and they're not familiar with that move. I'll walk over and in as nice a voice as possible I'll say, "Look, don't call traveling on that move again because I'm going to use it again."

They say, "You traveled."

"No, no, no, let me show you what I did. Look here." They watch my feet as I pace off the move in slow motion. "Okay, is this traveling? You tell me now if it's traveling." Of course I don't travel on this move, I have spent time in practice working this out so I can make this move and stay within the rules.

Their answer is always "But that's not what you did."

"I'm telling you this is what I did. I'm going to do it again. It just works."

The referees appreciate the time I've taken to explain it to them. It's like I am acknowledging their power. Before the game, after the game, they're the nicest guys. If you talk to them it will always be interesting, and they always say nice things about me. But it's like they're two different kinds of people; when the game starts they just don't give me a break.

Our team was coming together. Kenny Smith and Vernon Maxwell had been starting in the backcourt together for three years now. Otis Thorpe was starting his fifth year as a Rocket. He had been selected to the All-Star team in 1992 and was a strong power forward who could rebound and score. The new guy in the starting lineup was the first-round draft pick from the University of Alabama, Robert Horry. At 6'10" he was our small forward, a young, slashing, dunking forward who blocked shots and played good defense. On the bench we had Carl Herrera, Scott Brooks, Sleepy Floyd, Matt Bullard, and Winston Garland all playing solid minutes.

We didn't start playing well until January, then we clicked. We were 16–16 on January 12, then we went 39–11 the rest of the way and won the Midwest Division by six games over the Spurs.

We were confident. We had split our season series with the Knicks and we'd beaten Michael Jordan and the Chicago Bulls both times we'd played them that year, once in Chicago early in the season when we weren't playing our best and again at the Summit in January when we had just begun to jell. We matched up well against the Bulls. Vernon Maxwell did a good job defending against Michael, Otis Thorpe banged with Horace Grant, Robert Horry ran with Scotty Pippin, and Kenny Smith shot it out with B.J. Armstrong. I was matched against Bill Cartwright and both our benches were strong.

We were confident we could beat Chicago if we met them in the finals and we were confident we could beat the Phoenix Suns, even though they had the best record in the Western Conference. We had split our series with Phoenix, 2–2, but we had lost to them early in the season and beaten them the last two times we had met, the last being only three games from the end of the season, when we beat them by fourteen in their home arena.

Home-court advantage usually counts for so much in the playoffs. The fans are more excited than during the regular season, your own game is heightened, and you like to have everything familiar.

With two games to go in the regular season we were in place to finish with the second-best record in the west. All we had to do was win one of two games against Dallas at home or San Antonio on the road. It was a lock. Dallas was the worst team in the league and that win was almost guaranteed. There was no way we could lose to them; they had won only eleven games *all year!*

We played miserably against Dallas. We were not serious, we were looking ahead to the playoffs and not in front of us at the game at hand, we thought we had won this game just by showing up. We were careless. As soon as we got careless it cost us.

We lost to Dallas by five points *at home* and now we had to go and win in San Antonio in order to clinch home-court advantage into the Conference finals.

We were in San Antonio and had the game won, and in the last moment, when the clock had run out completely, the Spurs put back a miss and the refs ruled it good. There was no question that time had run out but the referee refused to change his call. We lost that game by two points in overtime, and we lost the home-court advantage. It was an outrage and I was furious. When I complained to the refs that their one terrible call had cost us so deeply, one of them said to me, "You should have beat Dallas."

We beat the Los Angeles Clippers in the first round of the playoffs and faced the Seattle Supersonics in the Western Conference semifinals. They had home-court advantage.

We'd had trouble all year with the Sonics because their style of play was not something we could ever really design a game plan for; their game was never really organized, they scrambled all over the place. They pressed, they pressured us, they jumped in front of me and made it difficult even to get the ball into the post to start our offense. It was scrappy, unorganized basketball but it worked for them. On offense all season long they got balanced scoring from Ricky Pierce, Sean Kemp, Eddie Johnson, Gary Payton, Derrick McKey, and Sam Perkins.

The first six games were all won by the home team. The series began in Seattle and they went up 2–0, we came back to Houston and tied them 2–2, we traded home victories, and game seven was played in the Seattle Superdome.

The game was close and in the last minutes the referees kept giving the ball to the Sonics. Seattle threw passes out of bounds several times but the refs kept ruling we had touched them. These phantom deflections gave the Sonics the ball and they finally won. If the game had been played in Houston, most likely we would have won it.

Everybody on the Rockets was tremendously disappointed. In the locker room afterward we weren't ready to stop playing. We had been thinking about a championship; that's what we always thought about at the beginning of a season, that's the goal. But there's a difference between saying you can win a championship and really seeing it in front of you. We really *saw* a championship. The winner of our series against Seattle would play Phoenix and then Chicago. It was clear in all of our minds that we were a better team than Seattle, and we felt we could beat both Phoenix and Chicago. I told my teammates, "We go from here."

I watched the NBA finals at home on TV and looked at the players and looked at the teams and knew we should have been there.

I decided to become an American citizen. It was a very tough call for me; Nigerians wanted to know why I would change my nationality. Was I no longer proud of my Nigerian heritage? I was, and still am, proud of having grown up in Nigeria. I love the culture I came from. I have not lost my Nigerian identity and certainly not my Nigerian accent. I simply found I was becoming more and more of an American.

I felt I owed America a great debt. For a long time I was classified as a permanent resident alien but my daughter had dual citizenship and except for that piece of paper she was completely American. I lived in America, I became an adult in America, I took advantage of the great opportunities afforded me and became a success in what I was doing in America. On a more personal level, I truly found Islam in America. People in America treated me like one of their own, and to show my gratitude and that I was honored to be treated so graciously, I wanted to become a citizen.

Another reason for my change was that the rulers of Nigeria had basically torn the country apart; the dignity of my country had been lost. The perception of Nigerians held by other countries, I found, was that we were scam artists, fake businessmen, or drug dealers. I was doing a lot of traveling and I found that with an American passport a person is more honored and trusted than with a Nigerian one. That was upsetting; the country I grew up in did not seem to exist anymore.

On April 2, 1993, I was officially sworn in as a citizen of the United States of America.

In July 1993 Charlie Thomas sold the Rockets to Les Alexander and his company, L.L.A. Ltd. Mr. Alexander had made his money on Wall Street. I was signed to a long-term contract so we didn't have any negotiating to do. I hoped this change in management and a thorough housecleaning in the front office would do great things for the Rockets.

I traveled that summer and played at Fonde, just like I did every summer, and when the Rockets got back together in the fall everyone in training camp was in his best shape. That was unusual; normally, players come to camp to try to get into shape. My teammates had played summer ball and they looked ready to go. I thought, Wow, I'm way behind, and I started working out by myself, just trying to keep up. This camp, right before the 1993–94 season, was very competitive. We had so many good players in camp that no one knew who would make the squad. Mario Elie arrived that year. I could tell from the dedication and concentration of everyone who came to camp that the team had matured. Vernon Maxwell, in particular, was extremely quick and ready to go. We *believed* we could win.

Rudy made an opening statement to the team, and the key was obvious in everybody's mind: Home-court advantage. If we had beaten Dallas or won in San Antonio, we all felt, we would have been in the finals and we might have been returning to camp as NBA champions. We had gotten careless, and we saw the results. The Rockets as a team made a commitment not to let that happen again.

The Chicago Bulls had won three NBA championships in a row but this year, 1993, Michael Jordan had retired and the teams around the league thought they had an opening. The Bulls had dominated, but now it was going to be someone else's turn. There was a rush to win.

We won eight games to start the season. Nine games. We have something going here, let's keep it up. Ten, eleven, twelve. The record for most games won to start a season was fifteen. Let's shoot for it.

Game fifteen, to tie the record, was against the New York Knicks at Madison Square Garden.

The game was nationally publicized, the whole league built it up. The Knicks had been hearing about this record we were chasing and they were on a crusade of their own. They had been beaten in the playoffs by the Chicago Bulls three years in a row, and now with Michael Jordan retired they were very outspoken that this was the Knicks' year to win the championship. Their coach, Pat Riley, who had coached the Lakers to their string of championships, was a great motivator. He got the most out of his players all season long. They weren't the most talented squad in the NBA but they played aggressive, hard-nosed, defensive basketball, they were intimidators, and we were coming into their gym to try to set an NBA record. We knew they weren't going to let us off without a fight. They couldn't wait to play us.

We ran them out of Madison Square Garden. They thought they were ready but they were not. It's amazing that sometimes when you sit for a few days and just practice, you lose your edge. We had been playing almost every other day, this was our fourth game in a week, they had been waiting for us, but they were the ones who were tired and we had the flow. We just ran them and took away the Garden for two hours.

We lost the next night in Atlanta and won seven straight after that.

We were 22–1. After that we'd lose a few, win a few. We had a couple of nice runs and finished the season 58–24.

The Rockets didn't have the greatest talent in the league. If you looked at us position by position we were good, but on paper we didn't dominate. Each of us had to play his best within the team concept, then we were an excellent team. Most of the time we did that. Kenny Smith ran the game as the point guard. He was our most accurate three-point shooter and he also got me the ball. Vernon Maxwell defended the opposition's toughest guard every night and also ran the floor and hit threes. Otis Thorpe posted up and scored and banged for rebounds. Robert Horry played active defense and started to take and make outside shots. We had a good bench with Carl Herrera, Sam Cassell, Scott Brooks, Mario Elie, Matt Bullard, Chris Jent, and Earl Cureton.

Horry and Bullard had been traded to Detroit for Sean Elliott in the middle of the season but the deal had been voided when Elliott failed his physical. Robert could have sulked the rest of the year but he used the trade as motivation and really picked up his game. The coaches wanted him to shoot more than he did — it's unusual for any coach to have to tell a player to shoot more — but Horry had been hesitant. When he came back to the team he was motivated to show his true value, so he started putting up his jump shot. He was successful and developed his confidence. Now we had *three* three-point shooters in the starting lineup, which meant that anytime the defense collapsed on me in the post the opposition was in danger of getting seriously burned.

Sometimes we lost sight of our team concept, and then this squad of Rockets became an average team. If we deceived ourselves and started thinking we could do it individually, that's when we would start to lose. If the guard holds the ball a moment too long looking for his own shot rather than looking for a teammate and making the right play, the whole game plan falls apart. A center has to fight hard to establish position down low, and he only gets it for a split second. The ball has to be there when he calls for it. If it's a moment late the defender can either cut in front of him or push him out. The center's competing with his man, it's a tough battle and he's fighting hard; when he's ready he's got to get the ball. I have to get the ball before the rest of the defenders get there so I can make a quick move to the basket or dish off.

Sometimes players forget that the glory comes from the team winning, not from one individual scoring a lot of points or making the last shot. If a guard finds himself in a bad position and moves the ball without hesitating, that's how we win. If the man in the post sees a guard open and chooses to shoot the ball himself instead of feeding him, or if the man on the fast break chooses to shoot with a defender in his face instead of dropping the ball to the man trailing, we don't score and we don't win. All these things take away our advantage.

The team concept demands unselfishness. It needs the guys on the bench not to complain about playing time, it needs guys who play hard when they are in there and who understand their role when they're not. The team concept needs the bench to jump up every time we score and share in the satisfaction and feel part of the victory, and it needs the starters to pull for the bench when they're in. A healthy team feels happy for one another. Once each guy wants the individual spotlight instead of the team floodlights, we are in trouble.

People always wonder why no lead is safe in the NBA, why a team can be up by twenty points in the first half and still have to fight it out at the last minute. It's because teams get careless and cocky, they stop feeling the anxiety and pressure, they stop doing all the things that got them the big lead in the first place. We were always doing that. We would concentrate in the beginning of the game, we would run our plays to perfection — and they would work because we were a good team with a good offense. On defense we would be intense and focused, we pressured the ball on the outside and denied it in the paint. And when we did what we were supposed to do we would be successful. For a while.

But then we would get a big lead and ease off. The guards would penetrate and try to shoot over the big man rather than dishing off, or they would settle for contested jump shots instead of working hard to get a better look. We can always get those shots; we have to get better each time down the court — and sometimes we don't. Many times these shots would miss and the other team would have a fast break. Okay, it's just a basket, we've still got a big lead, we can still feel comfortable and loose. This time the ball is thrown inside and instead of taking the right shot the big men try one-on-one moves they've been working on in practice. It doesn't work and the opposition is off the other way on a fast break again. Another score. But there's nothing to worry about, we're still ahead. Then we try to run our offense and the other team plays good defense, we lose the ball, they go down and score. The game has tightened up. Now we're back on our heels, they are excited and coming back, and where just a few minutes before they were demoralized now they believe they can win. Now it's hard for us to get back the momentum. Now it's a game again. And we were the ones who let them back in it.

That whole season was like one long game for us. We started out doing everything we should, we got cocky and let the league back in, then we pulled it together. We began with the winning streak but in January we hit a stretch where we lost five games out of six, and by mid-February the San Antonio Spurs had caught us. We regrouped and spent only a couple of days out of first place in the Midwest Division the whole season. We won the Midwest but the Seattle Supersonics had the best record in the Western Conference.

We met the Portland Trail Blazers in the first round of the playoffs. Portland had gone to the finals twice in the last four years, the last time only two seasons before. They were a tough, experienced team led by Clyde Drexler, Cliff Robinson, Buck Williams, Rod Strickland, and Kevin Porter. Not only was Portland a team of basketball players, they were a team of *athletes* and they challenged us in many ways. They were relentless rebounders, they had speed and good outside shooting. We realized that this wasn't going to be an easy series but we didn't even want to think about not getting out of the first round. It became a must. You could tell from the attitude of the players that we knew this was a big task. The whole season would be wasted if we let ourselves be beaten so early.

The first round of the playoffs was best-three-of-five, and in the first game, at home at the Summit, Clyde played wonderfully. It seemed like every time there was a key basket, Clyde was making it. We won by ten but they were no pushovers. They were a tough, physical team and the battling was brutal. We won the second game as well, keeping the home-court advantage. We lost by three in Portland, and we really didn't want to go home to Houston and have to play winner-take-all. That was too dangerous. We had to do it in four.

We beat them, 92–89, and went home to face the Phoenix Suns.

The next day, Seattle, which had won sixty-three games during the season, lost to Denver, which had won twenty-one games less, in a winner-take-all deciding game in overtime *at home*. They had been pointing toward the finals and now their season was over. It must have been devastating for them. I didn't even want to think about it. That's why when you have the knockout punch you throw it, you don't want to go home and face that kind of pressure so early in the playoffs.

We knew that now we had the best record of any team still playing; from then on we had home-court advantage throughout the playoffs.

Phoenix had an excellent team. Charles Barkley was their leader. They had Kevin Johnson, one of the best point guards in the league; they had Dan Majerle, A.C. Green, Oliver Miller. They were a tough team but we were confident we could beat them.

We were even more confident when we jumped on them early and went up by eighteen points in the first half. We did all the right things; we moved the ball and tossed it inside, we hit from outside, we shut off their offense and left them nothing at all. It seemed so easy. I remember thinking, Portland was tougher than this.

But just when we thought we had the game won in the second period, things turned around. A little selfishness here, a little carelessness there . . . it's okay, we're still up sixteen, no big deal. . . .

But they were playing hard and we were getting too comfortable. The lead was cut to twelve points. Then it was a different game, there was pressure. Now they were on the attack, they had momentum, they had hope. We felt the pressure, we were frustrated, we made more mistakes. They kept their eyes on that, scored again, came back. *Boom.* They were only down five, they were back in the game. We blew the lead and they saw that we were wild in the eyes. They attacked us some more. Charles Barkley made a three from the side, they came back and tied the game. They took the lead. We lost, 91–87.

We had been doing anything we wanted, and then all of a sudden we were going back to the locker room, having lost after being up eighteen points. I started running over in my head how the same kind of carelessness had cost us the games against Dallas and San Antonio the year before and here we were again in the same position. We thought we had the game won and we got comfortable. Guys started to take shots they never would take under pressure, and the lead and then the game disappeared quickly.

We lost the game with our heads down. Home-court advantage was gone. All we could do was hope we would play better next time.

Game two was close in the first half but we opened a nice lead in the third quarter, and with ten minutes left in the fourth quarter we were up by twenty. Okay, if the series was tied 1–1 we'd just have to win a game in Phoenix. No problem.

Then it happened again. The exact identical game. Someone just dropped the ball out of bounds. Turnover. Someone dribbled off his foot out of bounds. Turnover. We were throwing the ball around on crucial, crucial possessions and they were taking it and going the other way.

This time when they showed signs of coming back we panicked. I couldn't believe it. We had scored forty points in the third quarter, we scored eight in the fourth. We made one shot, a three-pointer by Sam Cassell, in the last ten minutes. They outscored us 24–4 — it was the biggest blown fourth-quarter lead in the history of the NBA playoffs — and sent the game into overtime. Overtime didn't help. We were shell-shocked. We lost the game by seven. We were down 0–2.

The Phoenix players themselves didn't believe it. They would have been very happy with a split. One victory would have been an accomplishment, they didn't come in expecting to win two games.

Choke City.

That was the headline: "Choke City." It wasn't any fun to see that in the papers.

We couldn't ignore the media. We had no choice, we had to pay attention, they were on our case. Houston takes its professional teams to heart and it had happened to the Oilers, it had happened to the Astros, now it was happening to us. When it came time to deliver, we choked. Choke City.

We understood how people were feeling. We ourselves were devastated. Blowing eighteen- and twenty-point leads in back-to-back games and losing both? At home? That was terrible. And now we were going to Phoenix. If we couldn't do it at home, we definitely couldn't do it over there.

We traveled directly to Phoenix after that game. That was a terrible flight. It was silent on the plane, as if somebody had died. Nobody was prepared for what had happened.

The next day's meeting was very constructive. Rudy T is the kind of coach who lets us talk. Many of the guys had their say. I spoke up, too. I was very blunt. First I said, "Coach, we are not utilizing all our talent to win the game. There are times that some guys on the floor are being too careless or not delivering and you've got guys on the bench who are hungry, they'll do something. If you don't use them now, when are you going to use them? Why do we have to go down with some players when at the time when they're needed the most they're not there? You have a team, you have twelve players, you must utilize everybody that can deliver. If somebody can come in and get one basket you've got to use him."

There was a player on our bench who I thought should be playing more, a small forward named Chris Jent. He was a good shooter and he was emotional. When we were getting panicky and the Suns were building up, we needed some new energy from somewhere, and Chris Jent was someone who could make the big play that could turn us around. Most of the time when we went down we went all the way down, there was no movement. I was very upset in the game when we began to stand around. I said, "Just use your resources to get the job done, it doesn't matter who."

I told the team, "We are here now. We don't have anybody but ourselves. The whole city is against us, we have no more room for mistakes, our back is against the wall. Everybody says that the pressure is on us now, but truly the pressure is on *them*. The pressure is now on Phoenix, it is not on us anymore, they took that pressure away when they came in and won two games. Now everybody expects them to win, so if we go and put our effort into winning the first game here in Phoenix that puts all the pressure back on them. Then they can't afford to lose the second game. If they do they're back where they were before. So *this* is the most important game, this first one in Phoenix."

We knew we had lost both games at the Summit not because they beat us but because we got careless again. We could beat this team if we did all the things we do when we're playing right.

"If we go out and win the first game here they will choke. They cannot afford to lose this game; then Phoenix will be Choke City."

Everybody around the room went, "Yeah, you're right. I think so!" They were seeing it differently now. We didn't feel pressure anymore.

Now we said, "For us to pull this out would be a miracle, so there's no more pressure." For Phoenix to have won this two-game home-court advantage *and then lose it* would be devastating.

At the end of the meeting we felt good. We shook hands and came together as a team. We didn't feel pressure, we just had a job to do.

The Phoenix fans showed up at the America West Arena with brooms, as if the Suns were going to sweep us. And for a while it looked like they might. They led by fourteen at the end of the first quarter. We were still down by nine at the half. But then Vernon Maxwell took over. He came out for the second half playing loose, hitting threes, driving, shooting beautifully. The whole team was cheering him on, rebounding, supporting him. Max brought us out of our funk. He hit four three-pointers in that game and scored thirty-one points in the second half, thirty-four points overall. Max made the difference and we won, 118–102.

Sure enough, the pressure shifted to Phoenix. In game four the first quarter was intense. We were rebounding, we were moving the ball, everybody was aggressive. The Suns saw that we were determined, we were not going to slow down, we meant business. Kevin Johnson scored thirty-eight points for Phoenix and Charles Barkley had nineteen, but we had six guys in double figures. Chris Jent played nine minutes. We outscored them in every quarter and won, 107–96.

Phoenix was very quiet that night. It seemed like we were the only ones in the whole city celebrating. Meanwhile Houston, which had been dead when we left, now became alive! "Choke City"? It was "Comeback City"! When the team flew back in its own chartered plane, the crowd who came to welcome us home at Hobby Airport was so huge it took the players an hour just to get out of the parking lot.

Game five at the Summit we jumped on them at the beginning and blew them out. Don't even think about it. So we went back to Phoenix. But the Suns were determined also and they beat us there, so it all came down to home-court advantage in game seven at the Summit.

Charles Barkley scored twenty-four points and got fifteen rebounds but Otis Thorpe was pounding him all night. Charles's back was killing him, and Otis, at 6'9", was bigger than he was, so this was a very strong effort. Throughout the series Barkley did his damage but the flow of the games was out of his control. Kevin Johnson really carried the team.

He scored thirty-eight points each in games three and four, he handled the ball, he ran the show.

I scored a lot of points that game, but the guy who came up big for us was Sam Cassell. He was a rookie out of Florida State University who had played his way into Rudy T's rotation in midseason, but he was exactly the kind of emotional player the Rockets needed. Sam gets excited, it's part of his game, and this was *big* excitement. He drove, he hit from outside, he scored twenty-two points — *nine* in the fourth quarter — he got seven assists and ran the offense at the end of the game like a veteran. We won, 104–94, in front of our screaming fans.

I was so excited. The team really came together as a unit that night. All the bitterness was gone, we had new life, great chemistry and unity. We had done something no one else thought we could do. I felt so happy and joyful.

Utah came in. They had just had a hard series against Denver and we jumped on them immediately and won the first game. Before the second game in the Summit the league presented me with the trophy for being the 1993–94 NBA Most Valuable Player.

I was very honored to be chosen. Shaquille O'Neal and David Robinson and Patrick Ewing had had excellent seasons and for me to be selected to win that award meant a lot. But I didn't want to go out and accept the trophy by myself because I had not won the award by myself. I told my teammates that they were the ones who did all the things — like winning our games together and getting me the ball in the post or hitting their shots when I passed back out to them — that added up to an MVP season for me. In the locker room I said, "I want to share this award with you. If not for you complementing me and making it happen, I would not be the MVP." To show my sincerity and my gratitude to them, and to get recognition for the fact that this was a collective effort, I asked my teammates to come on the floor and accept the trophy with me.

The Summit was cheering and I told the crowd I happily accepted the award for myself and the entire team. Everybody took pictures of us with our hands on the trophy and all the guys enjoyed being part of something special. They seemed to think that sharing the spotlight was something out of the ordinary for an MVP, but to me it was the right thing to do, the only thing to do. They were a big part of my success and I was sincerely thankful to have such a good group of players and guys with me. I felt very happy.

After that we felt much closer as a team. And this game was very, very important. We didn't want to turn over home-court advantage again and we knew Utah would give it their best shot, which was very good. The guard-forward pair of John Stockton and Karl Malone was as good as any in the league. They were two All-Stars and they had a strong team around them and they played us tough from the beginning. Some games you build a lead, they come back, it goes back and forth. This game was close and tough for forty-eight minutes. It was a two-point game at the half; we had a four-point lead after three quarters. No one could pull away. I scored forty-one points, made all thirteen of my free throws, got thirteen rebounds and six assists. I remember putting up a hook shot and being so tired I fell down. But I was so focused that the ball went in. When we won, 104–99, Utah was disappointed. They thought this was the one they could get, that if they had won one in Houston they could go home and build on that lead.

They did beat us the first game in Salt Lake City, and in the second Kenny Smith stepped up big. In Phoenix it was Maxwell and everybody was giving him five, encouraging him, so he was even more aggressive. In Utah Kenny Smith was the key, playing loose, hitting jumpers, driving, penetrating, and everybody was cheering him on. That was the beautiful part about our team, someone was always rising to the occasion and the rest of us were there supporting him.

Still, the game came down to the wire. We were up by two points with 13.5 seconds to go and the ball in Utah's hands. They had a chance to tie or win the game with the last shot. They worked the ball and worked the ball . . . and the time clock never moved. For ten seconds they worked for the game-winner and the clock stayed frozen. Our bench was screaming but the timekeeper didn't start it. (He said later that it was an oversight.) Even with this extra time we played excellent defense, didn't allow them to score, and when we finally got the ball we ran the clock down to zero.

Utah lost that game and they were quiet. We killed their morale. They did not want to come back to Houston, they knew what was going to happen. Game five was a blow-out.

We thought the Utah series might go seven games and we beat them in five. It was funny, we were still looking for battle, but the battle was over quicker than we thought. Then it sunk in for the first time. You could kind of feel it go around the locker room. We were going to the NBA finals!

That was a wonderful feeling. We had been playing for this moment all season long and now it was finally here! We were confident but not overconfident. We celebrated but the job was not done. A lot of things had to go right for us to win the NBA championship.

16

THE DREAM SEASON

THE EASTERN CONFERENCE finals were still going on. We beat Utah on a Tuesday, and on Wednesday the Indiana Pacers beat the New York Knicks, *in New York,* to take a 3–2 lead in their play-offs. When I started thinking about it, I didn't want to play Indiana for the title. People would say it wasn't a classic, the Pacers were a good team but they were a Cinderella team, they weren't supposed to win, the team to beat in the east was the New York Knicks. The Pacers had swept the young Orlando Magic and beaten the Atlanta Hawks to get to the Conference finals. The Knicks had eliminated the Nets and then dethroned the defending champion Chicago Bulls. With Patrick Ewing at center and Pat Riley coaching, they were dominators, intimidators. They were the natural heirs to the Eastern Conference crown.

But when I looked at it again I said, "I don't know, maybe I just want to win the championship and I don't care who I beat." There was no guarantee that we would win either way, but we felt confident that this was our year, that we could beat anybody.

I went back and forth between Indiana and New York, I really didn't know who I wanted to face. Finally I stopped caring. I thought, Whichever is best.

I watched some of the games on TV but not very many. It was difficult to stay focused. If we were not playing either of these teams then it would be okay to watch players individually and see what kinds of moves they were making. Usually I watch the moves of the man I will be guarding, but here I might be playing against either of the centers, Patrick Ewing or Rik Smits, and I had to watch the way the whole team played ball.

Sometimes when I watch two teams play I underestimate our own ability. I say, "Wow, these teams are tough!" They look so good and I look at their intensity and think they will blow us out. But when it comes time for us to play I start seeing we have an effect on them. They miss shots, they struggle.

If you look at our team on the level of individual talent we are not clearly superior to a lot of teams. If you look at players one-on-one, other teams are as tough. What gives us the confidence that we can go and win this game? It's more than individual match-ups, it's teamwork. There's a lot of individual talent but if the players don't complement one another they don't make a great team, the chemistry is not balanced. Someone may be very strong only in a particular area; if you hit him with a pass in a certain spot he will make nine out of ten shots but if you take him to a different spot he will have difficulty. The defensive team that recognizes this will keep him out of that spot; one man can't do it, it takes teamwork. If the player's teammates don't get him the ball where he is most effective, he loses his strength.

That's why sometimes when a player gets traded from one team to another he seems to lose his ability. You used to be so good, now you come to this team, what happened? It's because either he can't adjust to the team's system or the system can't adjust and put him in the exact spot where he's most effective. He's the same player he always was but he's not comfortable now because he is not put where he can do his best.

A good example of this is what happened to Rolando Blackman. When he was with the Dallas Mavericks he was tough, always on the All-Star team. When he played against us he always took crucial shots — big shots: penetrating, shooting — and he would make them. When he got traded to the Knicks I said, "Now New York is complete." I respected Pat Riley tremendously for making the right decision and picking the right player.

But Blackman went to New York and he didn't fit the system. He wasn't even the same player. Then he got injured, and now he's out of the league. The same thing happened to Alex English when he was traded from Denver to Dallas. More recently, Sean Elliott didn't do anything in Detroit but when he went back to San Antonio he became a big star again. It's the team that really makes the difference.

Some players are just athletes, they can play with any team because their game is individual, one-on-one. Ricky Pierce is a perfect example of this kind of player. He has been traded to a lot of teams and he is consistent. He's a talented player one-on-one. I like his game, it's very solid. If he gets the ball and you give him a wide-open shot, he will make it. If you trade him to a better team he looks better, to a worse team he stands out.

So I watched some of the Eastern Conference final and we practiced every day. We were going to be well prepared for the finals. When the Knicks came back and beat Indiana in both Indianapolis and Madison Square Garden I knew this was going to be a battle.

I was going up against Patrick Ewing. NBA games are not won on individual match-ups, it is team against team, but my part in this series would be largely concerned with rebounding, blocking shots, taking the ball to the basket with authority on offense, and making Patrick work for every shot on defense — no easy baskets.

I had been watching Ewing since college. I did not think he was better than I was but I also didn't think I was better than Patrick. I would watch him play and he would block shots. Well, I felt I would have blocked those shots too, but there weren't too many other players in the NBA who could match him. I thought, What I'm doing is not unique; he can do everything I can. He's a shot blocker, he's a rebounder, he has a jump hook, he has a turnaround jumper, he plays above the rim. We both can dominate a game, we have the same basic moves. He's tough. I like him and have tremendous respect for his game. He's a true big man.

The big difference between Patrick and me is that he is a classic big man, a center, and I don't picture myself as a center at all. Patrick has post moves, he takes up space and dominates in the middle. In college Patrick was a zone all by himself. I play the center position but I'm not truly a center. As I've said, I'm really an in-between player, more like a power forward. I'm usually the tallest man on my team so they put me at center but when I play center I'm almost always at a height disadvantage; other centers are bigger, so I have to make more moves and fade away and shoot my jump hook or go outside and make my man move. If I'm playing against one big guy with an inside game then I play inside and outside. If they guard me with a power forward and get physical, that's when I use my post moves inside to advantage: back up, call for the ball, make my basic move, and shoot over him. I like post moves. I also like to shoot other shots. I don't want to bring the ball down the court — that is not my territory — but anywhere inside the three-point line you have to respect me.

So Patrick and I matched up very evenly. The rest of the match-ups were also very even. Otis Thorpe and Charles Oakley were the same type of player, tough under the boards; they could battle each other. Robert Horry and Charles Smith were both long and lean, both could slash and shoot and score. Horry was now hitting three-point shots consistently, however, which gave him an advantage: He could run, post up, or hit from the outside. Vernon Maxwell and John Starks were both fast and emotional players with good outside shots and they would go at each other the whole series.

Kenny Smith and Derek Harper were similar only in that they both ran their team's offense. Kenny is a good outside shooter who relies on speed and quickness. Harper is bigger and stronger and more physical. He's hard-nosed and tough, he'll kill you if he can. Pat Riley had whittled their bench and was really playing only Anthony Mason, Greg Anthony, Hubert Davis, and Herb Williams. Rudy had Carl Herrera, Mario Elie, Matt Bullard, Chris Jent, Earl Cureton, Scott Brooks, and Sam Cassell.

The Knicks played physical basketball. They hand-checked all over the floor, they didn't let you get into your offense. They prided themselves on not letting teams score a hundred points against them. We had a physical team that we thought matched up well against them; we didn't mind playing physical if we had to but it wasn't our first choice. If we had our first choice we wouldn't get into a pounding match with a strong team. Our plan was to run them.

The plan didn't work out. From the beginning they took the running game away from us with tough defense and hard rebounding and it was clear very quickly, from the first few minutes of game one, that this was going to be a grind. Everybody had to work. We had been sitting for a week before the first game of the finals. We had been practicing but it was not like playing in a game, you don't have the emotion driving you, you lose your edge. For some reason, I don't know why, we came out tight. But the Knicks had just finished a long and draining seven-game series against Indiana and were even tighter than we were. We were ready to play them; they weren't ready to play us.

The game was low-scoring, rugged. The play in the post and all over the court was unrelenting. We shot only two for thirteen from the field in the fourth quarter but we played tough defense and didn't let them score much either. We were at each other all game, no team taking a big lead. It felt like we were all growling at each other. We won, 85–78.

They pass around a stat sheet in the locker room after each game and when I saw it I was amazed to see that we and the Knicks *combined* had scored sixty-three points in the second half. We were capable of doing that all by ourselves. We had scored only thirteen points in the whole fourth quarter and we'd still won. "When it gets to this point it's not going to be pretty," Rudy T told the press. "It's a war. And it's hard work."

We felt happy; we'd taken care of the first assignment, we'd held the home-court advantage.

The Knicks knew that in order for them to win the championship they would have to win one game in the Summit. Two days later they came out determined to make it game two. They knew if they lost this one they would definitely have to come back to Houston.

The Knicks' backcourt won this game for them. Derek Harper and John Starks played tough, and six Knicks scored in double figures. We had a one-point lead with a little more than five minutes remaining but Harper hit two threes, they outscored us 9–1, and we lost, 91–83.

On the sidelines after the game I saw Alonzo Mourning of the Charlotte Hornets and Dikembe Mutombo of the Denver Nuggets. They were there to support Patrick. All three had gone to Georgetown, all the big men. The Georgetown connection. This school produces centers. Their coach was there too, John Thompson, a big man. They had come to see the war of the centers and they were Patrick's supporters. I knew they were going to talk to Patrick, give him some tips about how to play me. I shook their hands when I saw them, they were NBA players, and they were pleasant to me.

Those guys saw a different ball game from everybody else. They were a special audience and were looking at it from a different angle. They were looking at post moves, they were looking at shot blocking, they were looking at rebounding, intimidation, control, they were looking at what *they* do as centers. They were watching the battle. They were watching the Big Man's Game.

This motivated me, gave me extra incentive. From now on I had to be even quicker, more flexible, more active. I had to sharpen up all my moves, everything had to be *real* sharp. The championship was at stake.

In the Summit's hallway this Georgetown reunion were all patting each other on the back and congratulating themselves. The way they were celebrating you'd think the championship was over.

These championship finals were being played 2–3–2: two games at the Summit, three at Madison Square Garden, two back at the Summit. The Knicks had tied the series and now were going home. They felt confident they were going to close us out. Now our backs were against the wall. If home-court advantage held we might not get another chance to play in Houston. The locker room was quiet, we were exhausted, and we looked at the task ahead of us, a big task: In order for us to climb out of this hole we had to win in New York. I was very worried.

The Garden is a tough place to play but we won game three when Vernon Maxwell set the tone with three straight early baskets, and Sam Cassell came up big down the stretch. The Knicks played strong but Sam scored seven points in the last 32.9 seconds and we won, 93–89. I was so relieved! We won the game we had to win.

The Knicks took games four and five. Kenny Smith, in particular, was having a hard time. Derek Harper was constantly in his face, hand-checking him, pressuring the ball, not letting him run our offense. The way the rules were that year Harper could put his hands all over Kenny and not get called for the foul. Harper played tough, tough defense and Kenny took a lot of criticism for not being fast enough to get away from him, and for missing his shots. I never blamed Kenny; Harper was a bigger, stronger, more physical player and he was having a great series. His advantage was his size.

Harper is also very mentally tough. He will challenge the big men. He feels if he had our size he could do what we do and more, he's that kind of guy. He would come in the paint and talk trash. He'd put up his shot and say, "You can't get that." Or he would come in and dish off to Patrick, Patrick would make it, and Harper would talk trash to me. He was always trying to psych me out and psych Patrick up. He would work the pick-and-roll and hit his shot and say, "If you come you're gonna pay the price." He was right. I had to run out there and try to block him and play defense inside at the same time. I was not very effective and most of the time he would still get the pass over.

We went back to Houston, down three games to two. We had to win the last two games or lose the championship, but they were on our court and this was what we had fought all year long to achieve: home-court advantage.

We focused on one game at a time. Game six was the one. The Knicks didn't want to play us in game seven in Houston, it's not the kind of game you want to play on the road if you have any choice in the matter. Game six was close but when I blocked John Starks's three-point shot at the buzzer we knew we would be playing one game for the championship.

There was a lot of talk during this series and all year long about some players' personalities on the court, but attitude doesn't come into play on the court very often. All this trash talk doesn't mean a lot to me, I just look at a guy's game. The game speaks for itself. If a player jumps into the key and steals a pass or tries to help on defense and draws a foul, if he is always creating problems for everybody, he's a tough guy. I don't care what he says when he's shooting or running the court. You're not tough with your mouth. If every time I look at a player he's doing something — getting a big steal or rebound, driving, "Why is he getting open?" — *that* is a tough player.

There were a lot of tough players on the court for game seven at the Summit. The game was tight and close all the way. No lead was large and no lead was safe. Kenny Smith and Vernon Maxwell both hit big threes and Max played excellent defense on John Starks. The whole team played together, the bench supported us, and we beat the Knicks. We were champions.

People came down from the stands in waves. It was a beautiful sight. We celebrated on the court, we celebrated in the locker room, we celebrated in the hallways. I gave thanks to Allah.

I went from interview to interview. Everyone wanted to know how it felt. It felt great! The team had worked hard all year for the honor of being champions and the team as a whole, as a unit, deserved the title.

Under the stands the Summit passageways were jammed with Rockets' family and friends and media and steamy with sweat and TV lights. The crush was so tight it was impossible to walk down the regular corridor to my car so I took a back way. I could still hear the celebration and I could hear my own footsteps on the concrete. As I reached the garage where all the players park I saw Patrick Ewing and Charles Smith walking slowly toward the Knicks' team bus. Patrick looked so disappointed. I felt sorry, I knew he wanted the championship and I saw how hard he worked throughout the series. To work that hard and still not come out on top, I understood how he felt.

I shook hands with Charles Smith. Ewing and I hugged. We had fought hard but we had fought clean and had shown each other mutual respect. I respected Patrick for his work and especially now, the way he carried himself in defeat. He was a big man. You can tell a real champion by how he handles losing. Patrick Ewing was a champion. I told him, "Maybe next year. Maybe *this* year." There was another game for anybody to grab; the 1994–95 season was only four months away. I was very happy we had won but I gave him words of encouragement. "Don't lose hope. It was a tough battle. You did all you could have done."

At the press conference the next day Commissioner David Stern congratulated me and the Houston Rockets on winning the NBA championship. Throughout my career I had been focused on winning the championship, I hadn't paid a lot of attention to statistics. I can remember individual plays that were important and individual games in which I scored a lot of points or played very poorly, but I couldn't tell you a list of my honors. Commissioner Stern noted them all — I was chosen 1994 Championship Series MVP and I was the only person ever given that honor and selected league MVP and Defensive Player of the Year in the same year — and he also said many personally complimentary things, not just about my basketball abilities but about me. I was very moved. Touched. I don't get that feeling often and I've never been a very emotional person, but this gave me goosebumps.

When it came time for me to talk about my awards and this dream season I paraphrased John S. Powell, SJ, who wrote the book *Happiness Is an Inside Job,* which has had a profound effect on the way I see the world. "Happiness is a by-product," I said. "You must be enjoying what you are doing in life, not trying to do something to enjoy life. I play because I enjoy playing. I play for fun. I try to learn from every game. I try to improve and do better. It's the journey, not the destination, that matters."

The Rockets were the center of a ticker-tape parade through downtown Houston and from the top of a fire truck I saw half a million Houstonians waving signs and yelling and feeling like champions. I felt the same way.

I was also feeling very sore. All my muscles were crying out at me. I had been so busy preparing for battle, and battling, that when it was finally over all the aches and pains descended on me. I had to do something.

I went to the gym. Three days after the finals, at the time of day that we usually went to practice, I was on the court at Second Baptist Church, one of the places the pros play in the summer.

There were a few guys there. They were surprised to see me. Hadn't I just won the NBA title?

Normally, when the season ends and summer starts and you stop practicing it takes about a week and you're already out of shape. You spend the rest of the summer trying to regain that cutting edge. But my game was sharp. I was jumping high, thinking about all the moves I'd made in the championships. I wasn't ready to stop.

17

MIKE TYSON WAS CRYING

I had heard that Mike Tyson had converted to Islam but the media was presenting it as if he were doing Islam a favor. That is a very wrong approach to the faith. I had never met Tyson and I wanted to tell him: No man does a favor for Allah; Allah favors you with the faith. All of a sudden I got a call saying Mike Tyson would like to talk with me. So my wish came true and I accepted the invitation with honor.

I visited Tyson at the Indiana youth facility where he was imprisoned for rape. The Rockets were on a road trip and we were playing the Indiana Pacers that night.

I didn't know what kind of Islamic teaching Tyson had been given but I did know that the Prophet Muhammad, PBUH, had perfected the message and any innovation was to be rejected. I specifically asked that we meet alone so I could find out what he had been taught. This was between Mike and me.

We met in a big room at the facility. There were families waiting to spend time with inmates but it was not crowded. I picked a nice spot in the corner for me and Mike to talk.

As soon as he came out I stood up and met him halfway. My hands were out to hug him, to make him feel comfortable right away. We embraced and sat down.

Tyson said he had read an article that said I had not been practicing Islam and then all of a sudden had begun. He wanted to know what happened. I heard this question all the time. Many people have to go wrong, go to an extreme, to the brink, before they catch themselves and turn to religion to guide their lives. Not just Islam but many religions. People wanted to know what had been the turning point for me.

I tried to clarify that I had actually *returned* to the faith of my childhood, not found it or been introduced to it later in life. These were the basic principles of the home in which I'd been raised, I told him, but religion hadn't been my major concern. I'd had basic values but until I studied Islam as an adult I had been playing without rules. I had lost my most precious possession. I had been searching for it but I didn't know it was missing. I told Tyson how I had never really enjoyed studying, but when I studied the rules and regulations of pure Islam it was a new experience and I found that I loved to learn. There is so much confusion over what it means to be a Muslim. The Arabic word *Islam* means peace and also means the submission and obedience to the will of Allah. In Arabic the word *Muslim* means "one who has submitted." It became clear that this was the direction in which I wanted to lead my life, so I was excited and moved and happy.

As I was talking I could see Tyson absorbing everything. I could see that he loved the religion. It wasn't anything he said, I could just tell from the way he responded. His face, his manner. He knew the excitement I was talking about.

"But mine is a rare case," I told him, "where things were going right in my life and I started practicing Islam and wanted to show gratitude to Allah. The majority of the time it's a case like yourself. When people get to the top they feel arrogant, they don't humble themselves, and often they fall. Most people will look at your coming here to this place as a setback, but I say it to you differently: This is the best thing that can ever happen to you. Look what happened to you here, you discovered Islam and got your life back together. You can be very firm, very strong, and very knowledgeable."

Tyson began telling me about his experiences, how he used to be, how he had been arrogant and done all the things that Islam prohibits. He knew the difference between the lifestyle he and his friends had been living and the one that is acceptable to Allah. He saw clearly what he should be doing. He saw that he had a second chance.

"Don't come to Islam as a favor to Islam," I told him. "There is a verse in the Qur'an that says, 'They impress on Thee as a favor that they have embraced Islam. Say, "Count not your Islam as a favor upon me . . ." Nay, Allah has conferred a favor upon you that He has guided you to the faith, if you be true and sincere.'

"This is your opportunity to do God's work. People have seen Mike Tyson before Islam. When you go out they will see Mike Tyson *with* Islam. Then you can become a real hero to the people. The only problem now is you have to take responsibility. You have to go to public places and share your experiences, talk about Islam and how it can change your life. You have to go to schools and talk to kids. Let them know!"

He cried.

Mike Tyson is a very shy person. He pictured himself standing in front of an audience and talking to them. I know that's why he cried. I understood perfectly. It took me a long time before I could get up in front of a crowd of people listening to me. There is a big difference between performing in front of tens of thousands of screaming fans and speaking to forty listening individuals.

"I understand," I told him. "That's going to be the problem. But when you see the reward you get from Allah for sharing your experience, you can do that kind of work. In the Qur'an it says, 'Who is better in speech than one who invites people toward Allah?' This is the mission!"

Tyson was very moved and excited. He dried his eyes and told me his role model in Islam: Amza. Amza was one of the companions of the Prophet Muhammad, PBUH. Before his conversion he had been a truly terrifying fighter for evil. When he embraced Islam he brought a great horde of new believers with him. They said, "If Amza can embrace Islam I want to be on his side." He became a warrior for Islam. "I want to be like Amza," Tyson said. "A fighter. A true warrior."

I almost cried myself. I saw he was learning the genuine Islam. You must have two personalities: You must be hard against injustice and good toward fairness and justice for the people. Tyson loved that. You want to be a tough guy? Be a tough guy for the right cause. "When you said you were Iron Mike Tyson you were arrogant," I said. "As a Muslim you must humble yourself. In the ring you're a lion, but when you win you understand that Allah gave you the victory. So, you're humble but tough." He understood. Mike Tyson could be a soldier for Allah.

All human beings are servants of Allah and are responsible to Him. The faithful servants of Allah will always try to act in accordance with divine guidance: to encourage good and justice in society while discouraging evil and injustice. The most important thing in a person's life is his faith and how he translates his faith into practical deeds. Mere faith without practical works is meaningless and useless. Good deeds without faith are also meaningless. It is essential that one should put his faith into practice by doing good deeds. The Qur'an stresses that faith must be demonstrated by good and just actions. Faith and good deeds are always mentioned together in the Qur'an, two sides of the same picture.

Education is one of the most important ways to rid society of ignorance. I formed the Dream Foundation to improve educational opportunities for kids in Houston and across the U.S. We are offering at least five college scholarships to Houston high school seniors whose grades are good, who perform important community service, and who show personal drive and are recommended by people in their communities. One of these five students will attend the University of Houston.

I will also visit schools and speak with students in each NBA city. It's important that kids hear from athletes that school is important. Every individual student and the whole country will be stronger if we are all educated. Kids should pursue their dreams, but their dreams should be realistic. There are twelve Rockets in Houston each year; there are thousands of doctors and teachers. It's not realistic for everyone to dream of playing in the NBA someday, but everyone can go to class. It takes a lot of discipline. It takes studying and making time to study, and it is completely worth it.

We all live in a world that is becoming smaller and smaller. Unnecessary conflict and brutality are making this a dangerous place to live. One reason for this conflict is our tendency to stereotype one another. Promotion of better mutual understanding between people is our sacred duty. All members of the human family should live together in brotherhood and peace.

As a Muslim, I recall the Qur'an: "O mankind! We [Allah] created you from a male and a female and made you into nations and tribes that you may know one another, not to despise one another. Verily, the most honorable of you in the sight of Allah is the most righteous of you. Verily, Allah is All-knowing, All-aware."

This divine call is not directed to Muslims alone but to everyone. It reminds us that we are, all of us, descendants of the same parents; we are brothers and sisters, diverse as we may be. It explains why Allah made us different in language, complexion, and ethnic background: to know one another, to complement one another, and to constitute together a beautiful mosaic, united in diversity and diverse in unity. That divine call is a powerful statement against all forms of racism, narrow nationalism, and false claims of superiority. Its only criteria for superiority are righteousness, moral behavior, and benevolence to fellow human beings.

My sincere suggestion to the reader who would like to learn more about Islam, the universal faith of all the prophets, is to learn about it from its authentic sources, especially the Qur'an and the *ahadeeth*.

May peace, justice, love, and human brotherhood prevail, and may Allah, the sole creator, cherisher, and sustainer of the universe, guide us all to His straight path, the path of happiness in this life and in the life to come. May the peace, mercy, and blessings of Allah be with us all.

18

BELIEVE IT AGAIN!

THE DREAM WAS OVER.

In June I had held the game ball, leaned on the scorer's table, and watched as Houston Rockets fans roared onto the court in jubilation, a frenzy of grins and shouts and bodies and colors, to celebrate our winning the 1993–94 NBA championship. It had been real then, a dream come true. But by the following January we were losing three times a week and it seemed out on the court that we were just sleepwalking.

Our Houston Rockets were falling apart. We began the season playing the same championship-quality basketball that had won us the playoffs. We won our first nine games, including five on the road, and we felt like we were unbeatable. Maybe we started believing it.

But the Rockets weren't the best team in the league on paper. Our success depended on our playing together and accepting our roles, on doing the little things like finding the man with the best shot on each play, or setting the pick that freed someone for a three-point shot, or making the right decision at the end of a drive and dishing off for the easy score instead of one guy trying to finish it himself and forcing up a tough shot in traffic. We had won by playing team defense, but little by little we had drifted apart.

Every team we played wanted to beat the NBA champs and we were not meeting the challenge. We were all over the place and on any given night our opponents didn't know which Rockets team was going to show up, the one with team unity or the one that was all individuals. When we played a quality team we came together, everybody did the right thing. But when we thought we could beat a team regardless of how we played, then everyone would go off on his own and we would lose. We would beat Charles Barkley and the Phoenix Suns one night and get beat by the Los Angeles Clippers, the team with the worst record in the league, four nights later. The core of the team had been together for five years and we were playing like we didn't know each other.

We weren't seeing the big picture: If we win, we *all* win. And winning has always been my goal.

You never know what individual players are thinking. One guy's contract could be coming up and he wants to score more points and get more money, so he's not dishing off inside. Another might just want to get his hands on the ball more on offense and complain when he doesn't get it. A third might want more playing time and feel he has to go one-on-one each time down the court just to get the coach's attention. Fans wonder why teams can be so inconsistent; it's the players.

We were fast and smart and tough and had a deep bench, we had good shooters and rebounders and defensive players, we should have been taking advantage of teams. We should have been dominating. Instead, other teams were taking advantage of us.

Our team couldn't handle success. And by mid-February 1995 we weren't having much of it. There was a lot of concern that we, the defending NBA champions, would not even make the playoffs.

Every time I played against the Portland Trail Blazers and when we saw each other at All-Star games, Clyde Drexler and I would talk about playing together. It was a shared dream but it didn't look like it was ever going to happen. Clyde was a longtime All-Star, one of the important members of the Trail Blazers, and they were never going to let him go. I had been in the league eleven years, Clyde had played for twelve, but NBA players don't really have a say in who their teammates are or even where they themselves play. But still, in early February, after a game in Portland where they had beaten the Rockets by thirty-eight points, we got together in the hotel lounge and dreamed about being teammates.

"You would take care of the inside," Clyde said, "I would take care of the outside . . ."

Just thinking about all the things Clyde could do — steal passes, run the floor, rebound, shoot — made me excited. "Wow," I said, "that would be wonderful." He would make my job so much easier!

It was just a dream. What were the chances?

"It doesn't look good."

Portland had had their chances to be champions. They had been to the NBA finals twice in the last five years but that winter they knew they weren't heading toward the title, and management was looking toward the future. Clyde's contract was almost up and it would cost the Trail Blazers a lot to re-sign him; perhaps he wasn't the ideal player to have on a rebuilding team.

Clyde wanted to play in Houston, where he grew up and his family still lived and the fans loved him.

A few days later Rockets' coach Rudy Tomjanovich came to me and asked, "How would you feel playing with Clyde again?" That's Coach Tomjanovich's way, he gets people involved in decision-making and he is always very concerned about his players. He granted me the privilege to express my opinion. The Rockets' guard situation was extremely unsettled and the team management was happy to have the opportunity to get Clyde. He didn't go into details about who might be traded, he just asked me my feelings.

I'd told him, "There's no way you can pull that deal off. If you can, I dare you to do it."

On February 14, right after the All-Star game, the Rockets traded our power forward Otis Thorpe and the rights to a European player to the Trail Blazers for Clyde and forward Tracy Murray.

This was unreal. We had talked about playing together for years but it had just been talk, now it was going to happen.

Otis Thorpe was well liked on the Rockets, he loved Houston and made the city his home. It wasn't that management was displeased with Otis, not at all; in fact, it was because he was so valuable to our team that Portland wanted him. Otis was a relentless rebounder and a good scorer in the post. He had been an NBA All-Star. In order to get a player of Clyde's magnitude we had to give up someone of real stature, and that was Otis. He didn't want to leave but at times when he could have been openly bitter or critical he said all the right things. I really admired Otis for how he handled the situation.

The trade was made near the final trading deadline after which teams had to maintain their rosters, and I was led to believe the dealing was not yet done. Otis had been a major rebounder and there was a big hole in our rebounding without him. Word got around that the Rockets were trying to get another strong power forward, Mark Bryant, from the Trail Blazers. However, because of financial complications around the salary cap it couldn't be done. So now the Rockets had no heavyweight rebounding power forward; we would have to go with what we had.

We had been playing against Clyde for many years so we all knew him. Clyde is a natural player, a very flexible ballplayer, and he can play several positions, all of them excellently. He can bring the ball up, he can play shooting guard, he can play small forward, and whatever he does he does it to win. He has only one style of playing: all out. He plays hard all the time, he doesn't know any other way to play, he's always going to do his best. It's one of the things I admired about him all those years.

It's tough coming to a new team in midseason, particularly when you're replacing a popular player and are going to take away playing time from several of your new teammates. The three players Clyde's presence would affect most were Mario Elie, Robert Horry, and Vernon Maxwell. Mario knew Clyde from their having played together in Portland. He knew that now with himself and Maxwell and Clyde at the off-guard, his playing time would be cut down, there wasn't enough time for him in that position. Clyde would be on the floor at times when it would have been Mario.

I understood his concern. I loved Mario's game. He is a very structured player, he plays hard and tough and consistent and he knows what he can do: shoot or drive, penetrate and dish off, and take good shots. He deserved to play. But Mario is a role player and probably felt he wasn't getting enough minutes as it was, so why complain. He handled it well.

Robert Horry was very close with Otis and didn't like the trade at all. It took a little while to work that out, for everyone to understand that we were all out there with one single purpose: to win. For a while the team floundered.

I was feeling terrible out on the court. Usually I like to run, but by late March just running up and down the court felt like a punishment. Rebounds that I was used to grabbing were flying over my head, the simple act of putting one foot in front of another made me tired. I was used to being in excellent physical condition and now I couldn't even move. I couldn't explain it, everything was a struggle. My statistics were okay, I kept on scoring and getting rebounds, but everything was so much harder than it should have been.

I am a Muslim and I had fasted over the month of Ramadan, so maybe that had taken something out of me. I thought, Maybe I'm getting old. I had heard of that happening to players, not being able to do the things they had always been capable of doing. I was thirty-two. Maybe I *was* getting old, but my skills shouldn't drop off like I'd gone over a waterfall.

We were playing in Los Angeles against the Lakers and I called a time-out. Something was wrong. No way it should be so difficult for me to run the floor.

When the doctors tested my blood the next day they found I was anemic. I had been taking anti-inflammatory pills whenever I got a deep bruise on the court. Doctors prescribe them for lots of players. After a game you are sore and bruised and you take these pills and the next day you don't feel the pain. But the key is to not stay on these pills for a long time — during the season you're supposed to go on and off them — and I guess I had not been taking them properly. I had been fasting for Ramadan and there had not been enough food or fluid in me to flush out the chemicals so they had built up inside and sapped the iron from my body. I had iron-deficiency anemia.

When the doctor called before practice the next day he told me he couldn't believe my blood count was so low. Anyone just walking to his car or driving around in my condition would be exhausted. I said, "Thank God!" If they had said there was nothing wrong with me, *then* I would've been in trouble.

The team's place in the playoffs was just about set. We'd been playing such mediocre basketball that we had no chance to get home-court advantage and at that point there was very little we could do to go up or down in the standings. The doctors put me on iron supplements and sent me home for two weeks to rest up.

I didn't even go to the Summit. I rested and worked out with a weight trainer, Anthony, and slowly, as the iron got back in my body, I got back into shape. It was important for me to get healthy and it was important for the team to find another way to win. Without me in the lineup the rest of the Rockets formed a good new working relationship. Each of the players was called upon to play more minutes and provide his own strength and responsibility, and they all responded. Clyde showed his leadership and the team accepted and supported him. They developed a good chemistry and became a team unit.

I stretched and lifted weights and ran track and when I got back to the team right before the playoffs I felt so happy just to be on the basketball floor. It felt wonderful just to run without being tired. In fact I was strong and rested, I had spring, I bounced off the guys who were banging me.

Vernon Maxwell had taken the same anti-inflammatory pills I did and he was hit with the same anemia. He came back a little more slowly and when I saw him we had a talk. Maxwell and I had spoken seriously before. His nickname was Mad Max and everybody thought he was crazy but I knew he wasn't. He lived life carelessly, on the edge, but at heart he wanted to do the right thing.

Vernon, our starting shooting guard, was a very intense and excitable player. The same night Clyde and I had talked in Portland, Vernon had been ejected from the game for leaving the bench and going into the stands to punch a fan who was heckling him. Vernon had been suspended by the league for ten games and there were a lot of questions in the Rockets' management and on the team about whether he could come back and play at the level we needed him to achieve.

Maxwell took advice from everybody on the street but I came at him from a different angle, not telling him what to do but talking to him as a friend. When he had gone into the stands and hit a spectator I'd asked him, "Why would you do something in public like a tough guy when you go to your room and feel so sober and sad that you did it? You put this image out as a tough guy, that you don't care about anything, but you really care. You think if you show you care that makes you soft? No, that's strength." He felt he had to live up to the Mad Max image and be street-tough but I had the strong feeling he was stuck playing a role and he wanted to change. He said, "You're right."

Maxwell needed something to structure his life and give him the discipline he was lacking. He needed Islam.

"Maxwell," I said, "you have to be God-conscious. That is the foundation. If you don't have that foundation you will never be successful." And it wasn't just Maxwell, there are a bunch of players like that in the league. "You can live carelessly but that is not wise. You may seem to succeed temporarily but in the end you will be a loser. You have to live the right life, be God-conscious, so you can be truly happy."

When Clyde came to the team Maxwell felt very insecure. He had been suspended, then he was sick, then he had to come back to the team and see a future Hall of Famer in his starting spot. The Houston crowd loved Max because he showed such intensity and emotion on the court, but management was more than a little concerned. I asked Clyde to talk to him, to make him feel comfortable. Clyde told me, "You know I would do that anyway."

I went to Max again.

"Clyde is an eight-time All-Star," I told him, "you're not in competition with him. When you're on the floor together he'll play forward, there's going to be a rotation. Now you can come off the bench and use your speed to create instant offense and give us the spark we need. He's come to make your job easier, to relieve your burden.

"Maxwell," I said, "I understand your position and I respect you so much. Every night on defense you have to guard the toughest opponent, you have to shut him down. You have the toughest job in the league." The NBA had changed even from the time Max had entered; most guards were now bigger and stronger than he was, but Maxwell was faster. "They run you through picks and post you up," I told him. "Just hold him behind you. I'm coming." All he had to do was contain his man and I would come from the weak side. "Maxwell, I don't know how you do it."

I did know he liked to get even, and sometimes that in-your-face mentality worked against him. If his man beat him a couple of times, Max wanted to come right back and score on the guy, but often he would take the first shot he saw and it wasn't the best one. "Max," I said, "don't worry about that. The *team* wins or loses, if *we* score on them next time down *you* get your vengeance. You don't have to take that shot; by being patient for a second and doing the right thing you can get a better shot. Set him up. When you throw the ball in the middle he will drop down to guard me, then I'll give you a three *with a clear look.*" Max understood. Sometimes he would even act on it, and when he didn't he would come back down the court and thump his chest and say, "My fault, my fault."

Max also encouraged me. If he thought I was playing too passively he would throw the ball to me in the middle. When I tossed it back out he would dump it right back in and call, "Take him!" He had a lot of confidence in my moves. I liked that.

Max could use his speed to create problems for the other team. He was so quick when he drove across the lane it was as if he was climbing stairs that weren't there. At his best he had a lot of energy. "You're on the bench but you know you're a key player," I told him. "We won a championship with you. You belong. When somebody's going to war they have to take you along, you're a warrior." Max liked that.

But we were still losing. We played the Utah Jazz in Salt Lake City four days before the end of the season and they beat us by nineteen. On the last day of the regular season they came to the Summit. I didn't play, the coaches didn't want to risk my getting injured. I didn't even dress; I sat on the bench in street clothes while my teammates were warming up, and I watched the Jazz. I knew what they were thinking: This team is in trouble.

Utah was cocky. They had won sixty games during the season, second-best in the league, and they thought this was their year. They were strong everywhere, good guards, good forwards, a bit weak at center but strong everywhere else. They must have thought, These are the champions, but that was last year. They are done. They beat us again, 103–97, in front of a sold-out Summit, and nothing we did changed their attitude one bit.

We went down to Galveston, Texas, to practice and get ready for the first round. There are two seasons in the NBA: the regular season, that's for all the players; and the playoffs, that's when it counts. We had five guys on our team who hadn't been on the Houston Rockets when we'd won the championship the year before; it was very important that we all saw things the same way.

The Utah Jazz has the great inside/outside team of Karl Malone and John Stockton. Even though they haven't gotten a lot of national recognition, the Jazz is known around the league as a hard team to beat. Karl Malone is one of the fastest-running big men. He gets the ball off the boards on one end, gives it to Stockton right away while he speeds up-court, and gets it back on the other end for a dunk. It's a very simple game the way they play it, a straight line, like they're running track. Stockton is a find-the-open-man type of guard, he makes good decisions with the ball, he scores. He's not tall — he's a tough, small guy — but he plays big, he makes things happen. He hurries down the court. If you think he's going all the way and you wait for him, he will pull up for the jumper and make it. He will hit threes. If you come get him he will pass off and find Malone for the dunk. The combination is very well balanced, they complement each other perfectly. They remind me of Magic Johnson and James Worthy.

We lost the first game by two points on a Stockton drive with a few seconds remaining. We exploited the inside game and could have won it; they were lucky to get away. Maxwell played sixteen minutes. Unfortunately, after the game he left the team. He couldn't adjust to the lack of playing time and, I think, in his mind, the loss of stature. He lost sight of the big picture. I wish he had talked to me first. He was gone for the entire playoffs.

In game two our point guard Kenny Smith came up big, he hit seven three-pointers and scored thirty-two points. Clyde scored thirty and the team together made nineteen three-point shots and we had the game won by the third quarter. We went back home tied one-all. We didn't want to go back to Utah, we wanted to close them out in Houston. We had the home-court advantage again, so the pressure was on.

We lost game three badly. Now the pressure was back on the Jazz. No one expected us to beat this strong team. But we believed we were the better team. We knew we could beat them if we played our game — we had almost done it in game one — and we attacked them. Clyde scored forty-one, I scored forty, and we blew them out.

When we went back to Utah tied two-two we felt we had already won the round. Just to go to game five was satisfying. Unfortunately, our reserve forward, Carl Herrera, who was supposed to pick up some of the rebounding slack when Otis Thorpe was traded, separated his shoulder in the game and was out for the playoffs. We would have to play with only ten men on the squad.

Guys play mind games with each other out on the court. This was

the end of the line for one of us, and during the game I saw Karl Malone looking at me. I knew what he was looking for, I got the message in his eyes. We were on the free-throw line and he was smiling, searching my face, as if to ask, Are you concerned that this will be your last game? You will lose your title, you will no longer be champion.

I was concerned. We were down by seven points at the end of the third quarter but I wasn't worried about losing, I was concerned because the referee was making some calls that I didn't think were justified. I used to argue with the referees a lot; I still disagree with them but now I talk to them instead.

Some referees jump to the home crowd. When they make a call and the home crowd roars they feel like they're making plays. When they get booed it affects them. Referees can be influenced by a big crowd. That happens. Game five was on Sunday in Utah. After one particularly outrageous call I went over to the ref and said, "Be God-fearing!"

"I went to church this morning," he shot back. "Did you?"

"Then practice what you believe. Be God-conscious! Just because you go to church does not mean you can do whatever you want afterward. Be fair! Whatever has been taught there, *practice* it! Live it! Be just!"

But I didn't want the referee to think I was just complaining. Later, when he called a foul on me, I walked over to him. He saw me coming and tensed up a little, waiting for the confrontation. I stopped in front of him.

"Good call."

He was shocked.

"We agree on that one," I said.

The crowd in Utah can win games for the Jazz. The energy level in the Delta Center is so high that during the regular season sometimes you go in there knowing you're going to lose. Utah will be up by eight in the first quarter, and with the crowd screaming and the music going it will feel like eighteen. The Jazz know this and they try everything to jump out to early leads. You say, "It's impossible, there's no way we can win today." It's very easy to give up in the first quarter against the Jazz because they come from everywhere. But if you can stay with them for three quarters you have a good chance, because these guys are not used to playing games when it's close in the fourth quarter.

So Karl Malone was showing no sign of concern, but I wasn't buying it. For us to lose in the playoffs was expected, but for the Jazz to lose in the first round would be a disaster.

Malone did everything his team needed him to and with five minutes left they were still up seven. But we fought back. We scored ten points in a row and from then on it got to be a game of free throws. Whoever could make the free throws was going to keep playing.

When we got to the line I looked at Malone again. This time he was sweating. I knew he was worried. He had played a great game but he didn't look at me.

Malone hit a big three-point shot to bring them within two points with 6.5 seconds to go, but Clyde hit three of four foul shots and we won, 95–91.

I felt bad for Utah. They had an excellent team with a real chance to be NBA champions. They were seeded above us, but they were playing a championship series in the first round and now they were going home for the summer. I was happy to keep playing.

We didn't go home, we went right to Phoenix to play the Suns in the second round.

They had beaten the Portland Trail Blazers three straight and had been waiting for us. This was Charles Barkley, Kevin Johnson, Dan Majerle, and a full roster of quality players — A. C. Green, Wayman Tisdale, Danny Ainge, Wesley Person — and they blew us out. The game was over in the second quarter. The second game was about the same. We played hard but they led by sixteen in the first quarter and we never got back in the game.

The Suns had a bunch of scorers and came at us from all angles. K.J. would drive and every time I left my man, Joe Kleine, to help out he would dish off. They kept me honest. Joe Kleine was one of those University of Arkansas spot-up-shooting centers; if I left him alone he would hit the standing jumper, so I could not leave him, and if I stuck with Joe Kleine they penetrated all the way for a lay-up. I thought, Boy, how can we beat this Phoenix team?

We were going home. Home-court advantage had been big the year before, and we hoped it would make a difference again.

We won game three in the Summit by jumping on them at the beginning. We led by twenty-two at the half and won by thirty-three.

Everything that had gone wrong in Phoenix went right in Houston. We hit our shots, we played defense, we out-rebounded them. Then the next day it all fell apart. Playing back-to-back games Saturday and Sunday, we were up by seven points with four and a half minutes to play, but from there to the finish they out-scored us 15–4. We lost, 114–110.

We were the league champions and now we were down 3–1 in the best-of-seven series. We had to beat Phoenix three straight times, *twice in Phoenix,* to advance to the Western Conference finals. The press was saying there was no way we could do it.

It was a big loss. The team needed something to motivate us. I went to the guys with excitement and said, "Let's go out there and surprise them!" In the America West Arena hallway before we went on the floor the team gathered. We always get together right before we go out and talk to each other. Kenny Smith usually does most of the talking. This time I spoke up too. "All we have to do is win this game," I said. "This is the championship game. When we win this game we go back to Houston. We get them there, it's a tie. Game seven is anybody's game. They don't want to play game seven. This is the championship game." We didn't have to win three games, we had to win one.

Phoenix came out passive. They couldn't close us out. Sometimes a game can become too important, so important that a team can't afford to lose and it affects their overall performance. I looked at them and said to myself, They're not aggressive. These guys don't want to win! In the third quarter I was standing at the lane waiting for someone to take their foul shots and I said to Danny Ainge, "How come you guys don't want to win?"

"We're trying too hard," he told me.

Clyde was sick with the flu and could play only limited minutes. He scored only four points but the Suns could not take advantage.

Chucky Brown stepped up big. Chucky had joined the Rockets in midseason from the Continental Basketball Association, the CBA, the minor leagues, and he was happy just to be with us. I liked his game when he was with the Cleveland Cavaliers and I was happy to have him. Chucky is a very good guy, always happy-go-lucky, good for the spirit of the team, the kind of role player every championship team needs. He usually played three, small forward, but with Otis gone all of a sudden he had to guard all these tough and muscular power forwards. They used to put me on the power forwards, so I knew how strong they were. I'd look at his man and I'd chuckle and ask all the time, "Chucky, is he strong?" Chucky would roll his eyes and go *"Whoooooh!"*

"Just contain him," I said. "Don't give him inside position. I'll come from the weak side. Just stay behind him, it's okay. You're not by yourself."

Chucky scored fifteen points that game and played big.

Another good Rocket was the other power forward, Pete Chilcutt. A wonderful guy with an important role to play. I was so impressed with Pete; I didn't know he had that much talent. He came to the team after the season had started in late November as an eleventh- or twelfth-man free agent. Pete was 6'10" and when I watched him play I saw he had this funny, off-balance-looking three-point shot. Every time he took it I thought, He's not going to make it. But after a while I started believing in that shot because it went in! He would fight hard under the boards and when the opposing power forward would crash the boards with him, Pete would go outside and make the three. Pete had gone to the University of North Carolina and was well schooled in the fundamentals. He would work the pick-and-roll. He played hard in practice and in games. I liked playing with him because he was a threat, and the more he played the more respect he earned.

The playoffs are like a new season. You make a point of being in excellent shape, your conditioning level is high, you are playing at your peak and looking forward to each game. You're playing with a group of guys who just want to win, who want to run and play hard. All season long I go to sleep before every game and picture myself playing against the other team. I see myself challenging every shot, making them miss, snatching every rebound, *dominating*. I *see* that. When I wake up the game is in my head, my confidence level is high, I have a feel for the game that evening. When I get to the court I am happy to be there because all the things I saw in my mind now can happen. I *feel* it. Things may develop in the game that I did not see beforehand but I am prepared mentally so I can take advantage of it.

There are also some times when I don't concentrate enough before the game, when I try to picture the team I am playing against and I can't. I'm not prepared mentally, I haven't done my homework. Those are the games in which I struggle. I try to adjust, to see the play, but sometimes I struggle through the whole thing.

Game five at Phoenix began as a problem. The first few shots I took I missed. That can really throw a player off his game. Now you're self-conscious, you try not to miss again. That's when you miss, when you try not to. So now your shooting touch is way off. Some guys try to shoot their way out of it. That's one way of getting free, but it has its drawbacks; you can miss and miss and miss. It becomes mental. But if you understand the game you have other options.

I try to do something else for a while. If my turnaround jumper is missing I go to my jump hook. Or I face up. Or I dish the ball off to a three-point shooter. I mix it up. I have to find something positive to do for a while. Sometimes I go away from my own offense altogether. If I make a big steal or get a rebound or block a shot or make a good pass so somebody else scores I feel satisfaction, I feel I'm still contributing to the team. I may not have put the ball in the basket but I have given my team points, I have been effective. *Then* I take another shot, as a reward. I reward myself for doing good things on the floor. Then when I shoot I feel good about my game, and that positive feeling is likely to make me shoot better. If I miss, that's okay, at least I have helped my team, I'm not afraid to look bad. If I miss again, then I have to keep finding something else to do. I have to create an opportunity and earn my reward one more time.

In game five the Suns' other center, Danny Schayes, was playing good defense. I was not shooting well and I was giving the ball up a lot. Unfortunately, my teammates were missing shots too. I was passing up close jump hooks for outside shots and we were missing them. Finally the coach said, "You have to shoot it." The whole team told me I had to shoot.

The game came down to the last shot. We needed a basket to get into overtime. They got the ball to me in the post. Danny Schayes had been flopping on me the whole game. If I turned to the middle and tried to power the guy he would fall down as if I had barged into him. If I even leaned his way he fell down. The refs had already called five fouls on me. I had to be careful because I didn't want to get called for a charge on the last play of the game.

This was not a matter of skill anymore, it became technical. I gave him something he had not seen the whole game. I dribbled in the same way, to my left with my back to the basket. He had been cutting off my jump hook, so this time I went to the center, put my left hand up to fend him off, faded just a little, and put up a strong jump shot in the lane. He couldn't touch it. That shot sent the game into overtime.

The beauty of the Rockets was that we had so many players who could step up when they were needed. This game it was Robert Horry. He hit a big three-pointer that gave us the lead and we won, 103–97.

Game six in Houston we just beat them, 116–103.

So it came down to game seven back in Phoenix.

Charles Barkley was the Suns' most visible player, he was a superstar and his presence was felt. He was effective but with our defensive rotation we were making him pay. We put Robert Horry on him, and Robert is 6'10", active, and hard to shoot over, an excellent defender who gets key rebounds. Barkley is an excellent passer so he would find the open man, he did his damage, but we took that blow. Game seven was Kevin Johnson's.

K.J. finishes better than almost any guard in the league. He has one of the best crossover dribbles in the NBA. Tim Hardaway crosses over but then he has to hit his jump shot, K.J. crosses over and beats you and goes to the basket. That's different. He's coming full speed, then all of a sudden he changes direction and sees a clear path to the basket. When he's on his game, by the time I come over to block him I'm always a second too late, he's putting it on the glass before I get there. If I go too soon he draws the foul as well. He knows how to get you to foul him and how to make the basket at the same time. K.J. went to the foul line twenty-two times that night and hit twenty-one.

Every time I looked K.J. was driving. When he wasn't penetrating he was pulling up and hitting his jump shots. He was just incredible. It's a trial just being on the same court with someone who is playing so well. I tried to encourage Kenny Smith and Sam Cassell, who were guarding him. I said, "You've got to contain him. When he's crossing over I can't get there. If you can delay him for a second I can help you. Meet him way out front, don't just let him come. Make him play defense on the other end. Don't worry, you're not by yourself, he has to beat the whole team, he has to beat *us!*"

I was having a hard time. Just like in game five, Dan Schayes was defending me and although he was playing me very physically I had to be very delicate with him or risk getting called for a lot of fouls. Normally my strength is in the post-up game, where I can either score or pass off, but the only way I could be effective against Schayes was to go outside. This game, I was missing a lot of shots. He is a good defensive player and he was doing a good job. For the first three quarters I struggled.

I was in foul trouble and spent a good part of the third quarter on the bench. I sat there and watched my teammates, who were playing well. Clyde was having a fantastic game. We were down by ten at the half but by the time the fourth quarter started we were ahead by a basket. We had twelve minutes to play, that was all. I had to give it all. Now.

My concentration got even higher and my shots began to fall. I finally had the feel of the game.

The game was tied with about fifteen seconds left and we had the ball. Phoenix was pressing us and we swung the ball to Mario Elie in the corner. There was no one around him. That's his shot, the open three-pointer. It comes right off his shoulder like a set shot. He practices it every day.

Even though that was his shot I thought he was going to pass it in to me. I was set up underneath the basket and I thought he would go for something that was certain. When Mario pulled up for that three I said, "*Oooooooooh.*" I turned toward the basket for the rebound. The ball went right in.

That was a backbreaker. He could have come closer and taken a two-pointer but Mario went for the kill and it finished them off.

Mario was the hero.

That's one of the beautiful things I enjoyed about our team: Somebody different was always stepping up to be the hero. In Utah it had been Kenny Smith, in game five it was Chucky Brown coming off the bench to make a big difference, and Robert Horry; here it was Mario Elie. And we were all happy for them because we were a team.

We were celebrating in Phoenix. No one but us had thought we could pull this off, and we had done it! The media was counting the consecutive "do-or-die" games — games which, if lost, would end our season — and over the past two seasons the number was up to seven. But that's a statistic the media created, it wasn't something we thought about. Reporters would create these records and tell me. I said, "Oh, really?" I wasn't paying attention to that, we had to think ahead to the Western Conference finals and the San Antonio Spurs. They had beaten us five of the six times we had played that season, so we knew they were tough.

The first game of the Conference finals was two days later but the planning began immediately. The Spurs were saying they had beaten us five out of six but I was saying to myself, These people are not being realistic. They beat us but they forget that it was a break here, a rebound there. Three of those losses had been by three points or less. It was not like they beat us convincingly. The Spurs and the media were looking at the record, but that's deceiving.

San Antonio was definitely the team to beat. This was the toughest challenge for me and the team. They had the best record in the league, they felt like it was their year, and they had the NBA MVP, center David Robinson.

I respect David's game. He is active, blocking shots, and when I see a master shot blocker I recognize him. When I watch games on TV and someone goes in and David *doesn't* block the shot I am surprised. How come he didn't block that? I know he can. I see what I would do and I know he can do the same thing. Or when he pulls up for an outside jumper and makes it, I respect that shot.

My motivation is the challenge of meeting another center who is my equal, my match. In scoring, blocking shots, rebounding, all aspects of the game. He is the key to their team; most of the Spurs' plays go through him. There was somebody like myself on the other side. It was all mental toughness now. First of all, I had to accept the challenge. For me to play I had to be very loose, I had to play *my* game.

The key was not to get into a one-on-one competition in which I would do battle with David and lose the focus and team spirit of the Houston Rockets against the San Antonio Spurs.

Still, you cannot escape the one-on-one comparison; that is going to be there. When I look up at the scoreboard to find out how much time is left I can see how many points I've scored, but it's not like I'm counting; if I'm double-teamed I will find the open man. I'm not trying to outscore him, *we* are trying to outscore *them*.

As excellent a player as David Robinson is, there was more to the Spurs than him. A lot of talk had centered on their forward Dennis

Rodman. Rodman led the league in rebounding, he was tireless and relentless. I used to think he got all those rebounds just because he was in the right place at the right time, but he was there so often I had to believe in him.

Rodman is always moving and he's very strong. He's a position player; before the ball even goes up he's already taking a rebounding position. He's not taking a large part in the offense, he's only rebounding, so while most of the other guys are still worried about handling the ball he is positioning himself. It's easier when you only have to think about one thing, and he's a specialist. But you have to give him credit, he's the best at it and he gives his team many second chances. He does a lot of tipping the ball, tips it up and gives it back to the Spurs' guards to reset the offense. He gives them lots of opportunities, so he's always a factor.

Everybody was asking, "What are you going to do with Rodman?" Our strongest rebounding forward, Otis Thorpe, had been traded, and going into the series the popular wisdom was that without someone to put a body on Rodman we were going to get eaten up on the boards. But Otis would have been banging with Rodman, the middle would have been clogged, there would have been less room for me to work. That's Rodman's game. With the Rockets now, Rodman was more of a disadvantage to the Spurs than an advantage.

Because Rodman was always roaming around, the man he guarded, Robert Horry, would get a clear look at the basket for wide-open three-point shots all the time. And Horry could hit them. As the series started we could hear Spurs coach Bob Hill yelling at Rodman, "Stay with your man!" but Rodman's mentality and his instincts were to go to the basket for the rebound. He got some rebounds — during the season he got a ton of them against us — but he gave up more points than he gave them. I looked at it as an advantage for us, like playing five on four.

Before game one at the San Antonio Alamodome I pictured myself being effective. I got a good night's sleep and saw myself making a lot of moves, looking sharp, very active, very light. That gave me confidence. On game day when I was warming up I was loose, I didn't even want to sweat. I moved very slowly. I didn't need to stretch as much as usual because I felt very flexible.

And I was calm. I prayed to Allah for support, guidance, and victory as if I was going into battle. In the locker room I had been thinking, I *have* to win this game, but once I was on the floor I was not worried, not concerned, I just walked around the court feeling a level of confidence I could only have hoped for. *Today I'm here to play.*

The Alamodome is an athlete's gym, a shooter's gym. You get to the arena and you feel like playing. The place holds thirty-five thousand people, more than twice the capacity of the Houston Summit. It looks like a stage and feels like a set. I said, "Wow, this is a performance!"

I knew what it was going to be like from the jump ball to the end. They were going to attack us and we were going to attack them. David believed he could take me, I believed I could take him, the two teams believed we could beat each other. And we could, we just had to fight it out to see who would win. There was no way to escape the challenge, so you just had to accept it and face it and deal with it.

I didn't know how my teammates prepared individually. Each player has his own way. In the locker room we were talking to each other. "Let's get the first game! The pressure is on them, they have to win. This is *our* game." Sometimes people say things and it's just locker room talk, it doesn't sound believable. This was coming from the heart. Before we entered to thirty-five thousand screaming fans we put our hands together and said, "*Rockets!*" It boomed in the hallway like a take-off.

At each game, after the introduction of the starting lineups we stand together and raise our hands like a big tent and we talk. Kenny Smith usually talks the most. He's the one who controls the ball. "We're gonna run the floor from the beginning!" he shouted over the din. "We're gonna push it. Hakeem, you go for the first trailer. We're gonna play good defense. We're gonna start from the beginning."

Everybody offered something. Clyde said, "Make them go through our five-on-five defense. No easy fouls, no easy baskets."

"We're gonna push it!" Kenny said again.

Kenny looked hyper. While the Spurs were being introduced I went to him. "Kenny," I said, "just be patient. If you rush you'll make mistakes. Patience." That's what I stressed. "So you can make the right decisions."

Mario, Clyde, Robert, and I had speed. That's what made our team so different, our speed and how active we were on defense. We were a bunch of athletes put on the floor of a shooter's gym. The game was going to be very athletic, very competitive, it was going to be a battle. So I smiled. This was exactly what I had expected. The more I looked at the competition the better I felt.

The crowd was roaring, but we had been exposed to loud crowds on the road: game five against Utah, game seven against Phoenix. It had very little effect on our team by now. San Antonio had the home court but we had already been tested.

The game was close the whole way, the kind of game we had all expected. David played well, I played well, we were all *right there*. As the best games do, this one went down to the wire. We were down by one point with under ten seconds left to play. Mario ended up with the ball and drove to the basket. David moved to the middle to stop him and I spotted up in the corner. Mario made the right decision. David was going to block him and instead of trying to be the hero and force a shot, Mario passed me the ball.

David, with his great athletic ability, recovered. He ran out at me. He is a large man. I faked, took one bounce, and he was still coming. I knew if I took that shot I'd be forcing it.

Robert Horry's man ran at me, too; even if I beat David, he was there. Still, the game was on the line. I was going to shoot. Then I saw Robert standing on the other side of the three-point line at the top of the key. He was wide open. I quickly passed him the ball.

Everybody was waiting on Horry. Nobody was moving. David was in the middle, too far away to contest the shot; Robert's man was running away from Robert and toward me; Robert was standing in three-point range and everyone else was coming to the lane.

This was a big shot for Robert Horry. The whole tone of the series was riding on this jumper. He had some decisions to make.

We were only down by one point. Robert is a good three-point shooter but we didn't need three points to win. He had the shot but why would he take a three when he could get closer? Instead of giving in to the pressure and taking the first open shot available to him, Robert took one bounce and came a big step closer to the basket.

There was nothing you could do but watch it.

The ball went in. It was a backbreaker. We won game one!

From the beginning of the playoffs Robert Horry's confidence had gone way, way up. He was playing on a different level. This was a career-transforming shot. Robert went from thinking he could be counted on to *knowing* it. It was a great thing to watch.

In the locker room we were wildly happy but we knew the series was far from over. We told ourselves, "We've got them on the hook now. They have to win the second game, the pressure is on them. We're not going to relax." In order to take advantage of this win we had to win game two. It was almost like a must-win. If we went out and attacked and they lost, we felt they would panic. That could change the whole series.

In game two we came out strong just like we wanted to and built a big lead in the first quarter, but San Antonio is a tough team and they fought back. Robert Horry and Clyde carried the scoring load along with me, but a key Rocket that day was Charles Jones. Charles had been signed by the Rockets in March and had played only three games with us during the season, but he was a seasoned professional with twelve years in the league and he had a great attitude. He was a quiet kind of guy, a very good guy, a pleasant man to work with who fit in with the team immediately.

Charles was a big factor in the playoffs. He played excellent defense and when I got into foul trouble the coach could leave me on the floor and put Charles in to guard David. He was a defensive specialist and we would talk about how to play Robinson. "Give him his room. When he shoots, make him shoot over your hand." I have the instinct to gamble to steal passes and Charles said, "Once you gamble it leaves you vulnerable, pulls you out of position. Don't overcommit, don't gamble, just stay with him." If you look at the box score Charles's contribution doesn't seem impressive — he took no shots, scored no points, got four rebounds — but his role was so important. We won, 106–96.

We couldn't believe it. Win two games on the road? This was unreal. I was thinking, Can we really sweep these people? San Antonio is not a team that we can sweep. Can we?

Rudy T told us, "Stay humble, stay hungry." We had all seen teams win early and start talking trash. That motivates the other team, starts a controversy and makes them fight even harder. We were not that kind of team. We wanted to say all the right things, to set a good example.

We didn't incite them but the Spurs motivated themselves. From the beginning, game three, at home at the Summit in Houston, was close. The Spurs were fighting, they were tough. They played as if they were on a mission. They got good shots and shot the ball well, they were taking chances on every possession, they outplayed us, and they won.

That was a wake-up call. We had captured the home-court advantage and we still had it. Game four, the pressure was on us. People around the team were whispering about how devastating it would be to lose. Phoenix had taken two from us at home the year before and we had come roaring back to win the series; we were aware of that and we were concerned about its happening to us.

Our celebration and momentum was gone. They ran us out of game four, 103–81. Nothing we tried made any difference, they just beat us. Now we had to go back and win in San Antonio again, where the Spurs had lost only eight games all year.

The flight to San Antonio was quiet. The guy who put it all in perspective was Kenny Smith. In each city the team takes a shuttle bus from the airport to the hotel and as Kenny climbed the steps to get on the shuttle he looked at all of us and said, "Ah! It feels so good to be back home!"

Exactly! We had won in the Alamodome — twice. We had lost twice in the Summit. So this was our home, this was our gym, we were taking over again. He said it so casually. No one was in a joking mood and what he said made sense. We had blown a two-game advantage, we had blown the home-court advantage big-time, but the feeling ran around the bus: *We have the advantage.*

The Spurs did something very silly. Each game in the series so far had been won by the visiting team, so the Spurs didn't go home, the coaches had the team check into a hotel. The whole point of the home-court advantage, in addition to having the crowd behind you, is to be able to be with your family and sleep in your own bed; you feel comfortable in your own home and you relieve some of the game's anxiety and pressure. I thought they made a big mistake.

People didn't expect us to win. Maybe the two wins at the Alamodome were our dying gasp and now form would prevail. But we knew we had lost in Houston because the Spurs had played at a higher level, not because we were a lesser team. They had outplayed us but we didn't believe they could continue to do it. In order for us to win we had to not only match their intensity, we had to better it.

And that's exactly how it happened. When we got on the Alamodome court for game five, we had the intensity and they didn't. They became passive and we were the aggressors. Kenny Smith played only twelve minutes that game and didn't score, but he gave us the leadership when we needed it. "Ah! It feels so good to be back home!"

Sam Cassell came off the bench and scored thirty points. He also handed out twelve assists. Sam gets all keyed up, you can see it in his face, and when he is on his game he gives us great intensity. Sam talks to me a lot on the court and in the huddle. He bellows at me, "Gather yourself!" Some people think I might be offended, having a secondyear player instruct me on how to play, but I understand. Sam is saying I should put two feet down — *gather myself* — before I go up with my jump hook. He understands my strength. He loves the jump hook. Sam isn't instructing me, he's encouraging me to play to my strength. He and I have a good working relationship on the court because I know Sam wants to win.

Sam and Kenny alternate at point guard, Rudy starts Kenny and plays whoever is hot during each game. The difference in their styles of play is noticeable. With Kenny running the offense we have more speed. The ball gets pushed up the floor, it's a faster game. He also likes to shoot threes. Sam likes to walk the ball up the court and isolate his man one-on-one. Sam dribbles, he is creative, it's like he's actually playing with the ball. He involves the team, either shooting or driving and drawing fouls and dishing off. Sam makes big shots, too. When he's scoring and penetrating he makes it difficult for the opponent.

Sam is sensitive to criticism, he loses his cool easily, and sometimes he loses focus, but he and Kenny can both step up anytime and make a big difference to our ball club. In game five it was Sam.

This was the game where Dennis Rodman spent part of the fourth quarter down on the end of the bench with his shoes off. I was playing so I was only vaguely aware of the controversy, but I think he wanted to be on the floor; it was the coach who realized what they were giving up when he put him out there. Robert Horry hit a couple of three-pointers, so that may have had a lot to do with the coach's decision.

I scored forty-two points and had one of my best games. I played that well because of the competition, because David *made* me. Because David is a shot blocker and an excellent athlete I had to play beyond my best to get by him. On one play I faked him three times — once to the middle, then the spin to the outside, then finally up and under — before I could get a clear shot. He covered the first, he covered the second; finally I got free on the third option. I used moves I had never used before *because I had to;* without them David would have stopped me. It was not that he was not playing well, he was playing tremendously; that's why I had to play even better. David brought out the best in me, he made me work for every shot; if I made a mistake he was going to block it. He pushed me to a higher level.

David presents another very particular problem for me. Because he is left-handed, when I move to my right to shoot I am moving to his strength. He's right on top of me so I have to keep him guessing. Often I face up straight in front of him so he doesn't know what I'm going to do, or when or how I'm going to do it. I put the ball on the floor and make him move, I try everything to be effective against him.

In game five, in the whole series, I was having fun, it was natural, I was just playing the game. I credit David with making me play my best.

We won game five, 111–90. Now all we had to do was win a game at home.

The Summit was full and rocking for game six. People had come from everywhere to watch us win the Western Conference championship. The game was tied at the end of the first quarter, tied at the half; we led by one point after three quarters. Robert Horry's confidence level was so high he hit six three-point shots, including a very big one with less than two minutes left. It was a tough, tough game that we won at the very end, 100–95.

When the buzzer sounded people poured onto the floor as if we'd won the finals. San Antonio had the best record in the league so it was like a minifinals. No one expected us to be playing for the championship again. In the beginning we hadn't either, but as the playoffs went on we developed as a team. We were confident but not cocky going back to the NBA finals again.

David Robinson came to the locker room to congratulate us. He was very sad, very disappointed. His face was like stone, he seemed almost in a daze. I felt bad to see him so dejected. He had had a great year, he had won the MVP award, he had really thought this was the Spurs' year. For them to lose to us, the underdogs, must have been very, very tough. I told him, as a friend, "Don't be discouraged. Look forward. Work hard for next year. Work hard in the summer and come back!" What had happened and how he responded could have a large effect on his career.

The media had pitted David against me. The media is always looking for weakness and they were all set to say David was not a winner because his team had not won the championship. The media says you're a failure if you don't win a championship, but that is not true. Basketball is a team game, *teams* win championships. David is a future Hall of Famer. He is a champion, regardless. He had played beautifully and I respected him tremendously because he had brought the best out of me. It pained me to see him feel so bad. God willing, I hope he will win a championship before his career is over. I wish the same for Patrick and Shaquille.

I watched the last game of the Eastern Conference finals to see who I would be playing, the Orlando Magic or the Indiana Pacers. I thought Orlando was a better team and should win easily and I was surprised it went seven games. I watched the Pacers' center Rik Smits, a big man with nice fundamentals. He had a good touch outside, a nice jump hook, I liked his game. And he was being effective against Shaquille O'Neal. They both played the same kind of game, with power. Smits is 7'4", taller than Shaq and five inches taller than I am, so I would have to play a small man's game against him. I couldn't stand and try to push Smits, to be effective I would have to face him up, make him move laterally, get him off balance and shoot over him. My game against Rik Smits and the Pacers would require quickness and mobility.

When Orlando won the conference championship and entered the finals I tried to picture playing against them, but I couldn't. I lay in bed and tried to see my moves, but nothing came. That concerned me; when I can't visualize a game I usually don't play very well, and I didn't want to go into this series unprepared. I hoped it would take only the first game to understand how the series was going to unfold.

Against San Antonio I had been very calm, just ready to compete.

Nobody outside the Rockets expected us to get there, we weren't supposed to win. We'd been playing well and we didn't have anything to lose. But this was the finals. Now I *really* didn't want to lose and I began to feel the pressure. We'd come this far, we wanted to finish. Everybody on the team felt the same way.

We didn't practice much against the Orlando offense, we mostly practiced *our* game. We knew we could not take a bad shot against the Magic because with Anfernee Hardaway and Shaquille O'Neal and Nick Anderson and Dennis Scott they would run us out of the gym. We had to run them out instead. We had to make them work through our five-on-five defense, not give them any fast breaks. No easy dunks or lay-ups. We had to rebound, box out; when somebody drove we had to rotate and help out. It was a help defense; if the ball went down low we planned to rush down and contest the pass, make them beat us from outside.

Orlando had lost at home only twice all season and the first two games were in their arena. Once again we were the underdogs. We were confident but we knew it was going to be a tough series. The Magic were a very young, complete, high-energy team.

I looked at the match-ups. Kenny Smith and Penny Hardaway, Clyde Drexler and Nick Anderson, Robert Horry and Horace Grant, Mario Elie (who had been inserted into the starting lineup in game five of the San Antonio series), and Dennis Scott. They're bigger, but we can run them, I thought. Let's test their conditioning. We had been playing just about every other day for a month and we were in great game shape, conditioned, comfortable. It was going to be a battle and we had to *make* them beat us; we could not just assume they were better than we were and give them the games.

The man with the ball for the Magic was Penny Hardaway, a 6'7", 210-pound guard who has fantastic speed, is a very good athlete, and can handle the ball and shoot and drive and do it all. He was much bigger than Kenny Smith, who is 6'3", 170 pounds, which could cause us problems. I was going to have my hands full with Shaq and wouldn't be able to help out as much as usual.

Shaq was in his fourth year, a veteran. He was a hard worker, he ran the floor; now he had the jump hook, which had become a powerful weapon, and the drop step, which was unstoppable inside. And any-

thing around the basket he finished with a dunk. He had size and power. How do you stop that?

The 1994 finals against the Knicks were like a war. We went out there and did battle. They were a tough, physical team and they wore their hard game faces and talked some trash. Against the Magic we walked to center court before the tip-off and shook hands, we even hugged. There was a lot of mutual respect and we didn't have any trouble showing it. We would let our games do the talking.

I couldn't see the game at all, I had no sense beforehand of what it would be like. Even once it began I was not sure. The first time I got the ball I took one bounce. Normally when I take one bounce I go straight up, that's a jump hook; I establish my game so the opponent has to respect it, then later, after I've scored a basket or two, I throw in some fakes. But this time I faked. *I started out faking!*

Shaq had watched the series against San Antonio and he wasn't going for the fake, he stayed down. Somebody knocked the ball out of my hand. I was not comfortable. I hoped this was not the start of a long struggle.

The first quarter was a disaster. We were losing 30–15 even though Shaq had scored only two points. Shaq was using his strength to drive me away from the basket, he was contesting every shot, and I was not getting the rhythm on my fadeaway. When I spun to the middle they had someone there. I wanted to score but their defense was swarming and even my passes were being contested. Soon we were down by twenty. The crowd was wild. This was not good. This was setting the tone for the series.

When you're up by twenty points, basketball can be an easier game. You're free-stroking, you take more chances, you take shots you might not take in a close game, and there's no pressure so you make those shots.

When Shaq got position in the deep post I was in trouble. I picked up my third foul and sat on the bench and started thinking about all the opportunities I'd had to be effective. I thought, Okay, now I have to do my job, I have to play my part to cut this lead down.

That's when Clyde began making his move. Clyde is a brilliant open-court player and he was rebounding, stealing the ball, running the floor, converting circus lay-ups. He scored fifteen points in the second

quarter and we cut the lead to eleven at the half. Robert Horry stepped up, stealing the ball and making big plays. He was laughing, having fun, and playing aggressively. I was happy to see him in that mood.

In the second half I went back in the game and just played defense, scored every once in a while, and continued to try to find the open man. That's when Kenny Smith went off.

Kenny is a streak shooter with a very flat jumper that doesn't get much higher than the rim, and he was unconscious hitting threes. We ran a play for Clyde three times in a row and each time before Clyde could come around the pick and get the ball, Kenny had a clear look at the basket and bombed from the outside. Kenny couldn't miss. Clyde couldn't believe it! Kenny was hitting from five feet beyond the three-point line! Clyde had never seen anybody shooting like that when it was most needed. He went, "Whooooa!" Kenny talks a lot, he's our motivator, before the game he tells everybody what he's going to do. This time he proved it; he hit five threes in the third quarter alone.

We came all the way back and took a seven-point lead at the end of the third quarter. But the Magic were a good team, they counterattacked, and with ten seconds left they were up by three with their guard Nick Anderson on the foul line shooting two. Anderson is a good player, an excellent shooter. If he made even one of these foul shots it would be very hard for us to win.

I knew he was going to make at least one. I was standing at the lane praying he would miss!

He missed the first one. The pressure rose. He missed the second.

The ball bounced far out, straight back to him. He got fouled again.

I felt so bad. I had to get a rebound at this time of the game.

Anderson stood at the foul line. He missed the third one. His confidence was shaken. The fourth wasn't even close.

We fought for the rebound, grabbed it, and called time-out.

We were down by three, 110–107. On the bench the coaches designed the play. There were 5.6 seconds left.

We inbounded the ball to Kenny Smith. What a beautiful opening. He dribbled to his right and Hardaway came after him. Kenny head-faked. Hardaway went flying by. Kenny ducked under, and with 1.6 seconds on the clock he hit his seventh three-pointer of the game. It was an NBA playoff record. Game tied.

The Magic still had a chance to win. They called a time-out and set up a play for Dennis Scott. Robert Horry blocked his shot at the buzzer. We went into overtime.

I can't remember the overtime exactly. We were all operating on overdrive. Robert Horry hit two three-pointers to keep us in it. I hit a jump hook with a minute and a half to go and we went up by three. The ball changed hands several times, and with 5.5 seconds left Dennis Scott hit a three to tie the game.

We put the ball in Clyde's hands. He had been having an excellent game and many good things could happen if Clyde had his hands on the ball. The play was called for Clyde to penetrate.

Five seconds is a very long time in the NBA. Clyde was at the top of the key and had a beautiful opening in front of him. He beat his man and drove toward the basket. I was hoping he was going to settle this game with a dunk.

Shaq had to respect that drive. The way Clyde was coming he had an open score, so Shaq moved into the driving lane.

Shaq is 7'1", somewhere around 325 pounds. He went way, way up to make Clyde change his shot. Clyde did a fantastic job to get the ball off, he altered his release and put the ball high up over Shaquille.

As soon as Shaquille stepped out of the rebounding position I stepped in. Right there. I found myself wide open under the basket.

That was very unusual. If Shaq moves away from me in the post there is always a guard slapping at the ball or putting a shoulder into me, trying to move me out of the way. In that situation, with the game on the line, *nobody* is ever wide open under the basket.

Shaq made Clyde miss but he did not block the shot. It bounced on the rim and sat up for me like a trophy. I was so alone I went up and with my right hand steadied the ball and then tapped it back in the basket.

I heard nothing. There was no noise, there was no whistle, there was just quiet. I thought something was wrong. What happened? The crowd was silent. I turned back down the court. Had the clock run out? Was there a foul? Did it count? What had gone wrong?

I saw Kenny Smith by the three-point line. Kenny jumped. As soon as he got up in the air I realized the basket was good. That's when I reacted. There was 0:00.3 on the clock, not enough time for them to score. We had won game one.

Running back to the locker room I couldn't believe it. We won that game! They played well enough to beat us, they'd been up by twenty, but we came out ahead. If you look at the statistics, they outrebounded us so badly, we didn't have a chance. If you look at the scoreboard, we won. How we won it I can't tell you.

Orlando didn't expect to lose, especially not in their own gym. They had to win the second game, it was critical for them. If they did not win game two they would be in very big trouble. Now we put pressure on them. It was up to us to increase their doubts.

In game two we came out attacking. This time *we* were ahead by twenty-two late in the second quarter. It's always better to have a big lead than to be behind, but in some ways it can make you more nervous. A team that is trailing has a goal, they have something to motivate them and shoot for that's right in front of them: "Let's cut into this lead." A team that is far ahead can get anxious if their margin starts to shrink. If you're playing loose and your shots stop falling your lead can slip away in no time. It can make you very anxious. Fortunately, in game two we kept up the pressure.

Kenny Smith had played so well in game one that Sam Cassell spent most of his time on the bench, but game two belonged to Sam. He played a lot of minutes, scored thirty-one points, and was a big key. Robert Horry had seven steals, a record for the finals.

I was learning how to play Shaq. Because they are in the east and we are in the west we only play the Magic twice each season so we hadn't gone head-to-head very often. In 1994–95 the Magic had beaten us both times, each time pretty convincingly. I knew Shaq was going to score. He's too big, too powerful to shut down. We wanted to double-team him in the post so he would be forced to pass the ball out rather than shoot from in close. It was important to me to make him work for every point he was going to get. We weren't going to stop him but we wanted to limit his effectiveness. I understood Shaq's strength.

Shaq had one move that was very effective. He would get the ball, dribble once, and hit me in the chest as he moved. He was sixty-five pounds heavier than I was so he would get me off balance and then shoot over me. Very effective.

Just boxing him out was difficult. I found that anytime I turned my back to him and looked for a rebound he would just bump me off my position. Since I couldn't turn my back to him I began to face him. I forfeited the rebound — I definitely wasn't going to get it if my back was to the basket, I couldn't even *see* it — but *he* wasn't going to get it either. Somebody else would have to get the ball, and I relied on my teammates.

This technique worked, sometimes. I could prevent Shaq from getting position by getting in his way, but every time I faced him he would lock me with his arms, we'd get tangled, and sometimes the refs would whistle me for a foul. I argued with them — "Why are you calling the foul on me? We were both tangled!" — but they saw me in the unusual position of anti-rebounding and called it on me twice. I could use that tactic only once in a while.

But there is more to playing Shaquille than playing defense against him. Against Shaq or any opponent you must make him respect your game and you must make him expend energy trying to stop you.

My offense was my defense. That is my game plan against all the big men. I test their conditioning. I wanted to run Shaq down the floor and work him at both ends. He had to guard me and he could never relax. In a battle between finesse and power, power will beat finesse. But to play with finesse you must have power, you need power to carry out finesse. You must be strong enough to post up, strong enough to get the ball in position to use your moves. You need power for the explosion and quickness, you need to finish with power. That's why I trained so hard, to develop the power that I could combine with finesse.

We held the lead all the way through game two and won, 117–106.

Every team we had played throughout the playoffs, this was supposed to be their year. Utah, Phoenix, San Antonio, Orlando. All the media and most of the fans around the country considered them the four best teams in the NBA. Everybody except Houston. When we got home the fans were going crazy. People soaped the windows of their limousines and pickup trucks with "Go, Rockets!" signs, you'd see it up and down the freeways. Businesses from barbecue joints to law firms were hanging Rockets pennants in their windows. You could feel and hear the energy and happiness in the whole city.

Winning game three was critical. We had to win. We didn't want this to be like the San Antonio series and let the Magic think they had a chance to come back. We had three games at home, we didn't want to leave town again.

On the court all the players stepped up. Robert Horry got better as the playoffs got more intense. He was getting key rebounds and blocking shots. Robert has long arms and knows how to feed the post. He was active. He would cut to the basket and I'd spot him. Playing with Robert is so much fun. Mario Elie was very solid spotting up, a safety guard with his set shot. He was automatic.

Clyde Drexler is a winner, he just wants to win, and game three belonged to him. Clyde pushed the ball up the floor the whole game. It seemed like every time I looked he was stealing the ball and finishing on the other end of the court with a slam. Clyde set the tone, he made the difference.

But the Magic wouldn't go away. We didn't win this game until Anfernee Hardaway's last-second three-pointer missed at the buzzer.

One more game. We didn't want to play more than one. Don't even open the door to the possibility, don't even begin to worry about losing a 3–0 lead. This was the time to finish it. The Summit was packed full of raucous Rocket fans, the team was all together.

Game four was close for three quarters and then we broke it open. We won our second consecutive NBA championship!

People hadn't believed we could sweep the Magic. They hadn't believed we could win at all. But the Rockets won the championship because we were a team. And most of all because it was Allah's will.

The Rockets were a good example of what it takes to win a championship, not only in sports but in the corporate world or in any group of people working together. Every organization needs team unity, team chemistry, and a team concept. No egos. It's said that you need a lot of big names to win, but the Rockets proved you can win with two dominant players and a team full of people who play their roles beautifully. We came together, everybody accepted his role, everyone knew his limitations, we all respected each other, and we were happy to be there. We had come from different places — from Alabama and Houston and Lagos, from the draft and trades and the CBA — and we were all so happy to be in the league, in the playoffs, in the finals. We worked hard in practice, we played hard in the game, we respected the veterans and appreciated the younger players. We came together and we made it work. There was no trash talking. Even when we were up two games, three games, we were consistent and respectful, we were doing it the right way. As soon as you asked for the ball you got it, as soon as someone was open you hit them. We ran the floor and played together as a team. It was a fantastic environment in which to live and work and play.

Clyde and I had endured the disappointment of losing the college championship in the last second many years before and I was so happy that he had finally won a championship.

The Magic's forward Horace Grant congratulated us and showed a lot of class. I went to Shaq on the court immediately after the buzzer and hugged him and told him it had been a tough battle and that I respected him.

Rudy T defined our team. He had made each of us focus on the job we had to do, he took us from a disorganized squad in midseason to the NBA title. In the glare of TV lights he said, "Never underestimate the heart of a champion." We'd done something that would go down in history. We stayed humble, we stayed hungry, and we won.

I had thought the dream season was over and that, like most dreams, it wasn't likely to come again. I didn't know it was just the beginning.

All praise and thanks be to Allah, the lord of the universe.